GW00792485

Other Outstanding Books by MikeRothmiller

L.A. Secret Police. Inside the LAPD Elite Spy Network

A New York Times Bestseller & Kindle Besteller

My Hero. Military Kid's Write About Their Moms and Dads

Endorsed by Three Presidents. Forward by Norman Schwarzkopf

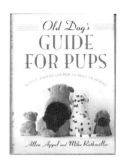

Old Dogs Guide For Pups. Advice and Rules for Human Training

Read by two Presidents and Queen Elizabeth

America. Words That Shaped The Nation. The First 50 years 1776-1826

A Highly Praised History Book

The Making of Adolf Hitler

Includes

The Complete Top-Secret Psychological Profile Of Hitler Compiled by the OSS

Hitler's Last Political Testament, Personal Will And Marriage Certificate

The Most Intimate Details Of Hitler's Life

Chilling Details Of His Childhood And His Rise To Power

Hitler Was Scolded In Front Of His Staff By Frau Hofman

His Bizarre Sexual Fantasies And Practices

Many Of Hitler's Close Associates Believed He Was Gay

Hitler Was Identified In Vienna Police Records As A Sexual Pervert

While In Vienna, Some Of his Closest Friends Were Jews

Two Women Close to Hitler Allegedly Committed Suicide with His Gun

His Insanity

Graphic, Shocking Photographs Of His Murderous Reign

Everything in this book is accurate. Nothing has been edited or changed

ISBN-13: 97816500254773

ISBN-10:1500254770

Library of Congress-1-1625961771

Dedication

For centuries scholars have debated the origin and date of the first written word. Most accept that the first word was inscribed in Mesopotamia (todays Iraq) or during the time of King Scorpion the First of Egypt; with dates ranging between 3,200 B.C.E and 3,500 B.C.E. In all likelihood we will never acquire unquestionable confirmation of the first writings. However, words are exceedingly important. They have power. They have shaped the world.

No one can deny that Adolf Hitler was a cunning genius when it came to word usage. He carefully managed his message and skillfully employed his superior oratory skills to manipulate minds, a nation, and much of the world. He masterfully understood the frailties of the human psychic and exploited those weaknesses at every opportunity. It took years of careful planning, mind manipulation on a massive scale and world events outside of Hitler's control to elevate him to the status of Germany's dictator. Hitler, as do today's politicians, understood a simple fact of human behavior; the political lie. He accurately stated, *"Make the lie big, make it simple, keep saying it, and eventually they will believe it."* Sadly, this simple philosophy is successfully employed by today's politicians.

In this book, I will not engage in word manipulation to articulate the true story of Adolf Hitler as known during his reign. I will use words to accurately focus a blinding light of clarity on the embryo of evil that was gestating within Adolf Hitler. An embryo so evil, it would eventually develop into a monster that slaughtered millions and bathed the world in blood.

Politicians believe in words when it benefits them. However, when words cannot stop an enraged monster from its murderous rampage extreme measures must be brought to bear. When this occurs it means the politician's pontificating has failed, and force must be utilized. However, politicians are not willing to engage the dragon themselves; they prefer to remain safe in the background so that a courageous few within a populous will step forward to sacrifice their lives in the ensuing battle. Politicians by their very nature are not willing to handle this brutal, dangerous and deadly task. They have an entrenched aversion to dirtying their hands or risking their lives. They prefer to sit back and order others to their death. The brave individuals who step forward and carry the burden are true heroes, which brings me to my point—words.

Hero--a small word with a currently ambiguous definition. Hearing that simple word our emotion ranges from modest to complex depending on the context in which it is used. Sadly, over use has diminished the impact of hero to a mere utterance.

In today's America, and perhaps the world, the word hero is used to label a football player who scores a touchdown, a baseball player hitting a home run, a basketball player making a shot, an actor receiving an award or a person simply performing a kind deed. These are not *heroes*.

A hero is a person who willingly risks their life to aid another; Period. Each day Americans perform heroic acts and should be commended. However, the true heroes of America are the men and women who serve in the military of our country. On a moment's notice these brave patriots are willing to leave their families, race to far off shores and engage an enemy in battle to protect America and people of other nations. They put country first and are willing to make the ultimate sacrifice. Unlike previous generations, in today's America few possess the courage to do so. These are the heroes who put country above all else, so that you and I can live in freedom.

Without our military and brave patriots the birth of this nation never would have occurred and the freedoms and prosperity Americans enjoy today would have been in doubt. Remember, the military doesn't start wars; politicians do. However, the military are the people called upon to fight the battles and make the sacrifice, not the politicians. There is much I could say about these brave patriots. However, I'll finish my thoughts with a few words; to the men and women who sacrificed so much to slay the dragon unleashed by Adolf Hitler, it is my pleasure to dedicate this book to you. All Americans and the world are indebted for your miraculous dedication to duty, extreme bravery and sacrifice. *You are America's finest. You are true heroes. I thank you. The world thanks you, and America thanks you.*

Table of Contents

Introduction

Throughout history various individuals have attained immense power. Some were considered virtuous; others were oppressors, tyrants and mass murders. In modern history, the case of Adolf Hitler is perhaps the best known and possibility the most studied. To understand Hitler, one must understand his mind and how various events shaped the man.

Adolf Hitler was born to working class parents on April 20, 1889. His early life was unimpressive. World War 1 German military records indicate that Hitler served as a low ranking soldier and exhibited courage under fire, was wounded and received several awards for gallantry. As with millions of soldiers during war, he apparently did his duty.

However, at some time during his adult life, his overall views became distorted and transformed the once aspiring artist into a fanatic. Something(s) drastically influenced him. Some historians believe it was the surrender of Germany during World War 1 and the conditions and punishment imposed on Germany in the Treaty of Versailles. Was it a single incident, mental illness or a confluence of events? No one can be certain. It is unlikely Hitler understood all the events which ultimately molded his mind. Nonetheless, what is certain is the fact that his life experiences placed him on the path of destruction and by a series of fortuitous events both large and small, including murder; he was thrust into the leadership of Germany.

Hitler's rise to power is an intriguing story. He was a simple, yet complex man. He was not highly educated, yet he possessed unique intelligence and more importantly, he understood the fine nuances of human behavior and mind manipulation. Hitler did possess an attribute which, without question, propelled him to the pinnacle of Germany. He was a *natural charismatic orator*. He knew what to say and how to say it. He brought unbridled emotion and carefully choreographed theatrics to his speeches and understood the value of employing cultural warfare.

Hitler was able to convince the German populace that its woes were the result of the Treaty of Versailles, communism (Marxist) and the Jews. If these forces could be defeated, and he could do it, the problems of the German people would be eliminated and its national pride and economy would be restored. In simple terms, he built a *straw man* to absorb the failures of government. It was the rich against the poor, and the communist and the Jews verses Germany. Simple targets the uniformed masses could identify and attack on numerous fronts.

This was not a new political tactic. To be successful, the *straw man* argument necessitates that the audience be illiterate or uninformed of the original argument or issues at large. This same ploy has been used successfully by politicians worldwide, including various Presidents of the

United States. Place the blame on easily identifiable targets and state to the masses that they are *victims* of these horrible entities.

Hitler successfully engaged this strategy to achieve his goal of ultimately becoming the dictator of Germany. Once achieved, he embarked on a journey of rewriting or ignoring laws which did not enhance his personal ambition. He used the power of the government to crush his perceived enemies, both large and small. More importantly, he used Germany's military in an attempt to accomplish his ultimate goal of dominating Europe and potentially the world.

In the end, Hitler's rise to power launched his nation on an immensely bloody path attesting to his arrogance and willingness to murder millions to satisfy his own self-aggrandize ego or to appease his insanity. In any event, he was a monster.

When writing a book on historic events the author must give serious consideration to the message and the facts they wish to convey. *The author must never impart their personal views or spin the facts to facilitate the storyline.* I have given this long and thoughtful consideration and believe I am presenting the most accurate, truthful and ethical approach in telling Hitler's rise to power. I will not impart my personal interpretation of issues or impose my personal judgments—except to say he was indeed a murderous monster.   The proper approach is to present the facts to the reader and allow them to form their own opinion.

With the passing of time, many historic events emerge from a blanket of fog to illuminate the truth, while others recede into the abyss and eventually from history. Memories of the event fade and eye witnesses die. Still, there are some events which are chronicled at the time of occurrence with such precise clarity; it is unlikely that the passage of time will unveil new, factual information that will alter the already known truth.   That is why I have elected to only present the most highly accurate information the various intelligence services developed and presented to the President of the United States and its allies during World War II.   Available to them was real time, first-hand knowledge and individuals who personally knew Hitler. This is their story, in their words, as compiled by the OSS. This extraordinary in-depth analysis of Hitler takes the reader inside his twisted mind.

On June 13, 1942, President Franklin Roosevelt ordered the establishment of the Office of Strategic Services (OSS) the predecessor of today's Central Intelligence Agency (CIA). One of its early undertakings was to assemble a top-secret team to clandestinely investigate and evaluate the mind of Adolf Hitler. They sought a deep understanding of his make-up and thought process in order to defeat his military machine and his quest for worldwide domination.

They began by dissecting his childhood, adolescence, early adult life and eventual rise to power. Every aspect of his life, including his bizarre sexual desires and practices were examined for his "weak" link. A link that would provide the US and its allies with an advantage that would allow them to be victorious.   Hitler had several strong points; however he had many inherent weaknesses which ultimately aided in Germany's defeat. He was a man so inured with his own intelligence and/or insanity; he was blind to the sage advice of others. Hitler wasn't the first political leader who failed to understand this deep-seated human flaw. But, the world paid a heavy price because of it.

This riveting formerly top-secret report will transport you into the White House with President Roosevelt. Imagine looking over his shoulder as he read page after page delving deeper and deeper into the psychic of Adolf Hitler. Ask yourself the following questions. How did it alter Roosevelt's and his general's minds? What battle plans and intelligence operations were undertaken, revised or eliminated based on this report? As you can appreciate, the questions are endless and unfortunately cannot be fully addressed. Except to say the report would certainly have provoked critical discussions at the highest levels.

After decades of secrecy the CIA finally declassified this revealing and thought provoking psychological analysis of Adolf Hitler. Compiled by Dr. Walter C. Langer, Prof. Henry A. Murray, Dr. Ernst Kris and Dr. Beltrand D. Lewin, this was one of the first and perhaps most extensive and critical forensic mental examinations undertaken without the advantage of interviewing the subject. Yet, these researchers were able to develop a vivid and accurate analysis of the making of Adolf Hitler. They accurately identified his strengths, weaknesses, deeply embedded human flaws and his fanatical passage into madness.

Adolf Hitler wasn't the first fanatical ruler to slaughter untold numbers of the innocent; sadly, he won't be the last. The world is only a military coup, revolution or election away from another monster rising to power to unleash their demented form of terror on the world.

Many good people foresaw the danger of Adolf Hitler. Many others elected to turn a blind eye.

On February 1, 1867, during his inaugural address as Lord Rector of the University of St. Andrews, England, John Stuart Mill said, *"Bad men need nothing more to compass their ends, than that good men should look on and do nothing."* The world must never forget those words.

Perhaps the most illuminating passage of this book is the final chapter. Not only does it close the book, but it closes the life of Adolf Hitler in his own words. In his last personal testament dictated just hours before his death, he continued to speak of his desire for world peace and places the blame for his actions and the war squarely on the shoulders of worldwide Jewry.

Adolf Hitler's Mother Klara

Adolf Hitler's Father Alois

Adolf the infant

Adolf the World War I soldier

Adolf the Man

The Dictator

The Monster

Hitler's Personal Standard

Men Who Were Essential in Hitler's Reign Of Terror

Hermann Goering

Born in Germany in 1893, Hermann Goering was an early and prominent member of the Nazi Party.

During World War I he became an ace fighter pilot, and was awarded the Pout le Merite, the *Blue Max* award. Goering was the last commanding officer of the fighter wing known as the Jagdgeschwader 1, or the famed "Red Baron."

Under Hitler he virtually directed the organizing of the Nazi police state and assisted in the development of the Nazi extermination camps. After the war he was convicted of war crimes and sentenced to death. He beat the executioner by taking a cyanide capsule.

Rudolph Hess

Born on April 26, 1894, Hess was a longtime friend and follower of Hitler. In 1933 he was appointed Deputy Fuhrer and became the third most-powerful man in Germany. Only Hitler and Goering possessed more power. Hess signed the legislation stripping all Jews in Germany of their rights.

In 1941 Hess undertook a secret mission (reportedly without the knowledge of Hitler) by flying to Scotland in a small aircraft to negotiate peace with Britain. He was taken into custody, convicted of war crimes and sentenced to life in Spandau Prison. In 1987, at the age of 93, Hess hung himself.

Heinrich Himmler

Born in Munich, Germany on October 7, 1900, Heinrich Himmler became Hitler's deputy propaganda chief. In 1929, Hitler appointed him commander of the Schutzstaffel—The SS and later assumed command of the feared Gestapo. He also commanded all German police and was also appointed minister of interior. After capture in 1945, he committed suicide via a cyanide capsule on May 23, 1945, in Lunberg, Germany.

Himmler oversaw the development and operation of the Nazi extermination camps.

Dr. Paul Joseph Goebbels

Dr. Paul Joseph Goebbels was born on October 29, 1897. He was an early and fanatical follower of Adolf Hitler. In 1933 he was appointed Reich Minister of Propaganda in Nazi Germany. It was his brilliant public relations skills which helped shape Hitler's public image. As one of Adolf Hitler's closest associates he was known as a stanch hater of the Jews and eagerly supported their extermination.

Just prior to Goebbels and his wife committing suicide, he had his six young children murdered with cyanide capsules.

Otto Adolf Eichmann

Otto Adolf Eichmann was born on March 19, 1906. He served as a Nazi SS Obersturmbannführer (lieutenant colonel). He was one of the major figures orchestrating the slaughter of over 6,000,000 Jews and others the Nazis deemed unworthy of life. Eichmann was charged with facilitating and managing the logistics of mass deportation of Jews to ghettos and extermination camps during World War II. In 1960, he was captured in Argentina by the Israel's intelligence service—the Mossad. He was tried for war crimes, found guilty and hanged in 1962.

Martin Bormann

Martin Bormann was born on June 17, 1900. Hitler appointed him the director of the Party Chancellery and he also served as Hitler's private secretary. He maintained Hitler's trust and in that position he was able to control access to Hitler. In many cases, Bormann personally conveyed Hitler's orders to military commanders and other high ranking Nazis.

The prolonged search for Martin Bormann came to an end in 1998. Using DNA analysis scientists determined that a skeleton unearthed in Berlin in 1972 is indeed Bormann.

DNA obtained from the skull was compared with a sample taken from a living Bormann relative and found to contain matching sequences.

Coupling the DNA results with eyewitnesses and dental records, the German government closed its case on this illusive Nazi and concluded he died on May 2, 1945. This puts an end to decades of speculation that he became a Soviet (Russian) spy, escaped to South America or lived under an alias.

The Enabling Act of 1933

The German Government Legally Elevates Hitler to Dictator Status

THE ENABLING ACT OF 1933

The official United States Department of State Translation

Law to Remove the Distress of the People and the State (The Enabling Act)

The Reichstag has passed the following law, which is, with the approval of the Reichsrat, herewith promulgated, after it has been established that it meets the requirements for legislation altering the Constitution.

Article 1. National laws can be enacted by the Reich Cabinet as well as in accordance with the procedure established in the Constitution. This also applies to the laws referred to in Article 85, Paragraph 2, and in Article 87 of the Constitution.

Article 2. The national laws enacted by the Reich Cabinet may deviate from the Constitution as long as they do not affect the position of the Reichstag and the Reichsrat. The powers of the President remain undisturbed.

Article 3. The national laws enacted by the Reich Cabinet shall be prepared by the Chancellor and published in the *Reichsgesetzblatt*. They come into effect, unless otherwise specified, the day after their publication. Articles 68-77 of the Constitution do not apply to the laws enacted by the Reich Cabinet.

Article 4. Treaties of the Reich with foreign states which concern matters of national legislation do not require the consent of the bodies participating in legislation. The Reich Cabinet is empowered to issue the necessary provisions for the implementation of these treaties.

Article 5. This law becomes effective on the day of its publication. It becomes invalid on April 1, 1937; it also becomes invalid if the present Reich Cabinet is replaced by another.

Reich President von Hindenburg
Reich Chancellor Adolf Hitler
Reich Minister of the Interior Frick
Reich Minister for Foreign Affairs Baron von Neurath
Reich Minister of Finances Count Schwerin von Krosigk

Source of English translation: Law to Remove the Distress of the People and the Reich (Enabling Act); reprinted in U.S. Department of State, Division of European Affairs, *National Socialism. Basic Principles, their Application by the Nazi Party's Foreign Organizations, and the Use of Germans Abroad for Nazi Aims*. Washington, DC: United States Government Printing Office, 1943, Appendix, Document 11, pp. 217-18. (Translation edited by GHI staff).

Adverse Consequences of the Enabling Act

The Enabling Act allowed the government, which was extensively Hitler, to pass laws without the consent of the Reichstag (Germany's Parliament) and to ignore their Constitution. The Act virtually relegated the Parliament to observers with no real power. It also eliminated all political parties, except the Nazi party. Effectively, Germany was now a one party country with Hitler being the supreme leader. In 1942 the Reichstag officially gave Hitler the right of life and death over all German citizens and people under Germany's control. As with ancient pharaohs, his word was the only law.

SECRET

OSS ARCHIVES

A PSYCHOLOGICAL ANALYSIS

OF

ADOLPH HITLER

HIS LIFE AND LEGEND

by

WALTER C. LANGER

M. O. Branch
Office of Strategic Services
Washington, D. C.

OSS ARCHIVE

Wash- MO- INT- 7   1943

With the collaboration of

PROF. HENRY A. MURRAY, Harvard Psychological Clinic
DR. ERNST KRIS, New School for Social Research
DR. BERTRAM D. LEWIN, New York Psychoanalytic Institute

SECRET

Approved For Release 1999/08/24 : CIA-RDP78-02646R000600240001-5

Approved For Release 1999/08/24 : CIA-RDP78-02646R000600240001-5

S E C R E T

C O N T E N T S

PREFACE

This study is not propagandistic in any sense of the term. It represents an attempt to screen the wealth of contradictory, conflicting and unreliable material concerning Hitler into strata which will be helpful to the policy-makers and those who wish to frame a counter-propaganda. For this reason the first three parts are purely descriptive and deal with the man (1) as he appears to himself, (2) as he has been pictured to the German people, and (3) as he is known to his associates. These sections contain the basic material for the psychological anaylses in sections IV and V in which an attempt is made to understand Hitler as a person and the motivations underlying his actions.

The material available for such an analysis is extremely scant and spotty. Fortunately, we have had at our disposal a number of informants who knew Hitler well and who have been willing to cooperate to the best of their abilities. The study would have been entirely impossible were it not for the fact that there is a relatively high degree of agreement in the descriptions of Hitler's behavior, sentiments and attitudes given by these several informants. With this as a basis it seemed worthwhile to proceed with the study filling in the lacunae with knowledge gained from clinical experience in dealing with individuals of a similar type. This is not an entirely satisfactory procedure, from a scientific point of view, but it is the only feasible method at the present time. Throughout the study we have tried to be as objective as possible in evaluating his strengths as well as his weaknesses.

All plain numbers in parentheses refer to the page of The Hitler Source-Book, a companion volume in which the original material is to be found together with the complete reference. Numbers in parentheses preceded by M. K. or M. N. O. refer to pages in Mein Kampf and My New Order, respectively. A detailed Index to the original material is to be found at the beginning of the Source-Book. A complete Bibliography is appended to this study.

It is hoped that the study may be helpful in gaining a deeper insight into Adolph Hitler and the German people and that it may serve as a guide for our propaganda activities as well as our future dealings with them.

Walter C. Langer
CONSULTANT, M. O. BRANCH, OSS

28

Chapter One

Hitler

As He Believes Himself To Be

"I follow my course with the precision and security of a sleep walker."

Adolf Hitler

PART I

HITLER — AS HE BELIEVES HIMSELF TO BE

30

HITLER — AS HE BELIEVES HIMSELF TO BE

At the time of the reoccupation of the Rhineland, in 1936, Hitler made use of an extraordinary figure of speech in describing his own conduct. He said:

> "I follow my course with the precision and security of a sleep-walker."

Even at that time it struck the world as an unusual statement for the undisputed leader of 67,000,000 people to make in the midst of an international crisis. Hitler meant it to be a kind of reassurance for his more wary followers who questioned the wisdom of his course. It seems, however, that it was a true confession and had his wary followers only realized its significance and implications they would have had grounds for far greater concern than that aroused by his proposal to reoccupy the Rhineland. For the course of this sleep-walker has carried him over many untravelled roads which finally led him unerringly to a pinnacle of success and power never reached before. And still it lured him on until today he stands on the brink of disaster. He will go down in history as the most worshipped and the most despised man the world has ever known.

Many people have stopped and asked themselves: "Is this man sincere in his undertakings or is he a fraud?" Certainly even a fragmentary knowledge of his past life warrants such a question, particularly since our correspondents have presented us with many conflicting views. At times it seemed almost inconceivable that a man could be sincere and do what Hitler has done in the course of his career. And yet all of his former associates, whom we have been able to contact, as well as many of our most capable foreign correspondents, are firmly convinced that Hitler actually does believe in his own greatness. Fuchs reports that Hitler said to Schuschnigg during the Berchtesgaden interviews:

> "Do you realize that you are in the presence of the greatest German of all time?"

It makes little difference for our own purpose whether he actually spoke these words or not at this particular time, as alleged. In this sentence he has summed up in a very few words an attitude which he has expressed to some of our informants in person. To Rauschning, for example, he once said:

> "Aber ich brauche sie nicht, um mir von ihnen meine geschichtiche Groesse bestaltigen zu lassen." (717)

And to Strasser, who once took the liberty of saying that he was afraid that Hitler was mistaken, he said:

> "I cannot be mistaken. What I do and say is historical." (378)

C02571145

Many other such personal statements could be given. Oechsner has summed up his attitude in this respect very well in the following words:

> "He feels that no one in German history was equipped as he is to bring the Germans to the position of supremacy which all German statesmen have felt they deserved but were unable to achieve." (669)

This attitude is not confined to himself as a statesman. He also believes himself to be the greatest war lord as, for example, when he says to Rauschning:

> "Ich spiele nicht Krieg. Ich lasse mich nicht von 'Feldherrn' kommandieren. Den Krieg fuehre *i c h*. Den eigentlichen Zeitpunkt zum Angriff bestimme *i c h*. Es gibt nur einen guenstigen. Ich werde auf ihn warten. Mit eiserner Entschlossenheit. Und ich werde ihn nicht verpassen . . ." (701)

And it seems to be true that he has made a number of contributions to German offensive and defensive tactics and strategy. He believes himself to be an outstanding judge in legal matters and does not blush when he stands before the Reichstag, while speaking to the whole world, and says:

> "For the last twenty-four hours *I* was the supreme court of the German people." (255)

Then, too, he believes himself to be the greatest of all German architects and spends a great deal of his time in sketching new buildings and planning the remodeling of entire cities. In spite of the fact that he failed to pass the examinations for admission to the Art School he believes himself to be the only competent judge in this field. A few years ago he appointed a committee of three to act as final judges on all matters of art, but when their verdicts did not please him he dismissed them and assumed their duties himself. It makes little difference whether the field be economics, education, foreign affairs, propaganda, movies, music or women's dress. In each and every field he believes himself to be an unquestioned authority.

He also prides himself on his hardness and brutality.

> "I am one of the hardest men Germany has had for decades, perhaps for centuries, equipped with the greatest authority of any German leader . . . but above all, I believe in my success. I believe in it unconditionally." (M.N.O. 871)

This belief in his own power actually borders on a feeling of omnipotence which he is not reluctant to display.

> "Since the events of last year, his faith in his own genius, in his instinct, or as one might say, in his star, is boundless. Those who surround him are the first to admit that he now thinks himself infallible and invincible. That explains why he can no longer bear either criticism or contradiction. To contradict him is in his eyes a crime of 'lese majeste'; opposi-

C02571145

> tion to his plans, from whatever side it may come, is a definite
> sacrilege, to which the only reply is an immediate and strik-
> ing display of his omnipotence." (French Yellow Book, 945)

Another diplomat reports a similar impression:

> "When I first met him, his logic and sense of realities had im-
> pressed me, but as time went on he appeared to me to become
> more and more unreasonable and more and more convinced
> of his own infallibility and greatness . . ." (Henderson, 129)

There seems, therefore, to be little room for doubt concerning
Hitler's firm belief in his own greatness. We must now inquire into the
sources of this belief. Almost all writers have attributed Hitler's confidence to the fact that he is a great believer in astrology and that he is
constantly in touch with astrologers who advise him concerning his
course of action. This is almost certainly untrue. All of our informants
who have known Hitler rather intimately discard the idea as absurd.
They all agree that nothing is more foreign to Hitler's personality than to
seek help from outside sources of this type. The informant of the Dutch
Legation holds a similar view. He says:

> "Not only has the Fuehrer never had his horoscope cast, but
> he is in principle against horoscopes because he feels he
> might be unconsciously influenced by them." (655)

It is also indicative that Hitler, some time before the war, forbade the
practice of fortune-telling and star-reading in Germany.

It is true that it looks as though Hitler might be acting under
some guidance of this sort which gives him the feeling and conviction
in his own infallibility. These stories probably originated in the
very early days of the Party. According to Strasser, during the early
1920's Hitler took regular lessons in speaking and in mass psychology
from a man named Hanussen who was also a practicing astrologer and
fortune-teller. He was an extremely clever individual who taught Hitler a
great deal concerning the importance of staging meetings to obtain the
greatest dramatic effect. As far as can be learned, he never had any
particular interest in the movement or any say on what course it should
follow. It is possible that Hanussen had some contact with a group of
astrologers, referred to by von Wiegand, who were very active in
Munich at this time. Through Hanussen Hitler too may have come in
contact with this group, for von Wiegand writes:

> "When I first knew Adolph Hitler in Munich, in 1921 and
> 1922, he was in touch with a circle that believed firmly in
> the portents of the stars. There was much whispering of the
> coming of 'another Charlemagne and a new Reich.' How far
> Hitler believed in these astrological forecasts and prophecies
> in those days I never could get out of Der Fuehrer. He neither
> denied nor affirmed belief. He was not averse, however, to
> making use of the forecasts to advance popular faith in him-
> self and his then young and struggling movement."

It is quite possible that from these beginnings the myth of his associations with astrologers has grown.

Although Hitler has done considerable reading in a variety of fields of study, he does not in any way attribute his infallibility or omniscience to any intellectual endeavor on his part. On the contrary, he frowns on such sources when it comes to guiding the destiny of nations. His opinion of the intellect is, in fact, extremely low, for in various places he makes such statements as the following:

> "Of secondary importance is the training of mental abilities."
> "Over-educated people, stuffed with knowledge and intellect, but bare of any sound instincts."
> "These impudent rascals (intellectuals) who always know everything better than anybody else . . ."
> "The intellect has grown autocratic, and has become a disease of life."

Hitler's guide is something different entirely. It seems certain that Hitler believes that he has been sent to Germany by Providence and that he has a particular mission to perform. He is probably not clear on the scope of this mission beyond the fact that he has been chosen to redeem the German people and re-shape Europe. Just how this is to be accomplished is also rather vague in his mind, but this does not concern him greatly because an "inner voice" communicates to him the steps he is to take. This is the guide which leads him on his course with the precision and security of a sleep-walker.

> "I carry out the commands that Providence has laid upon me." (490)
> "No power on earth can shake the German Reich now, Divine Providence has willed it that I carry through the fulfillment of the Germanic task." (413)
> "But if the voice speaks, then I know the time has come to act." (714)

It is this firm conviction that he has a mission and is under the guidance and protection of Providence which is responsible in large part for the contagious effect he has had on the German people.

Many people believe that this feeling of Destiny and mission have come to Hitler through his successes. This is probably false. Later in our study (Part V) we will try to show that Hitler has had this feeling for a great many years although it may not have become a conscious conviction until much later. In any case it was forcing its way into consciousness during the last war and has played a dominant role in his actions ever since. Mend (one of his comrades), for example, reports:

> "An eine eigenartige Propheseiung errinere ich nich noch in diesem Zusammenhang: Kurz vor Weihnachten (1915) aeusserte er sich, dass wir noch vieles von ihm hoeren werden. Wir sollen nur abwarten, bis seine Zeit gekommen ist." (208)

Then, too, Hitler has reported several incidents during the war which proved to him that he was under Divine protection. The most startling of these is the following:

> "I was eating my dinner in a trench with several comrades. Suddenly a voice seemed to be saying to me, 'Get up and go over there.' It was so clear and insistent that I obeyed automatically, as if it had been a military order. I rose at once to my feet and walked twenty yards along the trench carrying my dinner in its tin can with me. Then I sat down to go on eating, my mind being once more at rest. Hardly had I done so when a flash and deafening report came from the part of the trench I had just left. A stray shell had burst over the group in which I had been sitting, and every member of it was killed." (Price, 241)

Then, also, there was the vision he had while in hospital at Pasewalk suffering from blindness allegedly caused by gas:

> "Als ich im Bett lag kam mir der Gedanke, dass ich Deutschland befreien wuerde, dass ich es gross machen wuerde, und ich habe sofort gewusst, dass das verwirklicht werden wuerde." (429)

These experiences must later have fit in beautifully with the views of the Munich astrologers and it is possible that underneath Hitler felt that if there was any truth in their predictions they probably referred to him. But in those days he did mention any connection between them or dwell on the Divine guidance he believed he possessed. Perhaps he felt that such claims at the beginning of the movement might hinder rather than help it. However, as von Wiegand has pointed out, he was not averse to making use of the forecasts to advance his own ends. At that time he was content with the role of a "drummer" who was heralding the coming of the real savior. Even then, however, the role of drummer was not as innocent or as insignificant in Hitler's mind as might be supposed. This was brought out in his testimony during the trial following the unsuccessful Beerhall Putsch of 1923. At that time he said:

> "Nehmen Sie die Ueberzeugung hin, dass ich die Erringung eines Ministerpostens nicht als erstrebenswert ansehe. Ich halte es eine grossen Mannes nicht fuer wuerdige seinen Namen der Geschichte nur dadurch ueberliefern zu wollen, dass er Minister wird. Was mir vor Augen stand, das war vom ersten Tage tausendmal mehr: ich wollte der Zerbrecher der Marxismus werden. Ich werde die Ausfgabe loesen, und wenn ich sie loese, dann waere der Titel eines Ministers fuer mich eine Laecherlichkeit. Als ich zum ersten Mal vor Richard Wagners Grab stand, da quoll mir das Herz ueber vor Stolz, dass hier ein Mann ruht, der es sich verbeten hat, hinaufzuschreiben: Hier ruht Geheimrat Musikdirektor Excellenz Baron Richard von Wagner. Ich war stolz darauf, dass dieser Mann und so viele Maenner der deutschen Geschichte sich damit begnuegten, ihren Namen der Nachwelt zu ueber-

C02571145

liefern, nicht ihren Titel. Nicht aus Bescheidenheit wollte ich 'Trommler' sein. Das ist das Hoechste, das andere ist eine Kleinigkeit."

After his stay in Landsberg Hitler no longer referred to himself as the "drummer." Occasionally he would describe himself in the words of St. Matthew, "as a voice crying in the wilderness," or as St. John the Baptist whose duty was to hew a path for him who was to come and lead the nation to power and glory. More frequently, however, he referred to himself as "the Fuehrer", a name chosen by Hess during their imprisonment. (901)

As time went on, it became clearer that he was thinking of himself as the Messiah and that it was he who was destined to lead Germany to glory. His references to the Bible became more frequent and the movement began to take on a religious atmosphere. Comparisons between Christ and himself became more numerous and found their way into his conversation and speeches. For example, he would say:

"When I came to Berlin a few weeks ago and looked at the traffic in the Kurfuerstendamm, the luxury, the perversion, the iniquity, the wanton display, and the Jewish materialism disgusted me so thoroughly, that I was almost beside myself. I nearly imagined myself to be Jesus Christ when He came to His Father's temple and found it taken by the money-changers. I can well imagine how He felt when He seized a whip and scourged them out." (903)

During his speech, according to Hanfstaengl, he swung his whip around violently as though to drive out the Jews and the forces of darkness, the enemies of Germany and German honor. Dietrich Eckart, who discovered Hitler as a possible leader and had witnessed this performance, said later, "When a man gets to the point of identifying himself with Jesus Christ, then he is ripe for an insane asylum." The identification in all this was not with Jesus Christ, the Crucified, but with Jesus Christ, the furious, lashing the crowds.

As a matter of fact, Hitler has very little admiration for Christ, the Crucified. Although he was brought up a Catholic, and received Communion, during the war, he severed his connection with the Church directly afterwards. This kind of Christ he considers soft and weak and unsuitable as a German Messiah. The latter must be hard and brutal if he is to save Germany and lead it to its destiny.

"My feeling as a Christian points me to my Lord and Saviour as a fighter. It points me to the man who once in loneliness, surrounded by only a few followers, recognized these Jews for what they were and summoned men to fight against them and who, God's truth! was greatest not as a sufferer but as a fighter. In boundless love, as a Christian and as a man, I read through the passage which tells us how the Lord rose at last in His might and seized the scourge to drive out of

36

C02571145

the Temple the brood of vipers and adders. How terrific was
the fight for the world against the Jewish poison." (M.N.O.
26)

And to Rauschning he once referred to "the Jewish Christ-creed with its
effeminate, pity-ethics."

It is not clear from the evidence whether the new State religion
was part of Hitler's plan or whether developments were such that it became feasible. It is true that Rosenberg had long advocated such a move,
but there is no evidence that Hitler was inclined to take such a drastic
step until after he had come to power. It is possible that he felt he needed
the power before he could initiate such a change, or it may be that his
series of successes were so startling that the people spontaneously adopted a religious attitude towards him which made the move more or less obvious. In any case, he has accepted this God-like role without any hesitation or embarrassment. White tells us that now when he is addressed
with the salutation, "Heil Hitler, our Savior," he bows slightly at the
compliment in the phrase — and believes it. (664)   As time goes on, it
becomes more and more certain that Hitler believes that he is really the
"Chosen One" and that in his thinking he conceives of himself as a second Christ who has been sent to institute in the world a new system of
values based on brutality and violence. He has fallen in love with the
image of himself in this role and has surrounded himself with his own
portraits.

His mission seems to lure him to still greater heights. Not content with the role of transitory savior it pushes him on to higher goals —
he must set the pattern for generations to come. Von Wiegand says:

"In vital matters Hitler is far from unmindful of the name
and record of success and failure he will leave to posterity."
(493)

Nor is he content to allow these patterns to evolve in a natural way. In
order to guarantee the future he feels that he alone can bind it to these
principles. He believes, therefore, that he must become an immortal to
the German people. Everything must be huge and befitting as a monument to the honor of Hitler. His idea of a permanent building is one which
will endure at least a thousand years. His highways must be known as
"Hitler Highways," and they must endure for longer periods of time than
the Napoleonic roads. He must always be doing the impossible and leaving his mark on the country. This is one of the ways in which he hopes
to stay alive in the minds of the German people for generations to come.

It is alleged by many writers, among them Haffner (418), Huss
(410) and Wagner (489), that he has already drawn extensive plans for
his own mausoleum. Our informants, who left Germany some time ago,
are not in a position to verify these reports. They consider them well
within the realm of possibility, however. This mausoleum is to be the

7

mecca of Germany after his death. It is to be a tremendous monument about 700 feet high, with all the details worked out so that the greatest psychological effect might be attained. It is also alleged that his first errand in Paris after the conquest in 1940 was a visit to the Dome des Invalides to study the monument to Napoleon. He found this lacking in many respects. For example, they had put him down in a hole which forced people to look down rather than high up.

> "I shall never make such a mistake," Hitler said suddenly. "I know how to keep my hold on people after I have passed on. I shall be the Fuehrer they look up at and go home to talk of and remember. My life shall not end in the mere form of death. It will, on the contrary, begin then." (410)

It was believed for a time that the Kehlstein had been originally built as an eternal mausoleum by Hitler. It seems, however, that if that was his original intention he has abandoned it in favor of something even more grandiose. Perhaps the Kehlstein was too inaccessible to enable large numbers of people to come and touch his tomb in order to become inspired. In any case, it seems that far more extravagant plans have been developed. His plan, if it is to be successful, needs constant emotional play on hysteric mass minds, and the more he can arrange the ways and means of achieving this, after he dies, the more assured he is of attaining his final goal.

> "He is firmly convinced that the furious pace and the epochal age in which he lived and moved (he really is convinced that he is the motivating force and the moulder of that age) will terminate soon after his death, swinging the world by nature and inclination into a long span of digestive process marked by a sort of quiet inactivity. People in his '1000 year Reich' will build monuments to him and go around to touch and look at the things he has built, he thought. He said as much on that glorified visit of his to Rome in 1938, adding that a thousand years hence the greatness and not the ruins of his own time must intrigue the people of those far-away days. For, believe it or not, that is how the mind of this man Hitler projects itself without a blush over the centuries." (410)

There was also a time a few years ago when he spoke a good deal about retiring when his work was done. It was assumed that he would then take up his residence in Berchtesgaden and sit as God who guides the destinies of the Reich until he dies. In July, 1933, while visiting the Wagner family, he talked at length about getting old and complained bitterly that ten years of valuable time had been lost between the Beer-hall Putsch in 1923 and his accession to power. This was all very regret-table since he predicted that it would take twenty-two years to get things in adequate shape so that he could turn them over to his successor. (936) It is supposed by some writers that during this period of retirement he would also write a book which would stand for eternity as a great bible of

National Socialism. (3) This is all rather interesting in view of Roehm's statement made many years ago:

> "Am liebsten taet er Heute schon in den Bergen sitzen und den lieben Gott spielen." (715)

A survey of all the evidence forces us to conclude that Hitler believes himself destined to become an Immortal Hitler, chosen by God to be the New Deliverer of Germany and the Founder of a new social order for the world. He firmly believes this and is certain that in spite of all the trials and tribulations through which he must pass he will finally attain that goal. The one condition is that he follow the dictates of the inner voice which have guided and protected him in the past. This conviction is not rooted in the truth of the ideas he imparts but is based on the conviction of his own personal greatness. (146) Howard K. Smith makes an interesting observation:

> "I was convinced that of all the millions on whom the Hitler Myth had fastened itself, the most carried away was Adolph Hitler, himself." (290)

We will have occasion in Part V to examine the origins of this conviction and the role it plays in Hitler's psychological economy.

Chapter Two

Hitler

As the German People Know Him

"How fortunate for governments that the people they administer don't think." Adolf Hitler

PART II

HITLER — AS THE GERMAN PEOPLE KNOW HIM

HITLER — AS THE GERMAN PEOPLE KNOW HIM

When we try to formulate a conception of Adolph Hitler as the German people know him we must not forget that their knowledge of him is limited by a controlled press. Many thousands of Germans have seen him in person, particularly in the past, and can use this experience as a basis for their individual conception of him.

Hitler, from a physical point of view, is not, however, a very imposing figure — certainly not the Platonic idea of a great, fighting Leader or the Deliverer of Germany and the creator of a New Reich. In height he is a little below average. His hips are wide and his shoulders relatively narrow. His muscles are flabby; his legs short, thin and spindly, the latter being hidden in the past by heavy boots and more recently by long trousers. He has a large torso and is hollow-chested to the point where it is said that he has his uniforms padded. From a physical point of view he could not pass the requirements to his own elite guard.

His dress, in the early days, was no more attractive. He frequently wore the Bavarian mountain costume of leather shorts with white shirt and suspenders. These were not always too clean and with his mouth full of brown, rotten teeth and his long dirty fingernails he presented rather a grotesque picture. (F. Wagner) At this time he also had a pointed beard, and his dark brown hair was parted in the middle and pasted down flat against his head with oil. Nor was his gait that of a soldier. "It was a very ladylike walk. Dainty little steps. Every few steps he cocked his right shoulder nervously, his left leg snapping up as he did so." (279) He also had a tic in his face which caused the corner of his lips curl upward. (483) When speaking he always dressed in a common-looking blue suit which robbed him of all distinctiveness. At the trial following the unsuccessful Beerhall Putsch Edgar Mowrer, who saw him for the first time, asked himself:

> "Was this provincial dandy, with his slick dark hair, his cutaway coat, his awkward gestures and glib tongue, the terrible rebel? He seemed for all the world like a traveling salesman for a clothing firm." (642)

Nor did he make a much better impression later on. Dorothy Thompson, upon her first meeting, described him in the following terms:

> "He is formless, almost faceless, a man whose countenance is a caricature, a man whose framework seems cartilaginous, without bones. He is inconsequent and voluble, ill poised and insecure. He is the very prototype of the little man." (307)

Smith (289) also found him "the apotheosis of the little man," funny looking, self-conscious and unsure of himself.

It may be supposed that this is only the judgment of American journalists who have a different standard of masculine beauty. However,

Hitler in Bavarian Costume

while testifying as a witness in the law court in 1923, Professor Max von Gruber of the University of Munich, and the most eminent eugenist in Germany, stated:

> "It was the first time I had seen Hitler close at hand. Face and head of inferior type, cross-breed; low receding forehead, ugly nose, broad cheekbones, little eyes, dark hair. Expression not of a man exercising authority in perfect self-command, but of raving excitement. At the end an expression of satisfied egotism." (575)

A great deal has been written about his eyes which have been described in terms of almost every color of the rainbow. As a matter of fact, they seem to be rather a bright blue — bordering on the violet. But it is not the color which has attracted people, but rather their depth and a glint which makes them appear to have a hypnotic quality. One finds stories like the following recurring over and over again in the literature. A policeman who is noted for his antipathy to the Nazi movement is sent to a Hitler meeting to maintain order. While standing at his post Hitler enters:

> "He gazed into the police officer's eye with that fatal hypnotizing and irresistible glare, which swept the poor officer right off his feet. Clicking to attention he confessed to me this morning: 'Since last night I am a National Socialist. Heil Hitler.'" (Fromm, 369)

These stories are not all from the Nazi propaganda agencies. Very reliable people, now in this country, have reported similar incidents among their own personal acquaintances. Even outstanding diplomats have commented on the nature of his eyes and the way in which he uses them when meeting people, often with disastrous effects.

Then there are others, like Rauschning, who find his look staring and dead — lacking in brilliance and the sparkle of genuine animation. (257) We need not dwell on his eyes and their peculiar quality, however, since relatively few Germans have come in such close contact with him that they could be seriously affected by them.

Whatever effect Hitler's personal appearance may have had on the German people in the past, it is safe to assume that this has been greatly tempered by millions of posters, pasted in every conceivable place, which show the Fuehrer as a fairly good-looking individual with a very determined attitude. In addition, the press, news-reels, etc., are continually flooded with carefully prepared photographs showing Hitler at his very best. These have undoubtedly, in the course of time, blotted out any unfavorable impressions he may have created as a real person in the past. The physical Hitler most Germans know now is a fairly presentable individual.

Hitler Entering Meeting in Hamburg

C02571145

The only other real contact the overwhelming majority of people have had with Hitler is through his voice. He was a tireless speaker and before he came to power would sometimes give as many as three or four speeches on the same day, often in different cities. Even his greatest opponents concede that he is the greatest orator that Germany has ever known. This is a great concession in view of the fact that the qualities of his voice are far from pleasant — many, in fact, find it distinctly unpleasant. It has a rasping quality which often breaks into a shrill falsetto when he becomes aroused. Nor is it his diction which makes him a great orator. In the early days this was particularly bad. It was a conglomeration of high German with an Austrian dialect which Tschuppik (317) describes as a "knoedlige Sprache." Nor was it the structure of his speeches which made him a great orator. On the whole, his speeches were sinfully long, badly structured and very repetitious. Some of them are positively painful to read but nevertheless, when he delivered them they had an extraordinary effect upon his audiences.

His power and fascination in speaking lay almost wholly in his ability to sense what a given audience wanted to hear and then to manipulate his theme in such a way that he would arouse the emotions of the crowd. Strasser says of this talent:

> "Hitler responds to the vibration of the human heart with the delicacy of a seismograph . . . enabling him, with a certainty with which no conscious gift could endow him, to act as a loudspeaker proclaiming the most secret desires, the least permissible instincts, the sufferings and personal revolts of a whole nation." (376)

Before coming to power almost all of his speeches centered around the following three themes: (1) the treason of the November criminals; (2) the rule of the Marxists must be broken; and (3) the world domination of the Jews. No matter what topic was advertised for a given speech he almost invariably would wind up on one or more of these three themes. And yet people liked it and would attend one meeting after another to hear him speak. It was not, therefore, so much what he said that appealed to his audiences as how he said it.

Even in the early days Hitler was a showman with a great sense for the dramatic. Not only did he schedule his speeches late in the evening when his audience would be tired and their resistance lowered through natural causes, but he would always send an assistant ahead of time to make a short speech and warm the audience up. Storm-troopers always played an important role at these meetings and would line the aisle through which he would pass. At the psychological moment, Hitler would appear in the door at the back of the hall. Then with a small group behind him, he would march through the rows of S.A. men to reach the speaker's table. He never glanced to the right or to the left as he came down the aisle and became greatly annoyed if anyone tried to accost him or hampered his progress. Whenever possible he would have a band present and they would strike up a lively military march as he came down the aisle.

When he began to speak he usually manifested signs of nervousness. Usually he was unable to say anything of consequence until he had gotten the feel of his audience. On one occasion, Heiden (499) reports, he was so nervous that he could think of nothing to say. In order to do something he picked up the table and moved it around on the platform. Then suddenly he got the "feel" and was able to go on. Price (241) describes his speaking in the following way:

> "The beginning is slow and halting. Gradually he warms up when the spiritual atmosphere of the great crowd is engendered. For he responds to this metaphysical contact in such a way that each member of the multitude feels bound to him by an individual link of sympathy."

All of our informants report the slow start, waiting for the feel of the audience. As soon as he has found it, the tempo increases in smooth rhythm and volume until he is shouting at the climax. Through all this, the listener seems to identify himself with Hitler's voice which becomes the voice of Germany.

This is all in keeping with Hitler's own conception of mass psychology as given in MEIN KAMPF where he says:

> "The psyche of the broad masses does not respond to anything weak or half-way. Like a woman, whose spiritual sensitiveness is determined less by abstract reason than by an indefinable emotional longing for fulfilling power and who, for that reason, prefers to submit to the strong rather than the weakling —the mass, too, prefers the ruler to a pleader."

And Hitler let them have it. NEWSWEEK (572) reported:

> "Women faint, when, with face purpled and contorted with effort, he blows forth his magic oratory. "

Flanner (558) says:

> "His oratory used to wilt his collar, unglue his forelock, glaze his eyes; he was like a man hypnotized, repeating himself into a frenzy."

Yeates-Brown (592):

> "He was a man transformed and possessed. We were in the presence of a miracle."

This fiery oratory was something new to the Germans and particularly to the slow-tongued, lower-class Bavarians. In Munich his shouting and gesturing were a spectacle men paid to see (216). It was not only his fiery oratory, however, that won the crowds to his cause. This

was certainly something new, but far more important was the serious-
ness with which his words were spoken.

> "Everyone of his words comes out charged with a powerful
> current of energy; at times it seems as if they are torn from
> the very heart of the man, causing him indescribable an-
> guish." (Fry, 577)

> "Leaning from the tribune, as if he were trying to impel his
> inner self into the consciousness of all these thousands, he
> was holding the masses and me with them under a hypnotic
> spell . . . It was clear that Hitler was feeling the exaltation of
> the emotional response now surging up toward him . . . his
> voice rising to passionate climaxes . . . his words were like a
> scourge. When he stopped speaking his chest was still heav-
> ing with emotion." (Ludecke, 164)

Many writers have commented upon his ability to hypnotize his audiences. Stanley High (453) reports:

> "When, at the climax, he sways from one side to the other
> his listeners sway with him; when he leans forward they also
> lean forward and when he concludes they either are awed
> and silent or on their feet in a frenzy."

Unquestionably, as a speaker, he has had a powerful influence
on the common run of German people. His meetings were always crowded and by the time he got through speaking he had completely numbed
the critical faculties of his listeners to the point where they were willing
to believe almost anything he said. He flattered them and cajoled them.
He hurled accusations at them one moment and amused them the next
by building up straw men which he promptly knocked down. His tongue
was like a lash which whipped up the emotions of his audience. And
somehow he always managed to say what the majority of the audience
were already secretly thinking but could not verbalize. When the audience began to respond, it affected him in return. Before long due to this
reciprocal relationship, he and his audience became intoxicated with the
emotional appeal of his oratory. (Strasser, 295)

It was this Hitler that the German people knew at first hand.
Hitler, the fiery orator, who tirelessly rushed from one meeting to another,
working himself to the point of exhaustion in their behalf. Hitler, whose
heart and soul were in the Cause and who struggled endlessly against
overwhelming odds and obstacles to open their eyes to the true state of
affairs. Hitler, who could arouse their emotions and channelize them
towards goals of national aggrandizement. Hitler the courageous, who
dared to speak the truth and defy the national authorities as well as the
international oppressors. It was a sincere Hitler that they knew, whose
words burned into the most secret recesses of their minds and rebuked
them for their own shortcomings. It was the Hitler who would lead them
back to self-respect because he had faith in them.

Hitler Addressing an Audience

18

49

C02571145

This fundamental conception of Hitler made a beautiful foundation for a propaganda build-up. He was so convincing on the speaker's platform and appeared to be so sincere in what he said that the majority of his listeners were ready to believe almost anything good about him because they wanted to believe it. The Nazi propaganda agencies were not slow in making the most of their opportunities.

Hitler, himself, had provided an excellent background for a propaganda build-up. From the earliest days of his political career he had steadfastly refused to divulge anything about his personal life, past or present. To his most immediate associates he was, in reality, a man of mystery. There was no clearing away of unpleasant incidents to be done before the building-up process could begin. In fact, the more secrecy he maintained about his personal life the more curious his followers became. This was, indeed, fertile ground on which to build a myth or legend.

The Nazi propaganda machine devoted all its efforts to the task of portraying Hitler as something extra-human. Everything he did was written up in such a way that it portrayed his superlative character. If he does not eat meat, drink alcoholic beverages, or smoke, it is not due to the fact that he has some kind of inhibition or does it because he believes it will improve his health. Such things are not worthy of the Fuehrer. He abstains from these because he is following the example of the great German, Richard Wagner, or because he has discovered that

Hitler's Meals are Very Simple. Only One Pot for Everybody.

50

it increases his energy and endurance to such a degree that he can give much more of himself to the creation of the new German Reich.

Such abstinence also indicates, according to the propaganda, that the Fuehrer is a person with tremendous will-power and self-discipline. Hitler himself fosters this conception, according to Hanfstaengl, for, when someone asked him how he managed to give up these things, he replied: "It is a matter of will. Once I make up my mind not to do a thing, I just don't do it. And once that decision is made, it is taken for always. Is that so wonderful?"

The same is true in the field of sex. As far as the German people know he has no sex life and this too is clothed, not as an abnormality, but as a great virtue. The Fuehrer is above human weaknesses of this sort and von Wiegand (494) tells us that he "has a profound contempt for the weakness in men for sex and the fools that it makes of them". Hanfstaengl reports that Hitler frequently makes the statement that he will never marry a woman since Germany is his only bride. However, Hitler with his deep insight into human nature, appreciates these weaknesses in others and is tolerant of them. He does not even condemn them or forbid them among his closest associates.

He is also portrayed in the propaganda as the soul of kindliness and generosity. Endless stories that illustrate these virtues are found over and over again in the literature. Price (236) cites a typical example: an attractive young peasant girl tries to approach him but is prevented from doing so by the guards. She bursts into tears and Hitler, seeing her distress, inquires into the cause. She tells him that her fiance had been expelled from Austria for his Nazi principles and that he cannot find work and consequently they cannot get married. Hitler is deeply touched. He promises to find the young man a job and, in addition, completely furnishes a flat for them to live in, even down to a baby's cot. Every attempt is made to present him as extremely human, with a deep feeling for the problems of ordinary people.

A great many writers, both Nazi and anti-Nazi, have written extensively about his great love for children and the Nazi press is certainly full of pictures showing Hitler in the company of little tots. It is alleged that when he is at Berchtesgaden he always has the children from the neighborhood visit him in the afternoon and that he serves them candy, ice cream, cake, etc. Phayre (225) says, "Never was there a middle-aged bachelor who so delighted in the company of children". Princess Olga reported that when she visited Hitler in Berlin and the topic of children came up during the conversation, Hitler's eyes filled with tears. The Nazi press had made extremely good use of this and endless stories accompany the pictures. Likewise, a great deal is written about his fondness for animals, particularly dogs. Here again, there are numberless pictures to prove it is so. As far as dogs are concerned, the propaganda build-up is Hitler's modesty and simplicity. His successes point in other respects. One writer even went so far as to attribute his vegetarianism to his inability to tolerate the thought of animals being slaughtered for human consumption (405). Hitler is pictured as an "affable lord of the manor", full of gentleness, kindliness and helpfulness, or, as Oechsner puts it, he is the Great Comforter—father, husband, brother or son to every German who lacks or has lost such a relative (668).

Another trait which has received a great deal of comment in the propaganda is probably fairly near the truth but it goes far beyond that have never gone to his head. At bottom he is still the simple soul he was when he founded the Party and his greatest joy is to be considered as "one of the boys". As proof of this they point to the fact that he has never sought a crown, that he never appears in gaudy uniforms or does a great deal of entertaining. Even after he came to power he continued to wear his old trench coat and slouch hat for a time and when he donned a uniform it was always that of a simple storm-trooper. Much was written about his fondness for visits from early acquaintances and how he loved to sit down in the midst of his busy day in order to talk over old times. There was really nothing he liked better than to frequent his old haunts and meet old friends while he was in Munich, or to take part in their festivities. At heart he was still a worker and his interests were always with the working classes with whom he felt thoroughly at home.

Hitler is also a man of incredible energy and endurance. His day consists of sixteen and eighteen hours of uninterrupted work. He is absolutely tireless when it comes to working for Germany and its future welfare and no personal pleasures are permitted to interfere with the carrying out of his mission. The ordinary man in the street cannot imagine a human being in Hitler's position not taking advantage of his opportunity. He can only imagine himself in the same position revelling in luxuries and yet here is Hitler who scorns them all. His only conclusion is that Hitler is not an ordinary mortal. Phillips (868) reports the case of a young Nazi who once confided to him: "I would die for Hitler, but I would not change places with Hitler. At least when I wake every morning I can say, 'Heil Hitler!', but this man, he has no fun in life. No smoking, no drinking, no women!—only work, until he falls asleep at night!"

A great deal is made of Hitler's determination. It is pointed out over and over again that he never gives up once he has made up his mind to attain a particular goal. No matter how rough the road, he plods along in unswerving determination. Even though he receives serious set-backs and the situation appears to be hopeless, he never loses faith and always gets what he goes after. He refuses to be coerced into compromises of any sort and is always ready to assume the full responsibility for his actions. The great trials and tribulations through which the Party had

Typical Picture Illustrating Hitler's Love for Children

Typical Picture Illustrating Hitler's Love for Children

to pass on its way to power are cited over and over again and all the credit is given to Hitler and his fanatical faith in the future. Even his refusal to permit ordinary scruples to get in his way is given as a sign of his greatness. The fact that he did not communicate with his family for over ten years becomes a great virtue since it meant a severe deprivation to the young man who was determined to make something of himself before he returned home!

A great deal of publicity has also been given to his breadth of vision, ability to penetrate the future and his ability to organize both the Party and the country in preparation for obstacles they will have to overcome. According to the propagandists, Hitler is the soul of efficiency and has an extraordinary power of resolving conflicts and simplifying problems which have stumped all experts in the past. In fact, his infallibility and incorruptibility throughout are not only implied but openly stated in no uncertain terms.

He is also a person of great patience who would never spill a drop of human blood if it could possibly be avoided. Over and over again one hears of his great patience with the democracies, with Czechoslovakia and with Poland. But here, as in his private life, he never loses control of his emotions. Fundamentally, he is a man of peace who desires nothing quite so much as to be left alone to work out the destiny of Germany in a quiet and constructive manner. For he is a builder at heart and an artist, and these prove that the creative and constructive elements in his nature are predominant.

This does not mean, however, that he is a coward. On the contrary, he is a person of outstanding courage. His way of life is proof of this, as well as his enviable record during the last war. A great many stories about his decorations for bravery have been circulated and particularly for his outstanding heroism when he was awarded the Iron Cross first-class. The fact that the stories of his performance vary from one time to another does not seem to disturb the people in the least.

Fundamentally, according to the Nazi press, Hitler is a man of steel. He is well aware of his mission and no amount of persuasion, coercion, sacrifices or unpleasant duties can persuade him to alter his course. In the face of all sorts of disasters and disagreeable happenings and necessary measures, he never loses his nerve for a moment. But he is not hard in human qualities. He places loyalty and justice as the two of the greatest virtues and observes them with scrupulous care. Loyalty means so much to him that the inscription over his door at Berchtesgaden reads, "Meine Ehre heisst Treue". He is the acme of German honor and purity; the Resurrector of the German family and home. He is the greatest architect of all time; the greatest military genius in all history. He has an inexhaustible fount of knowledge. He is a man of action and the creator of new social values. He is indeed, according to the

Nazi propaganda bureau, the paragon of all virtues. A few typical examples may illustrate the extent to which they are carried in their praise of him.

"Zunaechst Hitler selbst: Hitler is der Mann ohne Kompromiss. Vor allem kennt er keinen Kompromiss mit sicht selbts. Er hat einen einzigen Gedanken, der ihn leitet: Deutschland wieder aufzurichten. Diese Idee verdraengt alles um ihn. Er kennt kein Privatleben. Er kennt Familienleben ebensowenig, wie er ein Laster kennt. Er ist die Verkoerperung des nationalen Willens.

"Die Ritterschaft eines heiligen Zieles, das sich kein Mensch hoher steken kann: Deutschland! . . . Hitler . . . ueberracht (durch) seine warme Liebenswuerdigkeit. Ueber die Ruhe und Kraft, die beinahe physisch von diesem Mann ausstraht. Man waechst in der Naehe dieses Menschen . . . Wie er auf alle Dinge reagiert! . . . Eisern werden die Zuege und die Worte fallen wie Bein . . . Der klassische Ernst, mit dem Hitler und seine um den Fuehrer gescharten Mitarbeiter ihre Sendung nehmen, hat in der Geschichte dieser Welt nur wenige Paralellen." Czech-Jochberg: Adolph Hitler und sein Stab, 1933. (861)

". . . auch in den privaten Dingen des Lebens Vorbildlichkeit und menschliche Groesse . . . ob Hitler . . . umbraust wird vom jubelnden Zuruf der Strassenarbeiter, oder aufgewuehlt und erschuettert am Lager seine ermordeten Kameraden steht, immer ist um ihn diese Hoheit und tiefste Menschlichkeit . . . dieser einzigartigen Perseonlichkeit . . . ein grosser und guter Mensch. Hitler ist ein universaler Geist. Es ist unmoeglich der Mannigfaltigkeit seines Wesens mit 100 Aufnahmen gerecht zu werden. Auch auf diesen beiden Bebieten (Architecture and History) ist Hitler eine unangreifbare Autoritaet. Unsere Zeit wird diesen Ueberragenden vielleicht verehren und lieben, aber wird ihn nicht in seiner grossen Tief ermessen koennen." Hoffman: Hitler, wie ihn keiner kennt, 1932 (899)

"Hitler is a modest man — and the world needs modest men. Therefore the people love him. Like every good leader, he must be an efficient follower. He makes himself the humblest disciple of himself, the severest of all disciplinarians with himself. In fact, Hitler is a modern monk, with the three knots of Poverty, Chastity and Obedience tied in his invisible girdle. A zealot among zealots. He eats no meat, drinks no wine, does not smoke. I am told he takes for himself no salary but lives privately from the income of his book, "Mein Kampf" . . . Surplus funds he turns back to the S.A. His work day consists of eighteen hours, usually, and he often falls asleep in the last hour of his work. There have been four women in his life — but only to help him along with service and money . . . He once gave a lecture at Bayreuth on Wagner and "Deutsche Lieder" that astounded the musical critics and revealed him as a musical scholar of parts . . . Sheer opportunism never lured him as much as the opportunity to

25

> preach his doctrines. His quality is Messianic; his spiritual
> trend is ascetic; his reaction is medieval . . ." Phillips: Ger-
> many Today and Tomorrow.   (868)

Hitler not only knows about all these writings but since he has always been the guiding spirit in all German propaganda and usually plans the broad lines that are to be followed, it is safe to assume that he himself is responsible for the instigation and development of this mythical personality. When we look back over the development of this build-up we can see clearly that Hitler, from the very beginning, planned on making himself a mythological figure. He opens MEIN KAMPF with the following passage:

> "In this little town on the river Inn, Bavarian by blood and
> Austrian by nationality, gilded by the light of German mar-
> tyrdom, there lived, at the end of the '80's of the last century,
> my parents: the father a faithful civil servant, the mother
> devoting herself to the cares of the household and looking
> after her children with eternally the same loving kindness."

This is the classic way of beginning a fairy tale rather than a serious autobiography or a political treatise. In the very first sentence of the book he implies that Fate was already smiling on him at the time of his birth, for it reads:

> "Today I consider it my good fortune that Fate designated
> Braunau on the Inn as the place of my birth."

As soon as Hitler came to power new weapons for self-aggrand-izement were put into the hands of the propagandists and they made good use of them. Unemployment dropped off rapidly, roads that the Germans never dreamed of sprung up over night, new and imposing buildings were erected with astounding rapidity. The face of Germany was being lifted at an incredible speed. Hitler was keeping his promises; he was accomplishing the impossible. Every success in diplomacy, every social reform was heralded as world-shaking in its importance. And for each success, Hitler modestly accepted all the credit. It was always Hitler that did this, and Hitler who did that, provided these acts were spectacular and met with the approval of the public. If they happened to meet with disapproval, it was always one of his assistants who was to blame. Every effort was made to cultivate the attitude that Hitler was infallible and was carrying through his mission of saving Germany.

It was not long before the German people were prepared to take the short step of seeing Hitler, not as a man, but as a Messiah of Germany. Public meetings and particularly the Nurnburg took on a religious atmosphere. All the stagings were designated to create a supernatural and religious atmosphere and Hitler's entry was more befitting a god than a man. In Berlin one of the large art shops on Unter den Linden exhibited a large portrait of Hitler in the center of its display window. Hitler's portrait was entirely surrounded as though by a halo, with various copies of a painting of Christ (High, 453). Notes appeared in the press to the effect that, "Als er sprach, hoerte man den Mantel Gottes durch den Saal rauschen!" Ziemar reports that on the side of a hill in Odenwald, conspicious as a waterfall, painted on white canvas were the black words:

> "We believe in Holy Germany
> Holy Germany is Hitler!
> We believe in Holy Hitler! !" (763)

Roberts reports:

> "In Munich in the early autumn of 1936 I saw colored pictures of Hitler in the actual silver garments of the Knights of the Grail; but these were soon withdrawn. They gave the show away; they were too near the truth of Hitler's mentality." (876)

Teeling (565) writes that at the Nurnburg Nazi Party Rally in September, 1937, there was a hugh photograph of Hitler underneath which was the inscription, "In the beginning was the Word . . .". He also says that the Mayor of Hamburg assured him, "We need no priests or parsons. We communicate direct with God through Adolph Hitler. He has many Christ-like qualities." Soon these sentiments were introduced by official circles. Rauschning (552) reports that the Party has adopted this creed:

> "Wir alle glauben auf dieser Erde an Adolph Hitler, unseren Fuehrer, und wir bekennen, dass der National-sozialismus der allein seligmachende Glaube fuer unser Volk ist."

A Rhenish group of German "Christians" in April, 1937, passed this resolution:

> "Hitler's word is God's law, the decrees and laws which represent it possess divine authority." (550)

And Reichsminister for Church Affairs, Hans Kerrl, says:

> "There has arisen a new authority as to what Christ and Christianity really are — that is Adolph Hitler. Adolph Hitler . . . is the true Holy Ghost." (749)

This is the way Hitler hopes to pave his path to immortality. It has been carefully planned and consistently executed in a step by step fashion. The Hitler the German people know is fundamentally the fiery orator who fascinated them and this has gradually been embroidered by the propaganda until he is now presented to them as a full-fledged deity. Everything else is carefully concealed from them as a whole. How many Germans believe it we do not know. Some, certainly, believe it wholeheartedly. Dorothy Thompson writes of such a case:

> "At Garmisch I met an American from Chicago. He had been at Oberammergau, at the Passion Play. 'These people are all crazy,' he said. 'This is not a revolution, it's a revival. They think Hitler is God. Believe it or not, a German woman sat next to me at the Passion Play and when they hoisted

27

Jesus on the Cross, she said, 'There he is. That is our Fuehrer, our Hitler.' And when they paid out the thirty pieces of silver to Judas, she said: 'That is Roehm, who betrayed the Leader.' " (568)

Extreme cases of this kind are probably not very numerous but it would be amazing if a small degree of the same type of thinking had not seeped into the picture of Hitler which many Germans hold.

Chapter Three

Hitler

As His Associates Know Him

"All propaganda has to be popular and has to accommodate itself to the comprehension of the least intelligent of those whom it seeks to reach."   Adolf Hitler

PART III

HITLER — AS HIS ASSOCIATES KNOW HIM

HITLER — AS HIS ASSOCIATES KNOW HIM

The picture the Nazi propaganda machine has painted of Hitler certainly seems like an extravagant one. Even if we ignore the deifying elements, it seems like the fantasy of a superman — the paragon of all virtues. Extraordinary as it may seem, however, there are times at which he approximates such a personality and wins the respect and admiration of all his associates.

At such times he is a veritable demon for work and often works for several days on end with little or no sleep. His powers of concentration are extraordinary and he is able to penetrate very complex problems and reduce them to a few simple, fundamental factors. He prides himself on this talent and has said to various people:

> "I have the gift of reducing all problems to their simplest foundations . . . A gift for tracing back all theories to their roots in reality."

And he really has it. Unencumbered with abstract theories or traditional points of view and prejudices he is able to look at complex problems in a rather naive way and pick out the most salient and significant elements and apply them to the present situation in a fairly simple and workable manner. To be sure, he never solves the entire problem in this way but only the human elements involved. Since this is the part which interests him most and produces immediate results, it has been rated very highly and has won the admiration of his close associates from the earliest days of his political career.

During these periods of activity Hitler is completely absorbed in the task confronting him. Conference follows conference with great rapidity. His judgments are quick and decisive. He is impatient to get things done and expects everyone to apply himself with an ardor equal to his own. He, therefore, demands great sacrifices from his associates.

At such times, however, he is also very human. He shows an unusual degree of considerateness toward others and a certain tolerance of their weaknesses. When he calls a halt for meals he will not eat until his entire staff has been served. When an overzealous servant insists on serving him before others he will often get up and take the plate over to one of his lowly assistants. During all of this he is in the best of spirits and jokes with everyone around him.

He has an extraordinary memory and continuously recalls amusing incidents from the past lives of those around him. These he tells to his staff at large. He is an excellent mimic and often plays out the role of the individual involved to the great amusement of the staff while the individual must sit by and witness the performance much to his own embarrassment. Nevertheless he is thoroughly flattered that the Fuehrer should single him out and remember him and his actions in such detail. During these periods Hitler is also the soul of kindliness and generosity. He acts more like a big brother to his staff than as a Fuehrer and manages to endear himself to each and every one of them.

But, underneath, he is every inch the Fuehrer. He displays extraordinary courage and determination. He shows a great deal of initiative and is willing to assume full responsibility for the wisdom of the course he has mapped out. He is very persuasive and is able to muster and organize his people into an efficient smooth-running unit. Personal frictions disappear, for the time being, and everybody has but a single thought in mind: To do what the Fuehrer wishes.

He works with great certainty and security and appears to have the situation entirely in hand. All kinds of facts and figures relevant to the problem flow from him without the slightest hesitation or effort, much to the amazement of those about him. He can cite the tonnages of ships in various navies:

> "He knows exactly what kind of armament, the kind of armor plates, the weight, the speed and the number of the crew of every ship in the British Navy. He knows the number of rotations of airplane motors in every model and type existent. He knows the number of shots a machine gun fires a minute, whether it is a light, medium or heavy one, whether it was made in the United States, Czecho-Slovakia or France."
> (Russell, 747)

Then, too, his staff has learned from past experience, that when Hitler is in one of these moods he approximates infallibility particularly when the support of the people is needed to carry through the project on which he is engaged. This may seem like an unwarranted statement but, if our study is to be complete, we must appraise his strengths as well as his weaknesses. It can scarcely be denied that he has some extraordinary abilities where the psychology of the average man is concerned. He has been able, in some manner or other, to unearth and apply successfully many factors pertaining to group psychology, the importance of which has not been generally recognized and some of which we might adopt to good advantage. These might be briefly summarized as follows:

(1) Full appreciation of the importance of the masses in the success of any movement. Hitler has phrased this very well in MEIN KAMPF:

> "The lack of knowledge of the internal driving forces of great changes led to an insufficient evaluation of the importance of the great masses of the people; from this resulted the scanty interest in the social question, the deficient courting of the soul of the nation's lower classes . . . ." (p. 138)

(2) Recognition of the inestimable value of winning the support of youth; realization of the immense momentum given a social movement

C02571145

by the wild fervor and enthusiasm of young people as well as the importance of early training and indoctrination.

(3) Recognition of the role of women in advancing a new movement and of the fact that the reactions of the masses as a whole have many feminine characteristics. As early as 1923, he said to Hanfstaengl (902):

> "Do you know the audience at a circus is just like a woman (Die Masse, das Volk is wie ein Weib). Someone who does not understand the intrinsicly feminine character of the masses will never be an effective speaker. Ask yourself: 'What does a woman expect from a man?' Clearness, decision, power and action. What we want is to get the masses to act. Like a woman, the masses fluctuate between extremes .... The crowd is not only like a woman, but women constitute the most important element in an audience. The women usually lead, then follow the children and at last, when I have already won over the whole family — follow the fathers."

And in MEIN KAMPF, he writes:

> "The people, in an overwhelming majority, are so feminine in their nature and attitude that their activities and thoughts are motivated. less by sober consideration than by feeling and sentiment." (p. 237)

(4) The ability to feel, identify with and express in passionate language the deepest needs and sentiments of the average German and to present oportunities or possibilities for their gratification.

(5) Capacity to appeal to the most primitive, as well as the most ideal inclinations in man, to arouse the basest instincts and yet cloak them with nobility, justifying all actions as means to the attainment of an ideal goal. Hitler realized that men will not combine and dedicate themselves to a common purpose unless this purpose be an ideal one capable of survival beyond their generation. He has also perceived that although men will die only for an ideal their continued zest and enterprise can be maintained only by a succession of more immediate and earthly satisfactions.

(6) Appreciation of the fact that the masses are as hungry for a sustaining ideology in political action as they are for daily bread. Any movement which does not satisfy this spiritual hunger in the masses will not mobilize their whole-hearted support and is destined to fail.

> "All force which does not spring from a firm spiritual foundation will be hesitating and uncertain. It lacks the stability which can only rest on a fanatical view of life. (MK 222)
> "Every attempt at fighting a view of life by means of force will finally fail, unless the fight against it represents the form of an attack for the sake of a new spiritual direction. Only in the struggle of two views of life with each other can

the weapon of brute force, used continuously and ruthlessly, bring about the decision in favor of the side it supports." (MK 223)

(7) The ability to portray conflicting human forces in vivid, concrete imagery that is understandable and moving to the ordinary man. This comes down to the use of metaphors in the form of imagery which, as Aristotle has said, is the most powerful force on earth.

(8) The faculty of drawing on the traditions of the people and by reference to the great classical mythological themes evoke the deepest unconscious emotions of the audience. The fact that the unconscious mind is more intensely affected by the great eternal symbols and themes is not generally understood by most modern speakers and writers.

(9) Realization that enthusiastic political action does not take place if the emotions are not deeply involved.

(10) Appreciation of the willingness, almost desire, of the masses to sacrifice themselves on the altar of social improvement or spiritual values.

(11) Realization of the importance of artistry and dramatic intensity in conducting large meetings, rallies and festivals. This involves not only an appreciation of what the artist — the writer, musician and painter — can accomplish in the way of evoking emotional responses but also the leader's recognition of the necessity of his participation in the total dramatic effect as chief character and hero. Hitler has become master of all the arts of high-lighting his own role in the movement for a Greater Germany. Shirer (157) describes this very well:

"A searchlight plays upon his lone figure as he slowly walks through the hall, never looking to right or left, his right hand raised in salute, his left hand at the buckle of his belt. He never smiles — it is a religious rite, this procession of the modern Messiah incarnate. Behind him are his adjutants and secret service men. But his figure alone is flooded with light.

"By the time Hitler has reached the rostrum, the masses have been so worked upon that they are ready to do his will. . . ."

(12) A keen appreciation of the value of slogans, catchwords, dramatic phrases and happy epigrams in penetrating the deeper levels of the psyche. In speaking to Hanfstaengl on this point he once used the following figure of speech:

"There is only so much room in a brain, so much wall space, as it were, and if you furnish it with your slogans, the opposition has no place to put up any pictures later on, because the apartment of the brain is already crowded with your furniture." Hanfstaengl adds that Hitler has always admired the use the Catholic Church made of slogans and has tried to imitate it." (899)

Spectacular and Dramatic Effects in Meetings

Spectacular and Dramatic Effects in Meetings

Spectacular and Dramatic Effects in Meetings

(13) Realization of a fundamental loneliness and feeling of isolation in people living under modern conditions and a craving to "belong" to an active group which carries a certain status, provides cohesiveness and gives the individual a feeling of personal worth and belongingness.

(14) Appreciation of the value underlying a hierarchical political organization which affords direct contact with each individual.

(15) Ability to surround himself with and maintain the allegiance of a group of devoted aides whose talents complement his own.

(16) Appreciation of winning confidence from the people by a show of efficiency within the organization and government. It is said that foods and supplies are already in the local warehouses when the announcement concerning the date of distribution is made. Although they could be distributed immediately the date is set for several weeks ahead in order to create an impression of super-efficiency and win the confidence of the people. Every effort is made to avoid making a promise which cannot be fulfilled at precisely the appointed time.

(17) Appreciation of the important role played by little things which affect the everyday life of the ordinary man in building up and maintaining the morale of the people.

(18) Full recognition of the fact that the overwhelming majority of the people want to be led and are ready and willing to submit if the leader can win their respect and confidence. Hitler has been very successful in this respect because he has been able to convince his followers of his own self-confidence and because he has guessed right on so many occasions that he has created the impression of infallibility.

Spectacular and Dramatic Effects in Meetings

C02571145

(19) This was largely possible because he is naturally a tactical genius. His timing of decisions and actions has almost been uncanny. As Thyssen puts it:

> "Sometimes his intelligence is astonishing .... miraculous political intuition, devoid of all moral sense, but extraordinarily precise. Even in a very complex situation he discerns what is possible and what is not."

(20) Hitler's strongest point is, perhaps, his firm belief in his mission and, in public, the complete dedication of his life to its fulfillment. It is the spectacle of a man whose convictions are so strong that he sacrifices himself for the cause which appeals to others and induces them to follow his example. This demands a fanatical stubbornness which Hitler possesses to a high degree.

> "Only a storm of glowing passion can turn the destinies of nations, but this passion can only be roused by a man who carries it within himself."

(21) He also has the ability to appeal to and arouse the sympathetic concern and protectiveness of his people, to represent himself as the bearer of their burdens and their future, with the result that he becomes a personal concern to individuals and many, particularly the women, feel tenderly and compassionately about him. They must always be careful not to inflict undue annoyance or suffering on the Fuehrer.

(22) Hitler's ability to repudiate his own conscience in arriving at political decisions has eliminated the force which usually checks and complicates the forward-going thoughts and resolutions of most socially responsible statesmen. He has, therefore, been able to take that course of action which appeals to him as most effective without pulling his punches. The result has been that he has frequently outwitted his adversaries and attained ends which would not have been as easily attained by a normal course. Nevertheless, it has helped to build up the myth of his infallibility and invincibility.

(23) Equally important has been his ability to persuade others to repudiate their individual consciences and assume that role himself. He can then decree for the individual what is right and wrong, permissible or unpermissible and can use them freely in the attainment of his own ends. As Goering has said: "I have no conscience. My conscience is Adolph Hitler."

(24) This has enabled Hitler to make full use of terror and mobilize the fears of the people which he evaluated with an almost uncanny precision.

(25) He has a capacity for learning from others even though he may be violently opposed to everything they believe and stand for. The use of terror, for example, he says he learned from the Communists, the

use of slogans from the Catholic Church, the use of propaganda from the democracies, etc.

(26) He is a master of the art of propaganda. Ludecke writes:

"He has a matchless instinct for taking advantage of every breeze to raise a political whirlwind. No official scandal was so petty that he could not magnify it into high treason; he could ferret out the most deviously ramified corruption in high places and plaster the town with the bad news." (169)

His primary rules were: never allow the public to cool off; never admit a fault or wrong; never concede that there may be some good in your enemy; never leave room for alternatives; never accept blame; concentrate on one enemy at a time and blame him for everything that goes wrong; people will believe a big lie sooner than a little one; and if you repeat it frequently enough people will sooner or later believe it.

(27) He has the "never-say-die" spirit. After some of his severest set-backs he has been able to get his immediate associates together and begin making plans for a "come-back." Events which would crush most individuals, at least temporarily, seem to act as stimulants to greater efforts in Hitler.

These are some of Hitler's outstanding talents and capacities. They have enabled him to attain a position of unprecedented power in an incredibly short period of time, over a rarely used route. No other Nazi in a high position possesses these abilities in any comparable degree and consequently they could not displace him in the minds of the masses.

His associates recognize these capacities in Hitler and they admire and respect his extraordinary leadership qualities, particularly the influence he has over people. In addition they love him for his very human qualities when he is at his best and is engaged in some important undertaking. These are aspects of Hitler's personality we should never lose sight of when evaluating his hold on his associates or on the German people. He has a magnetic quality about him which, together with his past accomplishments, wins the allegiance of people and seems to rob them of their critical functions. It is a bond which does not easily dissolve even in the face of evidence that he is not always what he pretends to be — in fact is more often than not, the exact opposite.

We have reviewed Hitler's strength and briefly portrayed his character when he is at his best. It is now time to look at the other side of his personality — the side which is known only to those who are on fairly intimate terms with him.

Perhaps the truest words that Goebbels ever wrote are: "The Fuehrer does not change. He is the same now as he was when he was a boy." (387)

If we glance at his boyhood we find that Hitler was far from a model student. He studied what he wanted to study and did fairly well in these subjects. Things which did not interest him he simply ignored even though his marks were "unsatisfactory" or "failing." For over a year before his mother died, he did nothing, as far as can be determined, except lie around the house or occasionally paint a few water-colors. Although they were in difficult financial circumstances he did not seek work or try to improve himself in school. He was self-willed, shy and inactive. In Vienna, after his mother died, he continued this pattern even though he was frequently on the verge of starvation and reduced to begging on the streets. Hanisch, who was his flop-house buddy, reports that "he was never an ardent worker, was unable to get up in the morning, had difficulty in getting started and seemed to be suffering from a paralysis of the will." As soon as he had sold a picture and had a little money in his pocket he stopped work and spent his time listening to parliament, reading newspapers in the cafes, or delivering lengthy political dissertations to his fellows in the hostel. This behavior he justified on the grounds that "he must have leisure, he was not a coolie." When Hanisch asked him one day what he was waiting for, Hitler replied: "I don't know myself."

As an adult he is still this little boy except when he is in one of his active moods. In 1931. Billing wrote:

> "Die inneren Schwierigkeiten einer Regierung Hitlers werden in der Person Hitler selbts liegen. Hitler wird nicht umhin koennen, sich an eine geregelte Geistige Taetigkeit zu gewoehnen." (588)

Ludecke (168) also wrote:

> "He had a typical Austrian 'Schlamperei.' He suffered from an all-embracing disorderliness. Naturally this grew less in time but in the beginning it was apparent in everything."

It was indeed so apparent that early in the history of the movement the party engaged a secretary whose duty it was to keep track of Hitler and see to it that he fulfilled his duties and obligations. The move was only partially succesful, however: "Hitler was always on the go but rarely on time" (Ludecke, 168). He is still rarely on time and frequently keeps important foreign diplomats, as well as his own staff, waiting for considerable periods of time.

He is unable to maintain any kind of a working schedule. His hours are most irregular and he may go to bed any time between midnight and seven o'clock in the morning and get up anywhere from nine o'clock in the morning to two in the afternoon. In later years the hours tended to get later and it was unusual for him, just before the war, to go to bed before daybreak. The night, however, was not spent in working as his propaganda agents allege but in viewing one or two feature movies,

39

endless newsreels, listening to music, entertaining film stars or just sitting around chatting with his staff. He seemed to have a violent dislike for going to bed or being alone. Frequently, he would ring for his adjutants in the middle of the night, after his guests had gone home, and demand that they sit up and talk to him. It was not that he had anything to say and often the adjutants would fall asleep listening to him talk about nothing of importance. As long as one of them remained awake, however, he would not be offended. There was an unwritten law among

his immediate staff never to ask a question at these early morning sessions because to do so might get Hitler off on another subject and force them to remain for another hour.

Hitler sleeps very badly and has been in the habit for some years of taking a sleeping powder every night before retiring. It is possible that he demands someone to be with him in the hope that the powder will take effect and he will be overcome with sleep. His behavior, however, is not in keeping with this hypothesis for he carries on a monologue and frequently gets very much stirred up about the topic. This is hardly conducive to sleep and we must suppose that there is some other reason for his late hours. Even after he has dismissed his adjutants and goes to bed he usually takes an armful of illustrated periodicals with him. These are usually magazines with pictures concerning naval and military matters and American magazines are usually included. Shirer (280) reports that he has been informed that since the war broke out Hitler has been keeping better hours and regularly has his first breakfast at seven A.M. and his second breakfast at nine A.M. This may have been so during the early days of the war but it is very doubtful that Hitler could keep up this schedule for any length of time. Rauschning (275) claims that Hitler has a bed compulsion which demands that the bed be made in a particular way with the quilt folded according to a prescribed pattern and that a man must make the bed, before he can go to sleep. We have no other information on this subject but from his general psychological structure such a compulsion would be possible.

His working day before the war was equally disorderly. Rauschning reports, "He does not know how to work steadily. Indeed, he is incapable of working." He dislikes desk work and seldom glances at the piles of reports which are placed on his desk daily. No matter how important these may be or how much his adjutants may urge him to attend to a particular matter, he refuses to take them seriously unless it happens to be a project which interests him. On the whole, few reports interest him unless they deal with military or naval affairs or political matters. He seldom sits in a cabinet meeting because they bore him. On several occasions when sufficient pressure was brought to bear he did attend but got up abruptly during the session and left without apology. Later it was discovered that he had gone to his private theater and had the operator

C02571145

show some film that he liked particularly. On the whole, he prefers to discuss cabinet matters with each member in person and then communicate his decision to the group as a whole.

He has a passion for the latest news and for photographs of himself. If Hoffmann, the official Party photographer, happens to appear or someone happens to enter his office with a newspaper he will interrupt the most important meeting in order to scan through it. Very frequently he becomes so absorbed in the news or in his own photographs that he completely forgets the topic under discussion. Ludecke (165) writes:

> "Even on ordinary days in those times, it was almost possible to keep Hitler concentrated on one point. His quick mind would run away with the talk, or his attention would be distracted by the sudden discovery of the newspaper and he would stop to read it avidly, or he would interrupt your carefully prepared report with a long speech as though you were an audience...."

And Hanfstaengl reports that "his staff is usually in despair on account of his procrastination ... He never takes their protests in this respect very seriously and usually brushes them aside by saying, 'Problems are not solved by getting fidgety. If the time is ripe, the matter will be settled one way or another.'" (899)

Although Hitler tries to present himself as a very decisive individual who never hesitates when he is confronted by a difficult situation, he is usually far from it. It is at just these times that his procrastination becomes most marked. At such times it is almost impossible to get him to take action on anything. He stays very much by himself and is frequently almost inaccessible to his immediate staff. He often becomes depressed, is in bad humor, talks little, and prefers to read a book, look at movies or play with architectural models. According to the Dutch report (656) his hesitation to act is not due to divergent views among his advisors. At such times, he seldom pays very much attention to them and prefers not to discuss the matter.

> "What is known as the mastery of material was quite unimportant to him. He quickly became impatient if the details of a problem were brought to him. He was greatly adverse to experts' and had little regard for their opinion. He looked upon them as mere hacks, as brush-cleaners and color grinders...." (269)

On some occasions he has been known to leave Berlin without a word and go to Berchtesgaden where he spends his time walking in the country entirely by himself. Rauschning, who has met him on such occasions, says:

> "He recognizes nobody then. He wants to be alone. There are times when he flees from human society." (275)

C02571145

Roehm (176) frequently said, "Usually he solves suddenly, at the very last minute, a situation that has become intolerable and dangerous only because he vacillates and procrastinates."

It is during these periods of inactivity that Hitler is waiting for his "inner voice" to guide him. He does not think the problem through in a normal way but waits until the solution is presented to him. To Rauschning he said:

> "Unless I have the incorruptible conviction: *This is the solution,* I do nothing. Not even if the whole party tried to drive me to action. I will not act; I will wait, no matter what happens. But if the voice speaks, then I know the time has come to act." (268)

These periods of indecision may last from a few days to several weeks. If he is induced to talk about the problem during this time he becomes ill-natured and bad-tempered. However, when the solution has been given to him he has a great desire to express himself. He then calls in his adjutants and they must sit and listen to him until he is finished no matter what time it happens to be. On these occasions he does not want them to question him or even to understand him. It seems that he just wants to talk.

After this recital to his adjutants Hitler calls in his advisers and informs them of his decision. When he has finished they are free to express their opinions. If Hitler thinks that one of these opinions is worthwhile he will listen for a long time but usually these opinions have little influence on his decision when this stage has been reached. Only if someone succeeds in introducing new factors is there any possibility of getting him to change his mind. If someone voices the opinion that the proposed plan is too difficult or onerous he becomes extremely angry and frequently says:

> "I do not look for people having clever ideas of their own but rather people who are clever in finding ways and means of carrying out my ideas." (654)

As soon as he has the solution to a problem his mood changes very radically. He is again the Fuehrer we have described at the beginning of this section.

> "He is very cheerful, jokes all the time and does not give anybody an opportunity to speak, while he himself makes fun of everybody."

This mood lasts throughout the period when necessary work has to be done. As soon as the requisite orders have been given to put the plan into execution, however, Hitler seems to lose interest in it. He becomes perfectly calm, occupies himself with other matters and sleeps unusually long hours. (654)

C02571145

This is a very fundamental trait in Hitler's character structure. He does not think things out in a logical and consistent fashion, gathering all available information pertinent to the problem, mapping out alternative courses of action and then weighing the evidence pro and con for each of them before reaching a decision. His mental processes operate in reverse. Instead of studying the problem as an intellectual would do he avoids it and occupies himself with other things until unconscious processes furnish him with a solution. Having the solution he then begins to look for facts which will prove that it is correct. In this procedure he is very clever and by the time he presents it to his associates, it has the appearance of a rational judgment. Nevertheless, his thought processes proceed from the emotional to the factual instead of starting with the facts as an intellectual normally does. It is this characteristic of his thinking process which makes it difficult for ordinary people to understand Hitler or to predict his future actions. His orientation in this respect is that of an artist and not that of a statesman.

Although Hitler has been extremely successful in using this inspirational technique in determining his course of action (and we are reminded of his following his course with the precision of a sleep-walker) it is not without its shortcomings. He becomes dependent on his inner guide which makes for unpredictability on the one hand and rigidity on the other. The result is that he cannot modify his course in the face of unexpected developments or firm opposition. Strasser (297) tell us that:

"When he was then confronted by contradictory facts he was left floundering."

And Roehm says that there is:

"No system in the execution of his thoughts. He wants things his own way and gets mad when he strikes firm opposition on solid ground." (176)

This rigidity of mental functioning is obvious even in ordinary everyday interviews. When an unexpected question is asked, he is completely at a loss. Lochner (154) supplies us with an excellent description of this reaction:

"I saw this seemingly super-self-confident man actually blush when I broached the theme of German-American relations .... This evidently caught him off-guard. He was not used to having his infallibility challenged. For a moment he blushed like a schoolboy, hemmed and hawed, then stammered an embarrassed something about having so many problems to ponder that he had not yet had time to take up America."

Almost everyone who has written about Hitler has commented upon his rages. These are well-known to all of his associates and they have learned to fear them. The descriptions of his behavior during these rages vary considerably. The more extreme descriptions claim that at

C02571145

the climax he rolls on the floor and chews on the carpets. Shirer (279) reports that in 1938 he did this so often that his associates frequently referred to him as "Teppichfresser." Not one of our informants who has been close to Hitler, people like Hanfstaengl, Strasser, Rauschning, Hohenlohe, Friedelinde Wagner, and Ludecke, have ever seen him behave in this manner. Moreover they are all firmly convinced that this is a gross exaggeration and the informant of the Dutch Legation (655) says that this aspect must be relegated to the domain of "Greuelmaerchen."

Even without this added touch of chewing the carpet, his behavior is still extremely violent and shows an utter lack of emotional control. In the worst rages he undoubtedly acts like a spoiled child who cannot have his own way and bangs his fists on the tables and walls. He scolds and shouts and stammers and on some occasions foaming saliva gathers in the corners of his mouth. Rauschning, in describing one of these uncontrolled exhibitions, says:

"He was an alarming sight, his hair disheveled, his eyes fixed, and his face distorted and purple. I feared that he would collapse or have a stroke." (710)

It must not be supposed, however, that these rages occur only when he is crossed on major issues. On the contrary, very insignificant matters might call out this reaction. In general they are brought on whenever anyone contradicts him, when there is unpleasant news for which he might feel responsible, when there is any skepticism concerning his judgment or when a situation arises in which his infallibility might be challenged or belittled. Von Wiegand (492) reports that among his staff there is a tactic understanding:

"For God's sake don't excite the Fuehrer — which means do not tell him bad news — do not mention things which are not as he conceives them to be."

Voigt (591) says that:

"Close collaborators for many years said that Hitler was always like this — that the slightest difficulty or obstacle could make him scream with rage. . . ."

Many writers believe that these rages are just play acting. There is much to be said for this point of view since Hitler's first reaction to the unpleasant situation is not indignation, as one would ordinarily expect. He goes off into a rage or tirade without warning. Similarly, when he has finished, there is no aftermath. He immediately cools down and begins to talk about other matters in a perfectly calm tone of voice as though nohting had happened. Occasionally he will look around sheepishly, as if to see if anyone is laughing, and then proceeds with other matters, without the slightest trace of resentment.

77

C02571145

Some of his closest associates have felt that he induces these rages consciously to frighten those about him. Rauschning (261), for example, says it is a : —

"....technique by which he would throw his entire entourage into confusion by well-timed fits of rage and thus make them more submissive."

Strasser (377) also believes this to be the case for he says:

"Rage and abuse became the favorite weapons in his armory."

This is not the time to enter into a detailed discussion concerning the nature and purpose of the rages. It is sufficient, for the present time, to realize that his associates are well aware that Hitler can and does behave in this way. It is a part of the Hitler they know and are forced to deal with. We may point out, however, that they are not conscious acting alone since it is almost impossible for an actor to actually become purple in the face unless he really is in an emotional state.

There are many other aspects of Hitler's personality, as it is known to his associates, which do not fit into the picture of the Fuehrer as it is presented to the German people. A few of the more important of these merit mention. Hitler is represented as a man of great courage, with nerves of steel who is always in complete control of every situation. Nevertheless, he often runs away from an unpleasant, unexpected or difficult situation.

Bayles (2) reports two incidents that illustrate this reaction:

"Particularly noticeable is his inability to cope with unexpected situations, this having been amusingly revealed when he laid the cornerstone of the House of German Art in Munich. On this occasion he was handed a dainty, rococo hammer for delivering the three traditional strokes to the cornerstone, but not realizing the fragility of the rococo, he brought the hammer down with such force that at the very first stroke it broke into bits. Then, instead of waiting for another hammer, Hitler completely lost his composure, blushed, looked wildly about him in the manner of a small boy caught stealing jam, and almost ran from the scene leaving the cornerstone unlaid. His enjoyment of the Berlin Olympic Games was completely spoilt when a fanatical Dutch woman who had achieved a personal presentation suddenly clasped him in two hefty arms and tried to kiss him in plain view of 100,000 spectators. Hitler could not regain his composure or stand the irreverent guffaws of foreign visitors, and left the Stadium."

This type of behavior is illustrated even more clearly in relation to Gregor Strasser because the occasion was one of extreme importance to Hitler. Strasser threatened to split the Party if a definite program could not be agreed upon. Hitler avoided the situation as long as he possibly could in the hope that something might happen, that the situation would somehow solve itself. When it did not he agreed to Strasser's demand for a meeting in Leipzig at which their differences could be thrashed out. Strasser was in the restaurant at the appointed hour. Hitler came late. Hardly had he sat down to the table when he excused himself in order to go to the toilet. Strasser waited for some time and when Hitler did not return he began making inquiries. To his amazement he discovered that instead of going to the toilet Hitler had slipped out of the back door and driven back to Munich without discussing a single point. (378)

Heiden (527) also tells us that in 1923 he was in conference with Ludendorff when he suddenly rushed off without as much as an apology. In the spring of 1932 he ran out on a meeting of the Verband Bayrischer Industrieller before which he was to speak. This group was not kindly disposed to him but it was important for Hitler to win them over. He got up to speak:

> ". . . er stockt, sieht auf den Tisch, Schweigen alles sieht sich verbluefft an. Peinliche Minuten. Ploetzlich dreht sich Hitler auf dem Absatz um und geht ohne ein Wort an die Tuer."

The same thing happened a year later when, as Chancellor, he was to speak to the Reichsverband der Deutschen Presse. Again he sensed opposition in the group and again he fled from the scene. Olden (611) says:

> "Das ist ein Trick, den der Fuehrer noch oft anwenden wird: wenn die Situation peinlich wird, versteckt er sich."

At other times, when he finds himself in difficult situations, the great dictator who prides himself on his decisiveness, hardness, and other leadership qualities, breaks down and weeps like a child appealing for sympathy. Rauschning (267) writes:

> "In 1934 as in 1932 he complained of the ingratitude of the German people in the sobbing tones of a down-at-the-heel music-hall performer! A weakling who accused and sulked, appealed and implored, and retired in wounded vanity ('If the German people don't want me!') instead of acting."

Otto Strasser reports that on one occasion:

> "He seized my hands, as he had done two years before. His voice was choked with sobs, and tears flowed down his cheeks." (381)

Heiden (280) reporting a scene at which the Party leaders were waiting for the arrival of Gregor Strasser:

> " 'Never would I have believed it of Strasser,' he (Hitler) cried, and he laid his head on the table and sobbed. Tears came to the eyes of many of those present, as they saw their Fuehrer weeping. Julius Streicher, who had been snubbed by Strasser for years, called out from his humble place in the background: 'Shameful that Strasser should treat our Fuehrer like that!' "

C02571145

In extremely difficult situation he has openly threatened to commit suicide. Sometimes it seems that he uses this as a form of black-mail while at other times the situation seems to be more than he can bear. During the Beer Hall Putsch he said to the officials he was holding as prisoners:

> "There are still five bullets in my pistol—four for the traitors,
> and one, if things go wrong, for myself." (253)

He also threatened to commit suicide before Mrs. Hanfstaengl directly after the failure of the Putsch, while he was hiding from the police in the Hanfstaengl home. Again in Landsberg he went on a hunger strike and threatened to martyr himself — in imitation of the Mayor of Cork. In 1930, he threatened to commit suicide after the strange murder of his niece, Geli, (302) of whom we shall speak later. In 1932, he again threat-ened to carry out this action if Strasser split the (98) Party. In 1933 he threatened to do so if he was not appointed Chancellor (63), and in 1936, he promised to do so if the Occupation of the Rhineland failed. (255)

These, however, are relatively infrequent exhibitions although his associates have learned that they are always a possibility and that it is wise not to push the Fuehrer too far. More frequent are his depressions about which a great deal has been written. It is certain that he does have very deep depressions from time to time. During his years in Vienna (1907-1912), he undoubtedly suffered from them a great deal. Hanisch reports (64):

> "I have never seen such helpless letting down in distress."

It is probably also true that he suffered from depressions during the war as Mend (199) reports.

After the death of his niece, Geli (1930), he also went into a severe depression which lasted for some time. Gregor Strasser actually feared that he might commit suicide during this period and stayed with him for several days. There is some evidence (Strasser, 302) that he actually tried to do so and was prevented from carrying it out. It is also interesting to note that for several years after her death he went into a depression during the Christmas holidays and wandered around Ger-many alone for days on end (937).

Rauschning gives us a vivid description of his condition after the Blood Purge of 1934. He writes (716):

> "Aber zunaechst machte auch er nicht den Eindruck des
> Siegers. Mit gedunsenen, verzerrten Zuegen sass er mir
> gegenueber, als ich ihm Vortrag hielt. Seine Augen waren
> erloschen, er sah mich nicht an. Er spielte mit seien Fingern.
> Ich hatte nicht den Eindruck, dass er mir zuhoerte ... Wae-
> hrend der ganzen Zeit hatte ich den Eindruck, dass Ekel,
> Ueberdruss und Verachtung in ihm herumstritten, und dass
> er mit seinen Gedanken ganz wo anders war ... Ich hatte

> gehoert, er sollte nur noch stundenweise schlafen koennen
> .... Nachts irrte er ruhelos umher. Schlafmittel halfen nicht
> .... Mit Weinkraempfen sollte er aus dem kurzen Schlaf
> aufwachen. Er haette sich wiederholt erbrochen. Mit Schuet-
> telfrost habe er in Decken gehuellt im Sessel gesessen....
> Einmal wollte er alles erleuchtet und Menschen, viel Men-
> schen um sich haben; im gleichen Augenblick haette er
> wieder neimanden sehen wollen...."

These were major crises in his life and we can assume that they probably represent his worst depressions. Undoubtedly he very frequently has minor ones when he withdraws from his associates and broods by himself, or periods when he refuses to see anyone and is irritable and impatient with those around him. On the whole, however, it appears that the reports of Hitler's depressions have been grossly exaggerated. Not one of our informants who has had close contact with him has any knowledge of his ever retiring to a sanatarium during such times and there is only one source which indicates that he ever sought psychiatric help and that was not accepted. We must assume that the many reports that have flourished in the newspapers have been plants by the Nazi Propaganda agencies to lure us into false expectations.

There are a number of other respects in which Hitler does not appear before his associates as the self-confident Fuehrer he likes to believe himself to be. One of the most marked of these is his behavior in the presence of accepted authority. Under these circumstances he is obviously nervous and very ill at ease. Many times he is downright submissive. As far back as 1923, Ludecke (166) reports that:

> "In conference with Poehner, Hitler sat with his felt hat
> crushed shapeless in his hands. His mien was almost hum-
> ble...."

Fromm (371) writes that at a dinner:

> "Hitler's eagerness to obtain the good graces of the princes
> present was subject to much comment. He bowed and clicked
> and all but knelt in his zeal to please oversized, ugly Princess
> Luise von Sachsen-Meiningen, her brother, hereditary Prince
> George, and their sister, Grand Duchess of Sachsen-Weimar.
> Beaming in his servile attitude he dashed personally to
> bring refreshments from the buffet."

On his visit to Rome, Huss (406) writes:

> "When leading Queen Helene in Rome he was like a fish out
> of water. He didn't know what to do with his hands."

To Hindenburg, he was extremely submissive. Pictures taken of their meetings illustrate his attitude very clearly. In some of them it looks almost as though he were about to kiss the President's hand. Flannery (698) also reports that when Hitler first met Petain he took him by the arm and escorted him to his car. Hanfstaengl (912) reports that he found

Hitler Greeting President Hindenburg, March 1933

49

Hitler outside the door of the banquet hall in which a dinner and reception were being given to the former Kaiser's wife. He was unable to bring himself to go in and meet her Highness alone. When Hanfstaengl finally persuaded Hitler to go in he was so ill at ease that he could only stammer a few words to Hermine and then excused himself. Many other examples could be cited. From the weight of evidence it seems certain that Hitler does lose his self-confidence badly when he is brought face to face with an accepted authority of high standing, particularly royalty.

This subservient attitude is also obvious in his use of titles. This is well described by Lania (148) reporting on Hitler's trial:

avoids contact with them as much as possible. Fromm (369) describes his behavior at a diplomatic dinner in the following words:

> "The corporal seemed to be ill at ease, awkward and moody. His coat-tails embarrassed him. Again and again his hand fumbled for the encouraging support of his sword belt. Each time he missed the familiar cold and bracing support, his uneasiness grew. He crumpled his handkerchief, tugged it, rolled it, just plain stage-fright."

Many others have also commented on this tendency to use the full title. It also fits in with his very submissive behavior to his officers during the last war which has been commented upon by several of his comrades. It seems safe to assume that this is a fundamental trait in his character which becomes less obvious as he climbs the ladder but is present nevertheless.

The Fuehrer is also ill at ease in the company of diplomats and

> "In the course of his peroration he came to speak of Generals Ludendorff and von Seeckt; at such moments, he stood at attention and trumpeted forth the words 'General' and 'Excellency.' It made no difference that one of the generals was on his side, while the other, von Seeckt, Commander-in-Chief of the Reichswehr, was his enemy; he abandoned himself entirely to the pleasure of pronouncing the high-sounding titles. He never said 'General Seeckt,' he said 'His Excellency Herr Colonel General von Seeckt,' letting the words melt on his tongue and savoring their after-taste."

Henderson (124) writes:

> "It will always be a matter of regret to me that I was never able to study Hitler in private life, as this might have given me the chance to see him under normal conditions and to talk with him as man to man. Except for a few brief words at chance meetings, I never met him except upon official and invariably disagreeable, business. He never attended informal parties at which diplomats might be present, and when friends of mine did try to arrange it, he always got out of meeting me in such a manner on the ground of precedent....
> But he always looked self-conscious when he had to entertain

the diplomatic corps, which happened normally three times a year."

Hitler also becomes nervous and tends to lose his composure when he has to meet newspapermen. Being a genius of propaganda he realizes the power of the press in influencing public opinion and he always provides the press with choice seats at all ceremonies. When it comes to interviews, however, he feels himself on the defensive and insists that the questions be submitted in advance. When the interview takes place he is able to maintain considerable poise because he has his answers prepared. Even then he gives no opportunity to ask for further clarification because he immediately launches into a lengthy dissertation, which sometimes develops into a tirade. When this is finished, the interview is over (Oechsner, 665).

He is also terrified when he is called upon to speak to intellectuals (Wagner, 487) or any group in which he feels opposition or the possibility of criticism.

Hitler's adjustment to people in general is very poor. He is not really on intimate terms with any of his associates. Hess is the only associate, with the possible exception of Streicher, who has ever had the privilege of addressing him with the familiar "Du". Even Goering, Goebbels and Himmler must address him with the more formal "Sie" although each of them would undoubtedly be willing to sacrifice his right hand for the privilege of addressing him in the informal manner. It is true that outside of his official family there are a few people in Germany, notably Mrs. Bechstein and the Winifred Wagner family who address him as "Du" and call him by his nickname, "Wolf", but even these are few and far between. On the whole, he always maintains a considerable distance from other people. Ludecke, who was very close to him for a while, writes:

> "Even in his intimate and cozy moments, I sensed no attitude
> of familiarity towards him on the part of his staff; there was
> always a certain distance about him, that subtle quality of
> aloofness . . . ." (180).

And Fry (577) says:

> "He lives in the midst of many men and yet he lives alone."

It is well-known that he cannot carry on a normal conversation or discussion with people. Even if only one person is present he must do all the talking. His manner of speech soon loses any conversational qualities it might have had and takes on all the characteristics of a lecture and may easily develop into a tirade. He simply forgets his companions and behaves as though he were addressing a multitude. Strasser (297) has given a good, brief description of his manner:

> "Now Hitler drew himself erect and by the far-away look in
> his eyes showed plainly that he was not speaking merely to

me; he was addressing an imaginary audience that stretched
far beyond the walls of the living room."

This is not only true in connection with political matters. Even
when he is alone with his adjutants or immediate staff and tries to be
friendly he is unable to enter into a give-and-take conversation. At times
he seems to want to get closer to people and relates personal experiences,
such as, "When I was in Vienna," or "When I was in the Army." But
under these circumstances, too, he insists on doing all the talking and
always repeats the same stories over and over again in exactly the same
form, almost as though he had memorized them. The gist of most of these
stories is contained in MEIN KAMPF. His friends have all heard them
dozens of times but this does not deter him from repeating them again
with great enthusiasm. Nothing but the most superficial aspects of these
experiences are ever touched upon. It seems as though he is unable to
give more of himself than that (Hanfstaengl, 898).

Price (230) says: "When more than two people are present, even
though they are his intimate circle, there is no general discourse. Either
Hitler talks and they listen, or else they talk among themselves and
Hitler sits silent." And this is the way it seems to be. He is not at all
annoyed when members of the group talk to each other unless of course
he feels like doing the talking himself. But ordinarily he seems to enjoy
listening to others while he makes believe that he is attending to something else. Nevertheless, he overhears everything which is being said
and often uses it later on (Hanfstaengl, 914). However, he does not give
credit to the individual from whom he has learned it but simply gives it
out as his own. Rauschning (266) says:

> "He has always been a *poseur*. He remembers things that he
> has heard and has a faculty for repeating them in such a
> way that the listener is lead to believe that they are his own."

Roehm also complained of this:

> "If you try to tell him anything, he knows everything al-
> ready. Though he often does what we advise, he laughs in
> our faces at the moment, and later does the very thing as if
> it were all his own idea and creation. He doesn't even seem
> to be aware of how dishonest he is." (176)

Another one of his tricks which drives people and particularly
his associates to distraction is his capacity for forgetting. This trait has
been commented upon so much that it scarcely needs mentioning here.
We all know how he can say something one day and a few days later say
the opposite, completely oblivious of his earlier statement. He does not
only do this in connection with international affairs but also with his
closest associates. When they show their dismay and call his attention
to the inconsistency he flies off into a rage and demands to know if the
other person thinks he is a liar. Evidently the other leading Nazis have
also learned the trick, for Rauschning (266) says:

> "Most of the Nazis with Hitler at their head, literally forget, like hysterical women, anything they have no desire to remember."

Although Hitler almost invariably introduces a few humorous elements into his speeches and gives the impression of considerable wit, he seems to lack any real sense of humor. He can never take a joke on himself. Heyst (600) says, "He is unable to purify his gloomy self with self-irony and humor." Von Wiegand (492) says he is extremely sensitive to ridicule and Huss says (408), "He takes himself seriously and will flare up in a temperamental rage at the least impingement by act or attitude on the dignity and holiness of state and Fuehrer." When everything is going well he sometimes gets into a gay and whimsical mood in a circle of close friends. His humor then is confined almost wholly to a kind of teasing or ribbing. The ribbing is usually in connection with alleged love affairs of his associates but are never vulgar and only hint at sexual factors (Hanfstaengl, 910). Friedelinde Wagner provides us with an example of his teasing. Goering and Goebbels were both present at the time that he said to the Wagner family:

> "You all know what a volt is and an ampere, don't you? Right. But do you know what a goebbels, a goering are? A goebbels is the amount of nonsense a man can speak in an hour and a goering is the amount of metal that can be pinned on a man's breast." (632)

His other form of humor is mimicking. Almost everyone concedes that he has great talent along these lines and he frequently mimics his associates in their presence much to the amusement of everyone except the victim. He also loved to mimic Sir Eric Phipps and later Chamberlain.

Hitler's poor adaptation to people is perhaps most obvious in his relations to women. Since he has become a political figure, his name has been linked with a great many women, particularly in the foreign press. Although the German public seem to know very little about this phase of his life, his associates have seen a great deal of it and the topic is always one for all kinds of conjectures. Roughly speaking, his relations to women fall into three categories: (a) much older women; (b) actresses and passing fancies, and (c) more or less enduring relationships.

A. As early as 1920 Frau Carola Hofman, a 61 year old widow, took him under her wing and for years played the part of foster mother. Then came Frau Helena Bechstein, the wife of the famous Berlin piano manufacturer, who took over the role. She spent large quantities of money on Hitler in the early days of the Party, introduced him to her social circle and lavished maternal affection on him. She often said that she wished that Hitler were her son and while he was imprisoned in Landsberg she claimed that she was his adopted mother in order that she might visit him. Strasser (300) says that Hitler would often sit at

C02571145

her feet and lay his head against her bosom while she stroked his hair tenderly and murmured, "Mein Woelfchen". Since he came to power things have not gone so smoothly. She seemed to find fault with everything he did and would scold him unmercifully, even in public. According to Friedelinde Wagner (939), she is the one person in Germany who can carry on a monologue in Hitler's presence and who would actually tell him what she thought. During these violent scoldings Hitler would stand there like an abashed schoolboy who had committed a misdemeanor. According to Hanfstaengl, Mrs. Bechstein had groomed Hitler in the expectation that he would marry her daughter, Lottie, who was far from attractive. Out of sense of obligation, Hitler did ask Lottie, but was refused, (904). Mrs. Bechstein was disconsolate over the failure of her plans and began to criticize Hitler's social reforms as well as his actions. Nevertheless, Hitler made duty calls fairly regularly even though he postponed them as long as possible (939).

Then there was also Frau Victoria von Dirksen, who is alleged to have spent a fortune on him and his career (554), and a number of others. In more recent years, Mrs. Goebbels has taken over the role of foster-mother and looks after his comforts, supervises his household and bakes delicacies of which he is particularly fond. She, too, has been acting as a matchmaker in the hope that he might marry one of her friends and thereby draw the bond between them even tighter. To Ludecke, (177) she complained, "I am no good as a matchmaker. I would leave him alone with my most charming friends but he wouldn't respond." There was also his older half-sister, Angela, who kept house for him at Munich and Berchtesgaden and, for a time, seemed to play a mother's role.

Winifred Wagner, the daughter-in-law of Richard Wagner, has also caused a great deal of comment. She is English by birth, and, from all accounts, is very attractive and about Hitler's own age. She met Hitler in the early 1920's and since that time has been one of his staunch supporters. He became a frequent visitor at the Wagner home in Bayreuth and after his accession to power, built a house on the Wagner estate for himself and his staff. After the death of Siegfried Wagner, reports all over the world had it that she would become Hitler's wife. But nothing happened in spite of the fact that it seemed like an ideal union from the point of view of both parties.

Nevertheless, Hitler continued to be a frequent guest at the Wagner's. It probably was the nearest thing to a home he has known since his own home broke up in 1907. Mrs. Wagner undoubtedly did everything in her power to make him comfortable and Hitler felt very much at home. There were three small children, a boy and two girls (one of them is our informant, Friedelinde) which added considerably to the home atmosphere. The entire family called him by his nickname "Wolf" and addressed him as "Du". He felt so secure in this house that he often

C02571145

came and stayed without his bodyguard. He sometimes spent his Christmas holidays with the family and became very much a part of it. But further than that he was unwilling to go, even though the marriage would have been exceedingly popular with the German people.

B. Then there were a long line of "passing fancies". For the most part these were screen and stage stars. Hitler likes to be surrounded with pretty women and usually requests the moving picture companies to send over a number of actresses whenever there is a party in the Chancellory. He seems to get an extraordinary delight in fascinating these girls with stories about what he is going to do in the future or the same old stories about his past life. He also likes to impress them with his power by ordering the studios to provide them with better roles, or promising that he will see to it that they are starred in some forthcoming picture. Most of his associations with women of this type, and their number is legion, does not go beyond this point as far as we have been able to discover. On the whole he seems to feel more comfortable in the company of stage people than with any other group and often went down to the studio restaurants for lunch.

C. There have been several other women who have played a more or less important role in Hitler's life. The first of which we have any knowledge was Henny Hoffmann, the daughter of the official Party photographer. Henny, according to reports, was little more than a prostitute and spent most of her time among the students in Munich, who alleged that she could be had for a few marks. Heinrich Hoffmann, her father, was a member of the Party and a close friend of Hitler. By a queer twist of Fate, Hoffmann had taken a picture of the crowds in Munich at the outbreak of the last war. Later, when Hitler became prominent in Munich politics, Hoffmann discovered Hitler in the picture and called it to his attention. Hitler was delighted and a close relationship sprung up between them. Hoffmann's wife was also very fond of Hitler and played a mother role towards him for a time.

With the death of Mrs. Hoffmann, the home went to pieces from a moral point of view and became a kind of meeting place for homosexuals of both sexes. There was a good deal of drinking and great freedom in sexual activities of all kinds. Hitler was frequently present at parties given in the Hoffmann home and became very friendly with Henny. The relationship continued for some time until Henny, who was a very garrulous person by nature, got drunk one night and began to talk about her relationship to Hitler. Her father became enraged and for a time had little to do with Hitler.

Up to this time Hitler had steadfastly refused to have his photograph taken for publication on the grounds that it was better publicity to remain a mystery man and also, because if his picture appeared it would be too easy to identify him when he crossed Communist territories.

Shortly after the above described episode, Hitler named Hoffmann as the official Party photographer and gave him the exclusive right to his photographs. These privileges, so it is alleged, have, in the course of years, netted Hoffmann millions of dollars. Among Hitler's associates, it was supposed that Hitler had committed some kind of sexual indiscretion with Henny and bought Hoffmann's silence by granting him these exclusive rights. In any event, Henny was soon married to Baldur von Schirach, the Leader of the Nazi Youth Movement who is reputed to be a homosexual. His family were violently opposed to the marriage but Hitler insisted. All differences between Hitler and Hoffmann seem to have disappeared and today he is one of Hitler's closest associates and exerts a great personal influence on the Fuehrer. We shall consider the nature of Hitler's indiscretion later in our study since it is not a matter of common knowledge and would lead us too far afield at the present time.

After the Henny Hoffmann episode, Hitler began to appear in public with his niece, Geli, the daughter of his half-sister, Angela, who had come to keep house for Hitler in 1924. At the time this relationship matured her mother had gone to Berchtesgaden and Hitler and Geli were living alone in his Munich flat. They became inseparable companions and the subject of much comment in Party circles. Many of the members, particularly Gregor Strasser, felt that this was poor publicity and was creating a good deal of unfavorable talk. Other members had Hitler brought on the carpet to explain where he was getting the money to clothe Geli and sport her around if he was not using Party funds for this purpose.

Hitler became very jealous of Geli's attention and refused to let her go out with any other men. Some claim that he kept her locked in during the day when he could not take her with him. For several years the relationship continued over the opposition of the Party. Then one day Geli was found dead in Hitler's apartment — she had died from a bullet fired from Hitler's revolver. There was considerable commotion. The coroner's verdict was suicide but Geli was buried in hallowed ground by a Catholic clergy. There was much speculation whether she killed herself or was killed by Hitler. Whatever the facts may be, Hitler went into a profound depression which lasted for months. During the first days after the funeral, Gregor Strasser remained with him in order to prevent him from committing suicide. Ludecke (178) says: "The special quality of Hitler's affection (for Geli) is still a mystery to those closest to him."

For a few years after Geli's death, Hitler had little to do with women except in a very superficial way. Along about 1932, however, he became interested in Eva Braun, Hoffmann's photographic assistant. This relationship did not develop very rapidly but it has continued. In the course of time, Hitler has bought her many things including high-powered automobiles and a house between Munich and Berchtesgaden where,

C02571145

it is alleged, he frequently spends the night on the way to or from his country estate. Eva Braun is also frequently a guest at Berchtesgaden and in Berlin. Oechsner was told that after one of her visits in Berchtesgaden, some of her underwear was found in Hitler's bedroom. Wiedemann, according to Hohenlohe, says that she has sometimes spent the entire night in Hitler's bedroom in Berlin. It is reported by Norburt (605) that Eva moved into the Chancellory on December 16, 1939 and it is said that Hitler intends to marry her when the war is over. Beyond that, we know nothing about this affair except that Eva Braun has twice tried to commit suicide and that one of Hitler's bodyguards hurled himself from the Kehlstein because he was in love with her but could not trespass on the Fuehrer's domain.

The affair with Eva Braun was not exclusive, however. During this period he has also seen a good deal of at least two moving picture actresses. These have been more enduring than most of his associations with actresses and much more intimate. Both of these girls were frequently invited alone to the Chancellory late at night and departed in the early hours of the morning. During their stay they were alone with Hitler behind closed doors so that not even his immediate staff knew what transpired between them. The first of these relationships was with Renarte Mueller who committed suicide by throwing herself from the window of a Berlin hotel. The other was with Leni Riefenstahl who continued to be a guest at the Chancellory up to the outbreak of the war.

Hitler's associates know that in respect to women Hitler is far from the ascetic he and the Propaganda Bureau would like to have the German public believe. None of them with the possible exception of Hoffmann and Schaub (his personal adjutant), know the nature of his sexual activities. This has led to a great deal of conjecture in Party circles. There are some who believe that his sex life is perfectly normal but restricted. Others, that he is immune from such temptations and that nothing happens when he is alone with girls. Still others believe that he is homosexual.

The latter belief is based largely on the fact that during the early days of the Party many of the inner circle were well-known homosexuals. Roehm made no attempt to hide his homosexual activities and Hess was generally known as "Fraulein Anna." There were also many others, and it was supposed, for this reason, that Hitler, too, belonged to this category.

In view of Hitler's pretense at purity and the importance of his mission for building a Greater Germany, it is extraordinary that he should be so careless about his associates. He has never restricted them in any way except at the time of the Blood Purge in 1934 when his excuse was that he had to purge the Party of these undesirable elements. At all other times, he has been liberal to a fault. Lochner reports:

C02571145

> "The only criterion for membership in the Party was that the applicant be 'Unconditionally obedient and faithfully devoted to me.' When someone asked if that applied to thieves and criminals, Hitler said, 'Their private lives don't concern me.'" (157)

Ludecke (179) claims that in speaking of some of the moralists who were complaining about the actions of his S.A. men, Hitler said:

> He would rather his S.A. men took the women than some fat-bellied moneybag. "Why should I concern myself with the private lives of my followers … apart from Roehm's achievements, I know that I can absolutely depend on him …."

Rauschning says (264) that the general attitude in the Party was:

> "Do anything you like but don't get caught at it."

This attitude towards his associates certainly did not make for high standards in the Party. Capt. von Mueke resigned from the Party on the grounds that:

> "Die Voelkische Partei ist nicht mehr die Partei der anstaendigen Leute, sie ist herunter gekommen und korrupt. Kurz, das ist ein Saustall." (614)

Rauschning (276) expresses a similar sentiment:

> "Most loathsome of all is the reeking miasma of furtive, unnatural sexuality that fills and fouls the whole atmosphere around him, like an evil emanation. Nothing in this environment is straightforward. Surreptitious relationships, substitutes and symbols, false sentiments and secret lusts — nothing in this man's surroundings is natural and genuine, nothing has the openness of a natural instinct."

One of Hitler's hobbies which is carefully hidden from the public is his love for pornography. He can scarcely wait for the next edition of DER STUERMER to appear and when it reaches him he goes through it avidly. He seems to get great pleasure out of the dirty stories and the cartoons that feature this sheet. (658: 261). To Rauschning Hitler said that the STUERMER "was a form of pornography permitted in the Third Reich." In addition, Hitler has a large collection of nudes and, according to Hanfstaengl and others, he also enjoys viewing lewd movies in his private theater, some of which are prepared by Hoffmann for his benefit.

He also likes to present himself as a great authority and lover of good music. One of his favorite pastimes is to lecture on Wagner and the beauty of his operatic music. There can be no doubt concerning his enjoyment of Wagnerian music and that he gets considerable inspiration from it. Oechsner (675) reports that he has been able to observe Hitler closely while he was listening to music and saw, "grimaces of pain and pleasure contort his face, his brows knit, his eyes close, his mouth contract tightly." Hitler has said, "For me, Wagner is something godly, and his music is my religion. I go to his concerts as others go to church." According to Hanfstaengl, however, he is not a lover of good music in general (895). He says that about 85% of Hitler's preferences in music are the normal program music in Viennese cafes. This is probably why Hitler rarely attends concerts and in later years, seldom goes to the opera. His preferences now seem to run to musical comedies and cabarets in addition to the movies he sees at the Chancellory. Pope (229) says that Hitler frequently visited the MERRY WIDOW in which an American actress played the lead. He says, "I have seen Hitler nudge his gauleiter, Wagner, and smirk when Dorothy does her famous backbending number in the spotlight." In this number, Dorothy's costume consists of a pair of transparent butterfly wings, or sometimes nothing at all. Hitler watches the performance through opera glasses and sometimes has command performances for his private benefit.

Much has been written by the Nazi propaganda bureau about his modest way of living. This, through the eyes of his associates, has also been vastly overrated. Although he is a vegetarian, most of them feel that his meals are scarcely to be considered as a form of deprivation. He eats large quantities of eggs prepared in 101 different ways by the best chef in Germany and there are always quantities and a large variety of fresh vegetables prepared in unusual ways. In addition, Hitler consumes incredible quantities of pastries and often as much as two pounds of chocolates in the course of a single day. Nor are his personal tastes particularly inexpensive. Although his clothes are simple, he has an incredible number of each article of clothing. All are made of the finest materials that can be procured and made up by the best workmen. He also has a passion for collecting paintings and when he has his heart set on one, the sky is the limit as far as price is concerned. The only thing that is really modest about his living arrangements is his bedroom which is extremely simple and contains only a white metal bed (decorated with ribbons at the head), a painted chest of drawers and a few straight chairs. Friedelinde Wagner and Hanfstaengl, both of whom have seen the room with their own eyes, have described it in identical terms: namely, that it is a room that one would expect a maid to have and not a Chancellor.

Although he is presented to the German public as a man of extraordinary courage, his immediate associates frequently have occasion to question this. Several occasions have been reported on which he has not carried through his own program because he feared opposition. This is particularly true in connection with his Gauleiters. He seems to have a particular fear of these people and rather than meet opposition from them, he usually tries to find out on which side of an issue the majority have aligned themselves before he meets with them. When the meeting takes place, he proposes a plan or course of action which will fit in with the sentiments of the majority. (718)

According to Hohenlohe he also backed down before three Army generals when they protested against the rapid developments in the Danzig question, and that before Munich, he decided to postpone the War because he discovered that the crowds watching the troops marching under the Chancellory windows were unenthusiastic (661).

Furthermore, they must wonder about the necessity of the extreme precautions that are taken for his safety. Most of these are carefully concealed from the German public. When Hitler appears he looks for all the world like an extremely brave man as he stands up in the front seat of his open car and salutes. The people do not know of the tremendous number of secret service men who constantly mingle with the crowds in addition to the guards who line the streets through which he is to pass. Neither do they know of all the precautions taken at the Chancellory or at Berchtesgaden. Before the war his house at Berchtesgaden was surrounded with eight miles of electrified wire. . Pillboxes and anti-aircraft batteries were set up in the surrounding hills (Morrell, 462). When he visited at Bayreuth, troops were sent in weeks in advance to set up machine-gun nests and anti-aircraft batteries in the hills immediately adjoining (Wagner, 934). Lochner (156) reports that when he travels in a special train he is accompanied by 200 SS guards who are more heavily armed than the retinue of any German emperor. After the war started, his train was heavily armored and equipped with anti-aircraft fore and aft. And, yet, when the newsreels show him at the front, he is the only one who does not wear a steel helmet.

There is, consequently, a considerable discrepancy between Hitler as he is known to the German people and Hitler as he is known to his associates. Nevertheless, it appears that most of his associates have a deep allegiance to Hitler personally and are quite ready to forgive or ignore his shortcomings. In many cases, it seems as though his associates are quite oblivious to the contradictory traits in his character — to them he is still the Fuehrer and they live for the moments when he actually plays this role.

Nazi Victims

Nazi Victims

General Dwight D. Eisenhower viewing bodies of victims

Nazi victims

Nazi Victims

166TH SIGNAL PHOTO CO, DET 16
ORNITZ   23 APR 45

THIS TATTOO WAS PART OF A MANS
BODY UNTIL IT WAS SKINNED OFF BY
NAZIS SS MEN AND USED AS A DECORA-
TION ON THE WALL OF THEIR QUARTERS,
AT BUCHENWALD CONCENTRATION CAMP.

Chapter Four

Hitler

As He Knows Himself

"Make the lie big, make it simple, keep saying it, and eventually they will believe it." Adolf Hitler

PART IV

HITLER — AS HE KNOWS HIMSELF

C02571145

HITLER — AS HE KNOWS HIMSELF

Hitler has always been extremely secretive in all his dealings. Hanfstaengl tells us that this trait is carried to such a degree that he never tells one of his immediate associates what he has been talking about or arranged with another. His mind is full of compartments, Hanfstaengl says, and his dealings with every individual are carefully pigeon-holed. What has been filed in one pigeon-hole is never permitted to mix with that in another. Everything is scrupulously kept locked up in his mind and is only opened when he needs the material.

This is also true of himself. We have already seen how he has steadfastly refused to divulge anything about his past to his associates. This, he believed, was something which did not concern them in any way and consequently he has kept the pigeon-hole tightly closed. He talks almost continually about everything under the sun — except himself. What really goes on in his mind is almost as great a mystery as his past life.

Nevertheless, it would be helpful and interesting to open this pigeon-hole and examine its contents. Fortunately, a few fragments of information concerning his past life have been unearthed in the course of time and these are extremely valuable as a background for understanding his present behavior. Then, too, we have records of attitudes and sentiments expressed in speeches and writings. Although these utterances are confined to a rather limited area, they do represent the products of some of his mental processes and consequently give us some clue to what goes on behind those much discussed eyes, of which Rauschning writes:

> "Anyone who has seen this man face to face, has met his uncertain glance, without depth or warmth, from eyes that seem hard and remote, and has then seen that gaze grow rigid, will certainly have experienced the uncanny feeling: 'That man is not normal.'" (273)

In addition, we have descriptions of his overt behavior in the face of varied circumstances. We must assume that these, too, are the products of his psychological processes and that they reflect what is going on behind the scenes.

All of this, however, would be insufficient data for an adequate picture of Hitler, as he knows himself, in everyday life. Fortunately, patients with behavior patterns, tendencies and sentiments very similar to those that Hitler has expressed are not unknown in psychoanalytical practice. From our knowledge of what goes on in the minds of these patients, together with a knowledge of their past histories, it may be possible to fill in some of the gaps and make some deductions concerning his extraordinary mode of adjustment.

102

C02571145

We have learned from the study of many cases that the present character of an individual is the product of an evolutionary process, the beginnings of which are to be found in infancy. The very earliest experiences in the lifetime of the individual form the foundation upon which the character is gradually structured as the individual passes through successive stages of development and is exposed to the demands and influences of the world around him. If this is true, it would be well for us to review briefly Hitler's past history, as far as it is known, in the hope that it may cast some light upon his present behavior and the course he is most likely to pursue in the future. Such a review of his past is also pertinent to our study insofar as it forms the background through which Hitler sees himself. It is a part of him he must live with, whether he likes it or not.

THE HITLER FAMILY

Father.

There is a great deal of confusion in studying Hitler's family tree. Much of this is due to the fact that the name has been spelled in various ways: Hitler, Hidler, Hiedler and Huettler. It seems reasonable to suppose, however, that it is fundamentally the same name spelled in various ways by different members of what was basically an illiterate peasant family. Adolph Hitler himself signed his name Hittler on the first party membership blanks, and his sister usually spells her name as Hiedler. Another element of confusion is introduced by the fact that Adolph's mother's mother was also named Hitler which later became the family name of his father. Some of this confusion is dissipated, however, when we realize that Adolph's parents had a common ancestor (father's grandfather and mother's great-grandfather), an inhabitant of the culturally backward Waldviertel district of Austria.

Adolph's father, Alois Hitler, was the illegitimate son of Maria Anna Schicklgruber. It is generally supposed that the father of Alois Hitler was a Johann Georg Hiedler, a miller's assistant. Alois, however, was not legitimized, and bore his mother's name until he was forty years of age when he changed it to Hitler. Just why this was done is not clear, but it is generally said among the villagers that it was necessary in order to obtain a legacy. Where the legacy came from is unknown. One could suppose that Johann Georg Hiedler relented on his deathbed and left an inheritance to his illegitimate son together with his name. It seems strange, however, that he did not legitimize the son when he married Anna Schicklgruber thirty-five years earlier. Why the son chose to take the name Hitler instead of Hiedler, if this is the case, is also a mystery which has remained unsolved. Unfortunately, the date of the death of Hiedler has not been established and consequently we are unable to relate these two events in time. A peculiar series of events, prior to Hitler's birth, furnishes plenty of food for speculation.

Hitler's Father

104

There are some people who seriously doubt that Johann Georg Hiedler was the father of Alois. Thyssen and Koehler, for example, claim that Chancellor Dollfuss had ordered the Austrian police to conduct a thorough investigation into the Hitler family. As a result of this investigation a secret document was prepared which proved that Maria Anna Schicklgruber was living in Vienna at the time she conceived. At that time she was employed as a servant in the home of Baron Rothschild. As soon as the family discovered her pregnancy she was sent back to her home in Spital where Alois was born. If it is true that one of the Rothschilds is the real father of Alois Hitler, it would make Adolph a quarter Jew. According to these sources, Adolph Hitler knew of the existence of this document and the incriminating evidence it contained. In order to obtain it he precipitated events in Austria and initiated the assassination of Dollfuss. According to this story, he failed to obtain the document at that time since Dollfuss had secreted it and had told Schuschnigg of its whereabouts so that in the event of his death the independence of Austria would remain assured. Several stories of this general character are in circulation.

Those who lend credence to this story point out several factors which seem to favor its plausibility:

(a) That it is unlikely that the miller's assistant in a small village in this district would have very much to leave in the form of a legacy.

(b) That it is strange that Johann Hiedler should not claim the boy until thirty-five years after he had married the mother and the mother had died.

(c) That if the legacy were left by Hiedler on the condition that Alois take his name, it would not have been possible for him to change it to Hitler.

(d) That the intelligence and behavior of Alois as well as that of his two sons, is completely out of keeping with that usually found in Austrian peasant families. They point out that their ambitiousness and extraordinary political intuition is much more in harmony with the Rothschild tradition.

(e) That Alois Schicklgruber left his home village at an early age to seek his fortune in Vienna where his mother had worked.

(f) That it would be peculiar for Alois Hitler, while working as a customs official in Braunau, to choose a Jew named Prinz, of Vienna, to act as Adolph's godfather unless he felt some kinship with the Jews himself.

This is certainly a very intriguing hypothesis and much of Adolph's later behavior could be explained in rather easy terms on this

C02571145

basis. However, it is not absolutely necessary to assume that he has Jewish blood in his veins in order to make a comprehensive picture of his character with its manifold traits and sentiments. From a purely scientific point of view, therefore, it is sounder not to base our reconstruction on such slim evidence but to seek firmer foundations. Nevertheless, we can leave it as a possibility which requires further verification.

In any event, Maria Anna Schicklgruber died when Alois was five years of age. When he was thirteen he left the Waldviertel and went to Vienna where he learned to be a cobbler. The next twenty-three years of his life are largely unaccounted for. It seems probable that during this time he joined the army and had perhaps been advanced to the rank of non-commissioned officer. His service in the army may have helped him to enter the Civil Service as Zollamtsoffizial later on.

His married life was stormy. His first wife (born Glasl-Hoerer) was about thirteen years older than himself. She is alleged to have been the daughter of one of his superiors and seems to have been in poor health. In any event, the marriage turned out badly and they finally separated since, as Catholics, a complete divorce was not possible. His first wife died in 1883.

In January, 1882, Franziska Matzelsberger gave birth to an illegitimate son who was named Alois. After the death of his first wife on April 6, 1883, Alois Hitler married Franziska Matzelsberger on May 22, 1883 and legitimized his son. On July 28, 1883, his second wife bore him another child, Angela, and a year later, on August 10, 1884, she also died. During the time of his first marriage the couple had taken as a foster-daughter Klara Poelzl, Alois Hitler's second cousin once removed. He had reared her up to the time of the separation from his first wife when she went to Vienna as a servant. During the last months of the life of his second wife, Klara Poelzl returned to his home to look after the invalid and the two children. She remained in his home as housekeeper after the death of his second wife and on January 7, 1885 he married her. On May 17, 1885 she gave birth to a son who died in infancy. It is alleged by William Patrick Hitler, Adolph's nephew, that an illegitimate child was born previously, but we have no other record of this. In any event, at least one child was conceived out of wedlock. Four more children were born of this union. This is certainly a tempestuous married life for a customs officer—three wives, seven or possibly eight children, one divorce, at least one birth and possibly two before marriage, two directly after the wedding, one wife thirteen years older than himself and another twenty-three years younger, one the daughter of a superior, one a waitress, and the third a servant and his foster-daughter. All of this, of course, has never been mentioned by Hitler. In MEIN KAMPF he gives a very simple picture of conditions in his father's home.

Relatively little is known about Alois Hitler. It seems that he was very proud of his achievements in the Civil Service and yet he retired from this service at the astonishing age of fifty-six, four years after Adolph was born. In very rapid succession the family moved into several different villages and the father tried his hand at farming. It is said, however, that he always wore his customs official's uniform and insisted on being addressed as Herr Oberoffizial Hitler. According to reports, he liked to lord it over his neighbors whom he may have looked down upon as "mere" peasants. In any event, it seems quite certain that he enjoyed sitting in the tavern and relating his adventures as a customs official and also in discussing political topics. He died on his way to the tavern in Leonding from a stroke of apoplexy in 1903.

He is generally described as a very domineering individual who was a veritable tyrant in his home. William Patrick Hitler says that he has heard from his father, Adolph's elder half-brother, that he used to beat the children unmercifully. On one occasion it is alleged he beat the older son into a state of unconsciousness and on another occasion beat Adolph so severely that he left him for dead. It is also alleged that he was somewhat of a drunkard and that frequently the children would have to bring him home from the taverns. When he reached home a grand scene would take place during which he would beat wife, children and dog rather indiscriminately. Although this story is rather generally accepted it is probably an exaggeration. Heiden, who interviewed a number of the villagers in various places where the family had lived, could not find substantiating evidence. Many found the old man rather amusing and claimed that his home life was fairly happy and quiet except when his wife's sister came to visit with the family. Why this should be a disturbing factor is unknown. Heiden suspects that the legacy was a bone of contention.

There is also some doubt about the complexion of Alois Hitler's political sentiments. Hanisch reports: "Hitler heard from his father only praise of Germany and all the faults of Austria." According to Heiden, more reliable informants claim that the father, though full of complaints and criticisms of the government he served, was by no means a German nationalist. They say he favored Austria against Germany and this coincides with William Patrick Hitler's information that his grandfather was definitely anti-German just as his own father was.

Mother.

Klara Poelzl, as has been said, was the foster-daughter of her husband and twenty-three years his junior. She came from old peasant stock, was hard-working, energetic, pious and conscientious. Whether it was due to her years of domestic service or to her upbringing, her home was always spotlessly clean, everything had its place and not a speck of dust was to be found on the furniture. She was very devoted to her

67

108

children and, according to William Patrick Hitler, was a typical step-mother to her step-children. According to Dr. Bloch who treated her, she was a very quiet, sweet and affectionate woman whose life centered around her children and particularly Adolph, who was her pet. She spoke highly of her husband and the life they had had together. She felt it was a real deprivation for the children to have lost their father while they were still so young.

One could question her background. Her sister is married and has two sons, one of whom is a hunchback and has an impediment in his speech. When we consider that Klara Poelzl may have lost one child before her marriage to Alois Hitler, another son born in 1885 who died in 1887, another son born in 1894 who died in 1900, and a girl who was born in 1886 and died in 1888, one has grounds to question the purity of the blood. There is even cause for greater suspicion when we learn from Dr. Bloch that he is certain that there was a daughter slightly older than Adolph who was an imbecile. He is absolutely certain of this because he noticed at the time that the family always tried to hide the child and keep her out of the way when he came to attend the mother. It is possible that this is Ida who was born in 1886 and who is alleged to have died in 1888, except that Dr. Bloch believes that this girl's name was Klara. He may, however, be mistaken in this particularly since both names end in "a" and he never had any close contact with her. There is no other mention of a Klara anywhere in the records. The younger sister, Paula, is also said to be a little on the stupid side, perhaps a high-grade moron. This is certainly a poor record and one is justified in suspecting some constitutional weakness. A syphilitic taint is not beyond the realm of possibility. The mother died following an operation for cancer of the breast on December 21, 1907. All biographers have given the date of her death as December 21, 1908 but Dr. Bloch's records show clearly that she died in 1907 and John Gunther's record of the inscription on her tombstone corroborates this. The last six months of her life were spent in extreme pain and during the last weeks it was necessary to give her injections of morphine daily.

It is often alleged that she was of Czech origin and spoke only a broken German and that consequently Adolph may have been ashamed of her among his playmates. This is almost certainly untrue. Dr. Bloch reports that she did not have any trace of an accent of any kind nor did she show any Czech characteristics. Alois Hitler's first wife was of Czech origin and later writers may have confused her with Adolph's mother.

Siblings   *Alois, Jr.*

Alois Hitler, Jr., was born January 13, 1882, the illegitimate son of the father's second wife but was born during the lifetime of the first wife. He is the father of William Patrick Hitler, one of our informants. He seems to have taken very much after his father in some respects. He left the parental home before the death of his father because, according to his

C02571145

Approved For Release 1999/08/24 : CIA-RDP78-02646R000600240001-5

son, he could tolerate it no longer. His step-mother, according to the story, made life very difficult for him and continually antagonized her husband against him. It seems that Alois, Jr., had considerable talent for mechanical pursuits and his father had planned on sending him to a technical school for training as an engineer. Until his third marriage the father was very fond of his oldest boy and all his ambitions were wrapped up in him. But the step-mother systematically undermined this relationship and finally persuaded the father that Alois, Jr. was unworthy and that he should save his money for the education of her son, Adolph. She was finally successful and Alois, Jr. was sent away from home as an apprentice waiter.

Evidently the profession of waiter did not intrigue him, for in 1900 he received a five-months' sentence for thievery and in 1902 he was sentenced to eight months in jail for the same reason. He then went to London where he obtained a position as a waiter and, in 1909, married Bridget Dowling, an Irish girl. In 1911 William Patrick Hitler was born and in 1913 his father deserted the family and returned to Germany. The family was not a happy one and broke up several times in the course of these four years. It is alleged that the father drank quite frequently and would then come home and create tremendous scenes during which he frequently beat his wife and tried to beat the small infant. During these four years when his mother and father had separated for a time, his father did go to Vienna. This would agree with Hanfstaengl's conviction that Alois, Jr. was in Vienna at the same time that Adolph was there.

In 1924 Alois, Jr. was brought before the court of Hamburg charged with bigamy. He was sentenced to six months in prison but since his first wife did not prosecute the sentence was suspended. He has an illegitimate child by the second wife who lives in Germany. During all these years he has never sent any money for the support of his first wife or child. Up until the time of the inflation it is alleged that he had a very successful business in Germany. The business failed and he has had various jobs up until 1934 when he opened a restaurant in Berlin which became a popular meeting-place for S.A. men.

According to the son, Alois, Jr. heartily disliked Adolph as a boy. He always felt that Adolph was spoiled by his mother and that he was forced to do many of the chores that Adolph should have done. Furthermore, it seems that Adolph occasionally got into mischief which his mother would blame on Alois and Alois would have to take the punishment from his father. He used to say as a boy he would have liked to have wrung Adolph's neck on more than one occasion and considering the circumstances this is probably not far from the truth. Since Hitler came to power, the two brothers have practically no contact with each other. They have come together a few times but the meeting is usually unpleasant, with Adolph taking a very high-handed attitude and laying

110

down the law to the rest of the family. Alois, Jr. is not mentioned in MEIN KAMPF and only a few people in Germany know of his relationship to Hitler. According to a newspaper report he was sent to a concentration camp in 1942 because he talked too much.

William Patrick Hitler.

He is a young man of thirty-two, the son of Alois, Jr. who has not amounted to much. Before his uncle came to power he worked as a bookkeeper in London. When his uncle became famous he obviously expected that something would be done for his family. He gave up his job in London and went to Germany where he had some contact with Adolph Hitler. The latter, however, was chiefly interested in keeping him under cover and provided him with a minor job in the Opal Automobile Company. It is my impression that William Patrick was quite ready to blackmail both his father and his uncle but that things did not work out as planned. He returned to England and, as a British subject came to this country where he is a professional speaker. He is also engaged in writing a book about his associations and experiences in Hitler Germany.

Angela.

She is an elder half-sister of Adolph. She seems to be the most normal one in the family and from all reports is rather a decent and industrious person. During her childhood she became very fond of Adolph despite the fact that she had the feeling that his mother was spoiling him. She is the only one of the family with whom Adolph has had any contact in later years and the only living relative Hitler ever mentioned. When his mother died in 1907 there was a small inheritance which was to be divided among the children. Since the two girls had no immediate means of earning a livelihood the brothers turned over their share to help the girls along. Adolph turned his share over to Angela while Alois turned his over to a younger sister, Paula. Angela later married an official named Raubal in Linz who died not long afterwards. She then went to Vienna where, after the war, she was manager of the Mensa Academica Judaica. Some of our informants knew her during this time and report that in the student riots Angela defended the Jewish students from attack, and on several occasions beat the Aryan students off the steps of the dining hall with a club. She is a rather large, strong peasant type of person who is well able to take an active part.

After Adolph was discharged from the army at the close of the last war, it is alleged that he went to Vienna and visited Angela with whom he had had no contact for ten years. While he was confined in Landsberg she made the trip from Vienna to visit him. In 1924 she moved to Munich with her daughter, Geli, and kept house for Adolph. Later, she took over the management of Berchtesgaden. In 1936 friction developed between Adolph and Angela and she left Berchtesgaden and moved to Dresden where she married Professor Hamitsch. It is reported

Hitler with His Half-Sister Angela

by William Patrick that the cause of the break was the discovery by Hitler that she was in a conspiracy with Goering to purchase the land adjoining Hitler's house at Berchtesgaden. This enraged Hitler to the extent that he ordered her from the house and has had little contact with her since. In any case, Adolph did not attend her second wedding.

Geli Raubal.

Hitler's relationship with Geli, Angela's daughter, has already been described in the previous section. She died in 1930.

Leo Raubal.

It has been generally assumed that Geli was the only child of Angela. William Patrick Hitler, however, reports that there was also a son named Leo. Not much is known of him except that he refused to have anything to do with his uncle Adolph after the death of Geli. He had a job in Salzburg and frequently came to Berchtesgaden to visit his mother when Hitler was in Berlin, but would leave again just as soon as word was received that Hitler was on his way there. According to William Patrick, he openly accused Hitler of causing Geli's death and refused to speak to him again as long as he lived. Word has been received that he was killed in 1942 while in the Balkans.

Paula Hitler.

Paula Hitler, or Hiedler, is Adolph's real sister and is seven years younger. What happened to her after her mother's death is a mystery until she was discovered living very poorly in an attic in Vienna where she has a position addressing envelopes for an insurance company. She now lives under the name of Frau Wolf (Hitler's nickname is Wolf) and is alleged to be very queer and to receive no one in her home. Dr. Bloch went to visit her in the hope that she might intercede with her brother and obtain permission for him to take some money out of the country when he was exiled. He rapped on her door a number of times but received no answer. Finally, the neighbor on the same landing came to the door and asked who he was and what he wanted. The neighbor explained that Frau Wolf never received anyone and intimated that she was very queer (other writers have also reported this). She promised, however, to deliver any message he might give her. Dr. Bloch explained his predicament in detail. The next day when he returned, hoping that he would have an opportunity of speaking to Paula Hitler personally, the neighbor reported that Paula was very glad to hear from him and that she would do everything she could to help him. Nothing more.

During her childhood, according to William Patrick Hitler, she and Adolph did not get on very well together. There seems to have been considerable friction and jealousy between them, particularly since Alois, Jr. was always taking her side. As far as is known, Hitler had no contact with her whatever from the time his mother died until 1933 when he became Chancellor. He has never mentioned her anywhere, as far as can be determined. It is alleged that he now sends her a small allowance each month to alleviate her poverty and keep her out of the limelight. According to William Patrick Hitler, his uncle became more interested in her as the friction with Angela increased. It is said that he has had her visit him at Berchtesgaden and William Patrick met her at the Bayreuth Festival in 1939 where she went by the name of Frau Wolf, but Hitler did not mention to anyone that it was his sister. He said she is a little on the stupid side and not very interesting to talk to since she rarely opens her mouth.

This is Adolph Hitler's family, past and present. It is possible that there is another sister, Ida, an imbecile, who is still living, but if so we have no knowledge of her whereabouts. On the whole, it is nothing to be proud of and Hitler may be wise in keeping it well under cover.

If we let our imaginations carry us back into the early '90's it is not difficult to picture what life was like for Adolph in his earliest years. His father was probably not much company for his mother. Not only was he twenty-three years older but, it seems, he spent most of his spare time in the taverns or gossiping with the neighbors. Furthermore, his mother knew only too well the past history of her husband, who was also her foster-father, and one can imagine that for a twenty-five year old woman this was not what might be called a romantic marriage. Moreover, Klara Hitler had lost her first two children, and possibly a third, in the course of three or four years. Then Adolph arrived. Under these circumstances, it is almost inevitable that he became the focal point in her life and that she left no stone unturned to keep him alive. All of the affection that normally would have gone to her husband and to her other children now became lavished on this newly born son.

It is safe to assume that for five years little Adolph was the center of attraction in this home. But then a terrible event happened in Adolph's life — another son was born. No longer was he the center of attraction, no longer was he the king of the roost. The newcomer usurped all this and little Adolph, who was on his way to growing up, was left to shift more or less for himself — at least, so it probably seemed to him. Sharing was something he had not learned up to this time, and it was probably a bitter experience for him as it is for most children who have a sibling born when they are in this age period. In fact, in view of the earlier experiences of his parents it is reasonable to suppose that it was probably more acute in his case than it is with the average boy.

For two years he had to put up with this state of affairs. Then matters went from bad to worse — a baby sister was born. More competition and still less attention for the baby sister and the ailing brother were consuming all of his mother's time while he was being sent off to school

114

and made to take care of himself. Four years later tragedy again visited the Hitler household. When Adolph was eleven years old (in 1900) his baby brother, Edmund, died. Again we can imagine that Adolph reaped an additional harvest of affection and again became the apple of his mother's eye.

This is certainly an extraordinary series of events which must have left their mark on Adolph's immature personality. What probably went on in his mind during these years we shall consider later on. It is sufficient at the moment to point out the extraordinary sequence of events and the probable effects they had on the members of the family and their relations with each other.

When Adolph was six years old he was sent off to school. The first school was a very small Volkschule where three grades met in the same room and were taught by the same teacher. In spite of the fact that he had to change schools several times in the course of the next few years, due to the fact that his father kept buying and selling his property and moving from one place to another, he seems to have done quite well in his studies. When he was eight years old he attended a Benedict Monastery in Lamback. He was very much intrigued with all this — it gave him his first powerful impression of human achievement. At that time his ambition was to become an abbot. But things did not work out very well. He was dismissed from the monastery because he was caught smoking in the gardens. His last year in Volkschule was in Leonding where he received high marks in all his subjects with the occasional exception of singing, drawing and physical exercises.

In 1900, the year his brother Edmund died, he entered the Realschule in Linz. To the utter amazement of all who knew him his school work was so poor that he failed and had to repeat the class another time. Then there was a gradual improvement in his work, particularly in history, free-hand drawing and gymnastics. In these subjects he was marked "excellent" several times. Mathematics, French, German, etc., remained mediocre, sometimes satisfactory, sometimes unsatisfactory. On "Effort" he was frequently marked "irregular". When he was fourteen years of age his father died suddenly. The following year he left the Realschule in Linz and attended the one in Steyr. We do not know why this change was made. Dr. Bloch is under the impression that he was doing badly toward the end of the year in the Linz school and was sent to Styria because it had the reputation of being easier. But his performance there was very mediocre. The only two subjects in which he excelled were in free-hand drawing, in which he was marked "praiseworthy", and gymnastics, in which he received the mark of "excellent". In the first semester "German Language" was "unsatisfactory" and in "History" it was "adequate".

All this is beautifully glossed over in Hitler's description of these years. According to his story he was at odds with his father concerning his future career as artist and in order to have his own way he sabotaged his studies — at least those he felt would not contribute to an artist's career, and History which he says always fascinated him. In these studies, according to his own story he was always outstanding. An examination of his report cards reveals no such thing. History, even in his last year in Realschule is adequate or barely passing, and other subjects which might be useful to an artist are in the same category. A better diagnosis would be that he was outstanding in those subjects which did not require any preparation or thought while in those that required application he was sadly lacking. We frequently find report cards of this type among our patients who are very intelligent but refuse to work. They are bright enough to catch on to a few of the fundamental principles without exerting themselves and clever enough to amplify these sufficiently to obtain a passing grade without ever doing any studying. They give the impression of knowing something about the subject but their knowledge is very superficial and is glossed over with glib words and terminology.

This evaluation of Hitler's school career fits in with the testimony of former fellow students and teachers. According to their testimony he never applied himself and was bored with what was going on. While the teacher was explaining new material, he read the books of Karl May (Indian and Wild West stories) which he kept concealed under his desk. He would come to school with bowie knives, hatchets, etc., and was always trying to initiate Indian games in which he was to be the leader. The other boys, however, were not greatly impressed by him and his big talk or his attempts to play the leader. On the whole, they preferred to follow the leadership of boys who were more socially-minded, more realistic in their attitudes and held greater promise of future achievements than Hitler who gave every indication of being lazy, uncooperative, lived in a world of fantasy, talked big but did nothing of merit. He probably did not improve his standing with the other boys, when, in his twelfth year, he was found guilty of a "Sittlichkeitsvergehen" in the school. Just what the sexual indiscretion consisted of we do not know but Dr. Bloch, who remembers that one of the teachers in the school told him about it, feels certain that he had done something with a little girl. He was severely censured for this and barely missed being expelled from school. It is possible that he was ostracized by his fellow students and that this is the reason he changed schools the following year.

In September, 1905, he stopped going to school altogether and returned to Leonding where he lived with his mother and sister. According to his biographers, he was suffering from lung trouble during this period and had to remain in bed the greater part of the time. Dr. Bloch, who was the family doctor at this time is at a loss to understand how this story ever got started because there was no sign of lung trouble of any sort. Adolph came to his office now and then with a slight cold or a sore throat but there was nothing else wrong with him. According to Dr. Bloch, he was a very quiet boy at this time, rather slight in build but fairly wiry. He was always very courteous and patiently waited for his turn. He made no fuss when the doctor looked into his throat or when he swabbed it with an antiseptic. He was very shy and had little to say except when spoken to. But there was no sign of lung trouble.

During this time, however, he frequently went with his mother to visit his aunt in Spital, Lower Austria where he also spent vacations. The doctor who treated him there is alleged to have said to the aunt: "From this illness Adolph will not recover." It has been assumed that he referred to a lung condition but he may have been referring to something else entirely. In any event Dr. Bloch is convinced that there were no indications of lung trouble a few months later when Adolph returned to Leonding.

Although the mother's income was extremely modest, Adolph made no attempt to find work. There is some evidence that he went to a Munich art school for a short time during this period. Most of his time, however, was evidently spent in loafing around and daubing paints and water colors. He took long walks into the hills, supposedly to paint, but it is reported that he was seen there delivering speeches to the rocks of the countryside in a most energetic tone of voice.

In October, 1907, he went to Vienna to prepare himself for the State examinations for admission as student to the Academy of Art. He qualified for admission to the examination but failed to be accepted as a student. He returned home to Linz but there is no indication that he communicated to anybody the results of the examination. It was undoubtedly a severe blow to him for he tells us himself that he couldn't understand it, "he was so sure he would succeed." At this time his mother had already undergone an operation for cancer of the breast. She was failing rather rapidly and little hope was held for her recovery. She died on December 21, 1907, and was buried on Christmas Eve. To preserve a last impression, he sketched her on her deathbed. Adolph, according to Dr. Bloch, was completely broken: "In all my career I have never seen anyone so prostrate with grief as Adolph Hitler." Although his sisters came to Dr. Bloch a few days after the funeral and expressed themselves fully, Adolph remained silent. As the little group left, he said: "I shall be grateful to you forever." (29) After the funeral he stood at her grave for a long time after the sisters had left. The bottom had obviously fallen out of his world. Tears came into Dr. Bloch's eyes as he described the tragic scene. "His mother would turn over in her grave if she knew what he turned out to be." (21) This was the end of Adolph Hitler's family life.

C02571145

LATER EXPERIENCES

Vienna.

    Shortly after his mother's death the family broke up and Adolph went to Vienna to make his way in the world as his father had done before him. This was early in 1908. How much money he took with him, if any, is not known. The records here are very vague particularly since all biographers have gone on the supposition that his mother died a year later than she actually did. This leaves an entire year unaccounted for since the next thing we hear of Adolph, he has again applied for admission to the examinations for the Academy of Art. One of the conditions for reexamination was that he submit to the Board some of the paintings he had done previously. This he did but the Board was not impressed with them and refused to allow him to enter the examination. This, it seems, was even a greater shock than his failure to pass the examinations a year earlier.

    After he had received notification to the effect that his work was of such a nature that it did not warrant his admission to the second examination, he interviewed the Director. He claims that the Director told him that his drawings showed clearly that his talents lay in the direction of architecture rather than pure art and advised him to seek admission to the Architectural School. This he applied for but was not admitted, according to his story, because he had not satisfactorily finished his course in the Realschule. To be sure, this was one of the general requirements but exceptions could be made in the case of boys who showed unusual talent. Hitler's rejection, therefore, was on the grounds of insufficient talent rather than for failure to complete his school course.

    He was now without hope. All his dreams of being a great artist seemed to be nipped in the bud. He was without money and without friends. He was forced to go to work and found employment as a laborer on construction jobs. This, however, did not suit him. Friction developed between himself and his fellow workmen. It seems logical to suppose that he was working beneath his class and refused to mingle with them for he tells us that he sat apart from the others and ate his lunch. Further difficulties developed inasmuch as the workmen tried to convert him to a Marxian point of view. Their attitudes and arguments jarred him since they were far from the ideal Germany that had been portrayed by his favorite Linz teacher, Ludwig Poetsch, an ardent German nationalist. But Hitler found himself unable to answer their arguments. He made the unpleasant discovery that the workmen knew more than he did. He was fundamentally against everything they said but he was unable to justify his point of view on an intellectual level — he was at a terrible disadvantage. In order to remedy the situation he began reading all kinds of political pamphlets and attending political meetings but not with the idea of understanding the problem as a whole, which might have en-

118

abled him to form an intelligent opinion, but to find arguments which would support his earlier conviction. This is a trait that runs throughout his life. He never studies to learn but only to justify what he feels. In other words, his judgments are based wholly on emotional factors and are then clothed with an intellectual argument. Soon, he tells us, he knew more than they did about their own political ideology and was able to tell them things about it which they did not know themselves.

It was this, according to Hitler, which antagonized the workmen against him. In any case, he was run off the job with the threat that if he appeared again they would push him off the scaffold. This must have been during the first half of 1909 when he was twenty years old. Without a job, he sunk lower and lower in the social scale and at times must have been on the verge of starvation. At times he found an odd job such as carrying luggage, shoveling snow or running errands but a large part of his time was spent in breadlines or begging on the streets. In November, 1909, he was ousted from his room because he did not pay his rent and was forced to seek refuge in a flophouse. Here he met Reinhold Hanisch who was in much the same predicament. Years later, Hanisch wrote a long book about his associations with Hitler during this period. It is a gruesome story of unbelievable poverty. Hitler must have been a sorry sight during these days with a full black beard, badly clothed and a haggard look. Hanisch writes:

> "It was a miserable life and I once asked him what he was really waiting for. The answer: 'I don't know myself'. I have never seen such hopeless letting down in distress."

Hanisch took him in hand and encouraged him to do some painting. The difficulty was that neither one had the money with which to buy materials. When Hanisch discovered that Hitler had signed over his inheritance to his sister, he persuaded Hitler to write her and obtain a small loan. This was presumably his half-sister, Angela. When the money was received Hitler's first thought was to take a week's vacation in order to recuperate. At this time he moved into the Maennerheim Brigittenau which was slightly better than the flophouses in which he had been staying.

He and Hanisch went into business together. It was Hitler's job to paint post cards, posters and water colors which Hanisch then took around Vienna and peddled to art dealers, furniture stores, etc. In this he was quite successful but his difficulties were not at an end. The moment Hitler got a little money, he refused to work. Hanisch describes this vividly:

> "But unfortunately Hitler was never an ardent worker. I often was driven to despair by bringing in orders that he simply wouldn't carry out. At Easter, 1910, we earned forty

C02571145

> kronen on a big order and we divided it equally. The next morning, when I came downstairs and asked for Hitler, I was told he had already left with Neumann, a Jew, ... After that I couldn't find him for a week. He was sight-seeing Vienna with Neumann and spent much of the time in the museum. When I asked him what the matter was and whether we were going to keep on working, he answered that he must recuperate now, that he must have some leisure, that he was not a coolie. When the week was over, he had no longer any money."

At this time, Hitler was not a Jew-hater. There were a number of Jews living in the Men's Home with whom he was on excellent terms. Most of his paintings were sold to Jewish dealers who paid just as much for them as the Aryans. He also admired Rothschild for sticking to his religion even if it prevented him from entering court. During this time he also sent two post cards to Dr. Bloch, in Linz, who was a Jew. One of these was just a picture post card of Vienna; the other, a copy which he had painted. On both of them he wrote of his deep gratitude to the doctor. This is mentioned because it is one of the very few cases of which we have any record in which Hitler showed any lasting gratitude. During this time Hitler himself looked very Jewish. Hanisch writes:

> "Hitler at that time looked very Jewish, so that I often joked with him that he must be of Jewish blood, since such a large beard rarely grows on a Christian's chin. Also he had big feet, as a desert wanderer must have." (73)

In spite of his close association with Hanisch the relationship ended in a quarrel. Hitler accused Hanisch of withholding some of the money he had received for a picture. He had Hanisch arrested and appeared as a witness against him. We have little knowledge of what happened to Hitler after this time. According to Hanfstaengl the home in which Hitler lived had the reputation of being a place where homosexual men frequently went to find companions. Jahn said that he had information from a Viennese official that on the police record Hitler was listed as a sexual pervert but it gave no details of offenses. It is possible that the entry may have been made solely on suspicion. Simone (467) claims that the Viennese police file in 1912 recorded a charge of theft against Hitler and that he moved from Vienna to Munich in order to avoid arrest. This would fit in with Hanfstaengl's suspicion that Hitler's elder half-brother (who was twice convicted for theft) was in Vienna at that time and that they may have become involved in some minor crime. This would not be impossible for Hanisch tells us that Hitler frequently spent his time figuring out shady ways of making money. One example may be of interest:

> "He proposed to fill old tin cans with paste and sell them to shopkeepers, the paste to be smeared on windowpanes to keep them from freezing in winter. It should be sold . . . in the

summer, when it couldn't be tried out. I told him it wouldn't work because the merchants would just say, come back in the winter. . . . Hitler answered that one must possess a talent for oratory."

Since Hitler could only be brought to work when he was actually hungry he spent a good deal of time reading political pamphlets, sitting in cafe houses, reading newspapers and delivering speeches to the other inmates of the home. He became a great admirer of Georg von Schoenerer and the Viennese mayor, Karl Lueger. It was presumably from them that he learned his anti-Semitism and many of the tricks of a successful politician. According to Hanisch his companions were greatly amused by him and often ridiculed him and his opinions. In any event it seems that he got a good deal of practice in speech-making during these years which stood him in good stead later on. Even in these days, he talked about starting a new party.

It is not clear why he remained in Vienna and lived in such poverty for five years, when he had such a deep love for Germany and could have gone there with relatively little difficulty. It is also not clear why he went when he did unless there is some truth in the supposition that he fled Vienna to avoid arrest. His own explanation is that he could not tolerate the mixture of people, particularly the Jews and always more Jews, and says that for him Vienna is the symbol of incest.

But as far as Hitler is concerned this time was not lost. As he looks back over that period he can say:

"So in a few years I built a foundation of knowledge from which I still draw nourishment today." (MK 29)

"At that time I formed an image of the world and a view of life which became the granite foundation for my actions." (MK 30)

Pre-War Munich.

In Munich before the war, things were no better for him. As far as poverty is concerned he might as well have stayed in Vienna. He earned a little money painting post cards and posters and at times painting houses. Early in 1913 he went to Salzburg to report for duty in the army but was rejected on the grounds of poor physical condition. He returned to Munich and continued to work at odd jobs and sit in cafe houses where he spent his time reading newspapers. Nothing of which we have any knowledge happened during this time which is pertinent to our present study. The prospects of ever making anything out of himself in the future must have been very black at that time.

World War.

Then came the World War. He writes of this occasion:

"The struggle of the year 1914 was forsooth, not forced on the masses, but desired by the whole people."

"To myself those hours came like a redemption from the vexatious experiences of my youth. Even to this day I am not ashamed to say that, in a transport of enthusiasm, I sank down on my knees and thanked Heaven from an overflowing heart. . . ."

On August 3, 1914, Hitler joined a Bavarian regiment as a volunteer. During the first days of the war his regiment suffered very heavy losses and was not particularly popular among the Bavarian people. Hitler became an orderly in Regimental Headquarters as well as a runner. The one thing that all his comrades commented on was his subservience to superior officers. It seems that he went out of his way to court their good graces, offering to do their washing and other menial tasks much to the disgust of his comrades. He was not popular with the other men and always remained aloof from them. When he did join them he usually harangued about political matters. During the four years of war he received no packages or mail from anyone. In this he was unique. At Christmas time when everyone else was receiving gifts and messages he withdrew from the group and sulked moodily by himself. When his comrades encouraged him to join the group and share their packages he refused. On October 7, 1916, he was wounded by a piece of shrapnel and sent to a hospital. It was a light wound and he was soon discharged and sent to Munich as a replacement. After two days there he wrote his commanding officer, Captain Wiedemann, asking that he be reinstated in his regiment because he could not tolerate Munich when he knew his comrades were at the Front. Wiedemann had him returned to the regiment where he remained until October 14th when he was exposed to mustard gas and sent to a hospital in Pasewalk. He was blind and, according to Friedelinde Wagner, also lost his voice.

It seems that mystery always follows Hitler. His career in the army is no exception. There are several things that have never been satisfactorily explained. The first is that he spent four years in the same regiment but was never advanced beyond the rank of First Class Private or Lance Corporal. The second is the Iron Cross First Class which he constantly wears. This has been the topic of much discussion but the mystery has never been solved. There is no mention of the award in the history of his regiment. This is rather amazing inasmuch as other awards of this kind are listed. Hitler is mentioned in a number of other connections but not in this one, although it is alleged that it was awarded to him for capturing twelve Frenchmen, including an officer, singlehanded. This is certainly no ordinary feat in any regiment and one would expect that it would at least merit some mention, particularly in view of the fact that Hitler had considerable fame as a politician when the book went to press.

The Nazi propaganda agencies have not helped to clarify the

Hitler as a Soldier in World War I

82

situation. Not only have a number of different versions of the story appeared in the press, but each gives a different number of Frenchmen he is alleged to have captured. They have also published alleged facsimiles of his war record which do not agree. The Berlin Illustrierte Zeitung of August 10, 1939 printed a facsimile in which the date of award for this decoration was clearly August 4, 1918. Yet the Voelkische Beobachter of August 14, 1934 had published a facsimile in which the date of award was October 4, 1918. Although these alleged facsimiles mentioned other citations they did not include the date of award of the Iron Cross Second Class. From all that can be learned the First Class Cross was never awarded unless the recipient had already been awarded the Second Class decoration.

Just what the facts are it is impossible to determine. It is alleged that his war record has been badly tampered with and that von Schleicher was eliminated during the Blood Purge because he knew the true facts. Strasser who served in the same division has probably as good an explanation as any. He says that during the last months of the war there were so many First Class Crosses being given out that General Headquarters was no longer able to pass on the merits of each individual case. To facilitate matters a number of these decorations were allotted

Hitler as a Soldier in World War I

to each regiment every month to be issued by the Commanding Officers. They, in turn, notified the High Command of the award and the deed which merited it. According to Strasser, when the army began to collapse, the Regimental Headquarters had in their possession a number of decorations which had not been awarded. Since few members of the Headquarters Staff ever received an award of this type they took advantage of the general melee and gave them to each other and forged the signature of the commanding officer in sending it to the High Command. The thing that speaks in favor of this explanation is the curious bond which exists between Hitler and his regimental sergeant-major, Max Amann who was later to become the head of the Nazi Eher Verlag. This is one of the most lucrative positions in the entire Nazi hierarchy and Amann was called to the position by Hitler.

The only explanation for the lack of promotion that has been published is the comment of one of his officers to the effect that he would never make a non-commissioned officer "out of that neurotic fellow, Hitler." Rauschning (947) gives a different explanation. He claims that a high Nazi had once confided in him that he had seen Hitler's military record and that it contained an item of a court martial which found him guilty of pederastic practices with an officer, and that it was for this reason that he was never promoted. Rauschning also claims that in Munich Hitler was found guilty of a violation of paragraph 175 which deals with pederasty. No other evidence of either of these two charges has been found.

The mystery becomes even deeper when we learn from a great many informants that Hitler was quite courageous and never tried to evade dangerous assignments. It is said that he was unusually adept at running and then falling or seeking shelter when the fire became intense. It also seems that he was always ready to volunteer for special assignments and was considered exceedingly reliable in the performance of all his duties by his own officers.

It may be well to mention at this point that when Hitler entered the army he again became a member of a recognized and respected social institution. No longer did he have to stand in breadlines or seek shelter in flophouses. For the first time since his mother died did he really belong to a group of people. Not only did this provide him with a sense of pride and security but at last he had achieved his great ambition, namely, to be united with the German nation. It is also interesting to note a considerable change in his appearance. From the dirty, greasy, cast-off clothes of Jews and other charitable people he was now privileged to wear a uniform. Mend (209), one of his comrades, tells us that when Hitler came out of the trenches or back from an assignment he spent hours cleaning his uniform and boots until he became the joke of the regiment. Quite a remarkable change for one who for almost seven years refused to exert himself just a little in order to pull himself out of the pitiful conditions in which he lived among the dregs of society.

Post-War.

Then came the armistice and all this was over. Adolph Hitler, from a psychological point of view, was in exactly the same position as the one in which he found himself eleven years before when his mother died. He faced the future alone. The army, his home for four years, was breaking up. Again he stood alone before a dismal future — a world in which he could not find a niche, a world which did not care for him, a world of aimless existence fraught with hardships. It was almost more than he could bear and he went into a deep depression which continued for a considerable period of time.

Where to go and what to do. Having no home or family to greet him he returned to Munich not because it had been kind to him in the past but because he had no other place to go. He could take up his life again where he had left off four years earlier. He wandered around Munich for a short time "a stray dog looking for a master." Then it is reported that he went to Vienna to visit his half-sister, Angela, with whom he had had no contact for many years. If he actually made this trip he did not stay long for soon he was back in the reserve army, stationed at Traunstein. Here he could wear the uniform and eat the food of the army and he stayed on there until April, 1920, when the camp was broken up. He then returned to Munich still attached to the army and living in the barracks. During this time he seems to have continued his political discussions with his comrades siding with the Social Democrats against the Communists. According to the Muenchener Post he actually affiliated himself with the Social Democratic Party (483). After the counter-revolution every tenth man in the barracks was shot, but Hitler was singled out beforehand and asked to stand to one side. At the inquiry he appeared before the board with "charge-lists" against some of his comrades which can only signify denunciations for Communistic activities. He had been spying on his comrades and now assigned them to the executioner. In MEIN KAMPF he refers to this occupation as his "first more or less political activity."

The Army now undertook to educate its soldiers in the proper political philosophy and Hitler was assigned to such a course. He spoke so ably in this group that his talent for speaking impressed an officer who was present and Hitler was appointed "education officer." His hour had struck — he was discovered and appreciated, singled out for his talent. He threw himself into this work with great enthusiasm always speaking to larger groups. His confidence grew with his success in swaying people. He was on his way to become a politician. From here on his career is a matter of history and need not be reviewed here.

This is the foundation of Hitler's character. Whatever he tried to be afterwards is only super-structure and the super-structure can be

C02571145

no firmer than the foundations on which it rests. The higher it goes the more unstable it becomes — the more it needs to be propped up and patched up in order to make it hold together. This is not an easy job. It requires constant vigilance, strong defenses and heavy losses in time and energy.

There was unanimous agreement among the four psychoanalysts who have studied the material that Hitler is an hysteric bordering on schizophrenia and not a true paranoiac as so frequently supposed. This means that he is not insane in the commonly accepted sense of the term, but neurotic. He has not lost complete contact with the world about him and is still striving to make some kind of psychological adjustment which will give him a feeling of security in his social group. It also means that there is a definite moral component in his character no matter how deeply it may be buried or how seriously it has been distorted.

With this diagnosis established, we are in a position to make a number of surmises concerning the conscious mental processes which ordinarily take place in Hitler's mind. These form the nucleus of the "Hitler" he consciously knows and must live with. It is in all probability not a happy "Hitler" but one harassed by fears, anxieties, doubts, misgivings, uncertainties, condemnations, feelings of loneliness and of guilt. From our experience with other hysterics we are probably on firm ground when we suppose that Hitler's mind is like a "battle-royal" most of the time with many conflicting and contradictory forces and impulses pulling him this way and that.

Such a state of confusion is not easy to bear. A large part of his energies are usually wasted in wrestling with himself instead of being directed towards the external world. He can see possibilities for gratifications around him but only rarely can he muster enough energy to make a consistent effort. Fears, doubts and implications obstruct his thinking and acting and he becomes indecisive and he frequently ends up doing nothing. Vicarious gratifications through fantasies become substitutes for the satisfaction obtained from real achievements. We must suppose that this is the state that Hitler was in during the seven years that elapsed between the death of his mother and the outbreak of the war when he was wasting his time lying around in flophouses and sitting in cafes in Vienna. Only when his hunger became acute could he muster the energy necessary to apply himself to a few hours of work. As soon as this hunger was appeased he lapsed back into his former state of procrastination and indecision.

We must assume that the periods of procrastination at the present time have a similar origin. He withdraws from society, is depressed and dawdles away his time until "the situation becomes dangerous" then he forces himself to action. He works for a time and as soon as the job is underway "he loses interest in it" and slips back into his leisurely life in which he does nothing except what he is forced to do or likes to do. Now, of course, it is no longer hunger that drives him to work but another motive, even more powerful, of which he is not fully conscious. The nature of this motive will be discussed in the next section.

As one surveys Hitler's behavior patterns, as his close associates observe them, one gets the impression that this is not a single personality but two which inhabit the same body and alternate back and forth. The one is a very soft, sentimental and indecisive individual who has very little drive and wants nothing quite so much as to be amused, liked and looked after. The other is just the opposite—a hard, cruel and decisive person with considerable energy—who seems to know what he wants and is ready to go after it and get it regardless of cost. It is the first Hitler who weeps profusely at the death of his canary and the second Hitler who cries in open court: "Heads will roll." It is the first Hitler who cannot bring himself to discharge an assistant and it is the second Hitler who can order the murder of hundreds, including his best friends, and can say with great conviction: "There will be no peace in the land until a body hangs from every lamp-post." It is the first Hitler who spends his evenings watching movies or going to cabarets and it is the second Hitler who works for days on end with little or no sleep, making plans which will affect the destiny of nations.

Until we understand the magnitude and implications of this duality in his nature we can never understand his actions. It is a kind of "Dr. Jekyl and Mr. Hyde" personality structure in which two wholly different personalities oscillate back and forth and make the individual almost unrecognizable. This characteristic is common to many hysterics. Under these circumstances it is extremely difficult to predict from one moment to the next what his reactions to a given situation are going to be. An illustration may be helpful. According to Russell (746) extravagant preparations were made for the commemorative services for the Germans who died when the battleship Deutschland was bombed. Hitler spoke long and passionately to those attending, as well as over the radio. It was then arranged that he should walk down the line of survivors and review the infantry and naval units drawn up at attention. Newsreel cameramen were stationed at all crucial points:

> "The first widow to whom Hitler spoke a few words cried violently. Her child, who was 10 years old and who stood next to his bereaved mother, began to cry heartrendingly. Hitler patted him on the head and turned uncertainly to the next in line. Before he could speak a word, he was suddenly overcome. He spun completely around, left the carefully prepared program flat. Followed by his utterly surprised companions he walked as fast as he could to his car and had himself driven away from the parade grounds."

This sudden alternation from one to the other is not uncommon.

Close associates have commented on it time and time again. Ludecke (166) writes:

> "There were times when he gave an impression of unhappiness, of loneliness, of inward searching. . . . But in a moment, he would turn again to whatever frenzied task . . . with the swift command of a man born for action."

Rauschning (263):

> "Almost anything might suddenly inflame his wrath and hatred. . . . But equally, the transition from anger to sentimentality or enthusiasm might be quite sudden."

Huddleston (759) writes:

> "His eyes, soft and dreamy as he spoke to me, suddenly flashed and hardened . . . ."

Voight (591) says:

> "Close collaborators for many years said that Hitler was always like this—the slightest difficulty or obstacle could make him scream with rage or burst into tears."

Heiden has commented upon the duality of Hitler's character and has suggested that the procrastinating side is "Hitler" while the fiery personality which erupts from time to time is "the Fuehrer." Although this may not be strictly true from a psychological point of view, it may be helpful to think of them in these terms.

There is not, however, a complete dissociation of the personality. In such a case we would expect to find the personalities alternating with each other quite beyond the voluntary control of the individual. This is clearly not the case with Hitler who can adopt either role more or less at will. At least, he is able, on occasion, to induce the Fuehrer personality to come into existence when the occasion demands. This is what he does at almost every speech. At the beginning as previously mentioned he is nervous and insecure on the platform. At times he has considerable difficulty in finding anything to say. This is "Hitler." But under these circumstances the "Hitler" personality does not usually predominate for any length of time. As soon as he gets the feel of the audience the tempo of the speech increases and the "Fuehrer" personality begins to assert itself. Heiden says: "The stream of speech stiffens him like a stream of water stiffens a hose." As he speaks he seduces himself into believing that he is actually and fundamentally the "Fuehrer," or as Rauschning (268) says: "He doses himself with the morphine of his own verbiage." It is this transformation, of the little Hitler into the great Fuehrer, which takes place under the eyes of his audience which probably fascinates them. By complicated psychological processes they are able to identify themselves with him and as the speech progresses, they themselves are temporarily transformed and inspired.

C02571145

He must also undergo a transformation of this kind when he is expected to make a decision or take definite action. As we have seen, Hitler procrastinates until the situation becomes dangerous and intolerable. When he can procrastinate no longer, he is able to induce the Fuehrer personality to assert itself. Rauschning has put this well:

> "He is languid and apathetic by nature and needs the stimulus of nervous excitement to rouse him out of chronic lethargy to a spasmodic activity." (269)

> "Before Hitler can act he must lash himself out of lethargy and doubts into a frenzy." (262)

Having lashed himself into this state of mind he can play the "Fuehrer" to perfection. When the transformation takes place in his personality all his views, sentiments and values are also transformed. The result is that as "Fuehrer" he can make statements with great conviction which flatly contradict what "Hitler" said a few minutes earlier. He can grapple with the most important problems and in a few minutes reduce them to extremely simple terms, he can map out campaigns, be the supreme judge, deal with diplomats, ignore all ethical and moral principles, order executions or the destruction of cities without the slightest hesitation. And he can be in the best of humor while he is doing it. All of this would have been completely impossible for "Hitler."

Hitler likes to believe that this is his true self and he has made every effort to convince the German people that it is his only self. But it is an artifact. The whole "Fuehrer" personality is a grossly exaggerated and distorted conception of masculinity as Hitler conceives it. The "Fuehrer" personality shows all the ear-marks of a reaction formation which has been created unconsciously as a compensation and cover-up for deep-lying tendencies which he despises. This mechanism is very frequently found in hysterics and always serves the purpose of repudiating the true self by creating an image which is diametrically opposite and then identifying oneself with the image. The great difference between Hitler and thousands of other hysterics is that he has managed to convince millions of other people that the fictitious image is really himself. The more he was able to convince them, the more he became convinced of it himself on the theory that eighty million Germans can't be wrong. And so he has fallen in love with the image he, himself, created and does his utmost to forget that behind it there is quite another Hitler who is a very despicable fellow. It is his ability to convince others that he is what he isn't that has saved him from insanity.

This psychological manoeuvre, however, is never entirely successful. Secret fears and anxieties that belie the reality of the image keep cropping up to shake his confidence and security. He may rationalize these fears or displace them but they continue to haunt him. Some are at least partially justified, others seem to be groundless. For example, he has had a fear of cancer for many years. Ordinarily he fears that he

130

C02571145

has a cancer in his stomach, since he is always bothered with indigestion, and all the assurances of his doctors have not been sufficient to dispel this fear. A few years ago a simple polyp grew on his larynx. Immediately his fear shifted to the throat and he was sure that he had developed a throat cancer. When Dr. von Eicken diagnosed it as a simple polyp, Hitler at first refused to believe him.

Then he has fears of being poisoned, fears of being assassinated, fears of losing his health, fears of gaining weight, fears of treason, fears of losing his mystical guidance, fears of anesthetics, fears of premature death, fears that his mission will not be fulfilled, etc. Every conceivable precaution must be taken to reduce these dangers, real and imagined, to a minimum. In later years, the fear of betrayal and possible assassination by one of his associates seems to have grown considerably. Thyssen (308) claims that it has reached the point where he no longer trusts the Gestapo. Frank (652) reports that even the generals must surrender their swords before they are admitted into conferences with him.

Sleep is no longer a refuge from his fears. He wakes up in the night shaking and screaming. Rauschning claims that one of Hitler's close associates told him that:

> "Hitler wakes at night with convulsive shrieks; shouts for help. He sits on the edge of his bed, as if unable to stir. He shakes with fear, making the whole bed vibrate. He shouts confused, unintelligible phrases. He gasps, as if imagining himself to be suffocating. On one occasion Hitler stood swaying in his room, looking wildly about him. 'He! He! He's been here!' he gasped. His lips were blue. Sweat streamed down his face. Suddenly he began to reel off figures, and odd words and broken phrases, entirely devoid of sense. It sounded horrible. He used strangely composed and entirely un-German word-formations. Then he stood still, only his lips moving. . . . Then he suddenly broke out —'There, there! In the corner! Who's that?' He stamped and shrieked in the familiar way." (274)

Zeissler (923) also reports such incidents. It would seem that Hitler's late hours are very likely due to the fact that he is afraid to go to sleep.

The result of these fears, as it is with almost every hysteric, is a narrowing of the world in which he lives. Haunted by secret misgivings, he distrusts everyone, even those closest to him. He cannot establish any close friendships for fear of being betrayed or being discovered as he really is. As his world becomes more and more circumscribed he becomes lonelier and lonelier. He feels himself to be a captive and often compares his life with that of the Pope (Hanfstaengl, 912). Fry (577) says, "spiritual loneliness must be Hitler's secret regret," and von Wiegand (491) writes:

> "Perhaps the snow-crowned peaks of the Alps glistening in the moonlight remind Adolph Hitler of the glittering but

131

Hitler at Berchtesgaden

cold, lonely heights of fame and achievement to which he has climbed. 'I am the loneliest man on earth' he said to an employee of his household."

Hysterics, however, are not discouraged by all this. On the contrary, they interpret their fears as proof of their own importance rather than as signs of their fundamental weakness. As Hitler's personal world becomes smaller he must extend the boundaries of his physical domains. Meanwhile, his image of himself must become evermore inflated in order to compensate for his deprivations and the maintenance of his repressions. He must build bigger and better buildings, bridges, stadia and what not, as tangible symbols of his power and greatness and then use these as evidence that he really is, what he wants to believe he is.

There is, however, little gratification in all this. No matter what he achieves or what he does it is never sufficient to convince him that things are what they seem to be. He is always insecure and must bolster up his super-structure by new acquisitions and more defenses. But the more he gets and the higher he builds, the more he has to worry about and defend. He is caught in a vicious circle, like so many other hysterics, which grows bigger and bigger as time goes on but never brings them the sense of security they crave above everything else.

The reason for this is that they are barking up the wrong tree. The security they seek is not to be found in the outside world but in themselves. Had they conquered their own unsocial impulses, their real enemy, when they were young, they would not need to struggle with such subterfuges when they are mature. The dangers they fear in the world around them are only the shadows of the dangers they fear will creep up on them from within if they do not maintain a strict vigilance over their actions. Repudiation is not synonomous to annihilation. These unsocial impulses, like termites, gnaw away at the foundations of the personality and the higher the super-structure is built, the shakier it becomes.

In most hysterics, these unsocial impulses, which they consciously regard as dangers, have been fairly successfully repressed. The individual may feel himself to be despicable without being conscious of the whys and wherefores of this feeling. The origins of the feeling remain almost wholly unconscious or are camouflaged in such a way that they are not obvious to the individual himself. In Hitler's case, however, this is not so—at least not entirely. He has good cause for feeling himself to be despicable and he is partially aware of its origins. The repression has not been completely successful and consequently some of the unsocial tendencies do from time to time assert themselves and demand satisfaction.

Hitler's sexual life has always been the topic of much speculation. As pointed out in the previous section, most of his closest associates are absolutely ignorant on this subject. This has led to conjectures of all sorts. Some believe that he is entirely immune from such impulses. Some

C02571145

believe that he is a chronic masturbator. Some believe that he derives his sexual pleasure through voyeurism. Many believe that he is completely impotent. Others, and these are perhaps in the majority, that he is homosexual. It is probably true that he is impotent but he is certainly not homosexual in the ordinary sense of the term. His perversion has quite a different nature which few have guessed. It is an extreme form of masochism in which the individual derives sexual gratification from the act of having a woman urinate or defecate on him. (Strasser, 919; see also, 931, 932)

Although this perversion is not a common one, it is not unknown in clinical work, particularly in its incipient stages. The four callaborators on this study, in addition to Dr. De Saussure, who learned of the perversion from other sources, have all had experience with cases of this type. All five agree that the information as given is probably true in view of their clinical experience and their knowledge of Hitler's character. In the following section further evidence of its validity will be cited together with a consideration of the influence it has had on his personality and actions. At the present time it is sufficient to recognize that these tendencies represent a constant threat to him which disturbs the equilibrium of his conscious mental life. Not only must he be continually on his guard against any overt manifestation but he must struggle with the intolerable feelings of guilt which are generated by his secret and unwelcome desires. These, together with his fears, haunt him day and night and incapacitate him as far as consistent and constructive work is concerned.

Surely Hitler has externalized his own problem and its supposed solution when he writes:

> "Only when the time comes when the race is no longer over-shadowed by the consciousness of its own guilt, then it will find internal peace and external energy to cut down regardlessly and brutally the wild shoots, and to pull up the weeds."

Chapter Five

Hitler

Psychological Analysis and Reconstruction

"Humanitarianism is the expression of stupidity and cowardice." *Adolf Hitler*

PART V

PSYCHOLOGICAL ANALYSIS AND RECONSTRUCTION

PSYCHOLOGICAL ANALYSIS AND RECONSTRUCTION

The world has come to know Adolph Hitler for his insatiable greed for power, his ruthlessness, cruelty and utter lack of feeling, his contempt for established institutions and his lack of moral restraints. In the course of relatively few years he has contrived to usurp such tremendous power that a few veiled threats, accusations or insinuations were sufficient to make the world tremble. In open defiance of treaties he occupied huge territories and conquered millions of people without even firing a shot. When the world became tired of being frightened and concluded that it was all a bluff, he initiated the most brutal and devastating war in history — a war which, for a time, threatened the complete destruction of our civilization. Human life and human suffering seem to leave this individual completely untouched as he plunges along the course he believes he was predestined to take.

Earlier in his career the world had watched him with amusement. Many people refused to take him seriously on the grounds that "he could not possibly last." As one action after another met with amazing success and the measure of the man became more obvious, this amusement was transformed into incredulousness. To most people, it seemed inconceivable that such things could actually happen in our modern civilization. Hitler, the leader of these activities, became generally regarded as a madman, if not inhuman. Such a judgment, concerning the nature of our enemy, may be satisfactory to the man in the street. It gives him a feeling of satisfaction to pigeon-hole an incomprehensible individual in one category or another and having classified him in this way, he feels that the problem is solved. All we need to do is to eliminate the madman from the scene of activities, replace him with a sane individual, and the world will again return to a normal and peaceful state of affairs.

This naive view, however, is wholly inadequate for those who are delegated to conduct the war against Germany or for those who will be delegated to deal with the situation when the war is over. They cannot content themselves with simply regarding Hitler as a personal devil and condemning him to an Eternal Hell in order that the remainder of the world may live in peace and quiet. They will realize that the madness of the Fuehrer has become the madness of a nation, if not of a large part of the continent. They will realize that these are not wholly the actions of a single individual but that a reciprocal relationship exists between the Fuehrer and the people and that the madness of the one stimulates and flows into the other and vice versa. It was not only Hitler, the madman, who created German madness, but German madness which created Hitler. Having created him as its spokesman and leader, it has been carried along by his momentum, perhaps far beyond the point where it was originally prepared to go. Nevertheless, it continues to follow his

C02571145

lead in spite of the fact that it must be obvious to all intelligent people now that his path leads to inevitable destruction.

From a scientific point of view, therefore, we are forced to consider Hitler, the Fuehrer, not as a personal devil, wicked as his actions and philosophy may be, but as the expression of a state of mind existing in millions of people, not only in Germany but, to a smaller degree, in all civilized countries. To remove Hitler may be a necessary first step, but it would not be the cure. It would be analogous to removing a chancre without treating the underlying disease. If similar eruptions are to be prevented in the future, we cannot content ourselves with simply removing the overt manifestations of the disease. On the contrary, we must ferret out and seek to correct the underlying factors which produced the unwelcome phenomenon. We must discover the psychological streams which nourish this destructive state of mind in order that we may divert them into channels which will permit a further evolution of our form of civilization.

The present study is concerned wholly with Adolph Hitler and the social forces which impinged upon him in the course of his development and produced the man we know. One may question the wisdom of studying the psychology of a single individual if the present war represents a rebellion by a nation against our civilization. To understand the one does not tell us anything about the millions of others. In a sense this is perfectly true. In the process of growing up we are all faced with highly individual experiences and exposed to varying social influences. The result is that when we mature no two of us are identical from a psychological point of view. In the present instance, however, we are concerned not so much with distinct individuals as with a whole cultural group. The members of this group have been exposed to social influences — family patterns, methods of training and education, opportunities for development, etc.—which are fairly homogenous within a given culture or strata of a culture. The result is that the members of a given culture tend to act, think and feel more or less alike, at least in contrast to the members of a different cultural group. This justifies, to some extent, our speaking of a general cultural character. On the other hand, if a large section of a given culture rebels against the traditional pattern then we must assume that new social influences have been introduced which tend to produce a type of character which cannot thrive in the old cultural environment.

When this happens it may be extremely helpful to understand the nature of the social forces which influenced the development of individual members of the group. These may serve as clues to an understanding of the group as a whole inasmuch as we can then investigate the frequency and intensity of these same forces in the group and draw deductions concerning their effect upon its individual members. If the individual being studied happens to be the leader of the group, we can

C02571145

expect to find the pertinent factors in an exaggerated form which would tend to make them stand out in sharper relief than would be the case if we studied an average member of the group. Under these circumstances, the action of the forces may be more easily isolated and subjected to detailed study in relation to the personality as a whole as well as to the culture in general. The problem of our study should be, then, not only whether Hitler is mad or not, but what influences in his development have made him what he is.

If we scan the tremendous quantities of material and information which have been accumulated on Hitler, we find little which is helpful in explaining why he is what he is. One can, of course, make general statements as many authors have done and say, for example, that his five years in Vienna were so frustrating that he hated the whole social order and is now taking his revenge for the injustices he suffered. Such explanations sound very plausible at first glance but we would also want to know why, as a young man, he was unwilling to work when he had the opportunity and what happened to transform the lazy Vienna beggar into the energetic politican who never seemed to tire from rushing from one meeting to another and was able to work thousands of listeners into a state of frenzy. We would also like to know something about the origins of his peculiar working habits at the present time, his firm belief in his mission, and so on. No matter how long we study the available material we can find no rational explanation of his present conduct. The material is descriptive and tells us a great deal about how he behaves under varying circumstances, what he thinks and feels about various subjects, but it does not tell us why. To be sure, he himself sometimes offers explanations for his conduct but it is obvious that these are either built on flimsy rational foundations or else they serve to push the problem further back into his past. On this level we are in exactly the same position in which we find ourselves when a neurotic patient first comes for help.

In the case of an individual neurotic patient, however, we can ask for a great deal more first-hand information which gradually enables us to trace the development of his irrational attitudes or behavioral patterns to earlier experiences or influences in his life history and the effects of these on his later behavior. In most cases the patient will have forgotten these earlier experiences but nevertheless he still uses them as premises in his present conduct. As soon as we are able to understand the premises underlying his conduct, then his irrational behavior becomes comprehensible to us.

The same finding would probably hold in Hitler's case except that here we do not have the opportunity of obtaining the additional first-hand information which would enable us to trace the history of his views and behavioral patterns to their early origins in order to discover the premises on which he is operating. Hitler's early life, when his fundamental attitudes were undoubtedly formed, is a closely guarded secret, particularly as far as he himself is concerned. He has been extremely careful and has told us exceedingly little about this period of his life and even that is open to serious questioning. A few fragments have, however, been unearthed which are helpful in reconstructing his past life and the experiences and influences which have determined his adult character. Nevertheless, in themselves, they would be wholly inadequate for our purposes.

Fortunately, there are other sources of information. One of them is Hitler himself. In every utterance a speaker or writer unknowingly tells us a great deal about himself of which he is entirely unaware. The subjects he chooses for elaboration frequently reveal unconscious factors which make these seem more important to him than many other aspects which would be just as appropriate to the occasion. Furthermore, the method of treatment, together with the attitudes expressed towards certain topics, usually reflect unconscious processes which are symbolically related to his own problems. The examples he chooses for purposes of illustration almost always contain elements from his own earlier experiences which were instrumental in cultivating the view he is expounding. The figures of speech he employs reflect unconscious conflicts and linkages and the incidence of particular types or topics can almost be used as a measure of his preoccupation with problems related to them. A number of experimental techniques have been worked out which bear witness to the validity of these methods of gathering information about the mental life, conscious and unconscious, of an individual in addition to the findings of psychoanalysts and psychiatrists.

Then, too, we have our practical experience in studying patients whose difficulties were not unlike those we find in Hitler. Our knowledge of the origins of these difficulties may often be used to evaluate conflicting information, check deductions concerning what probably happened, or to fill in gaps where no information is available. It may be possible with the help of all these sources of information to reconstruct the outstanding events in his early life which have determined his present behavior and character structure. Our study must, however, of necessity be speculative and inconclusive. It may tell us a great deal about the mental processes of our subject but it cannot be as comprehensive or conclusive as the findings of a direct study conducted with the cooperation of the individual. Nevertheless, the situation is such that even an indirect study of this kind is warranted.

Freud's earliest and greatest contribution to psychiatry in particular and to an understanding of human conduct in general was his discovery of the importance of the first years of a child's life in shaping his future character. It is during these early years, when the child's acquaintanceship with the world is still meagre and his capacities are still undeveloped, that the chances of misinterpreting the nature of the world about him are the greatest. The mind of the child is inadequate for understanding the demands which a complex culture makes upon him or the host of confusing experiences to which he is exposed. In consequence, as has been shown over and over again, a child during his early years frequently misinterprets what is going on about him and builds his personality structure on false premises. Even Hitler concedes that this finding is true, for he says in MEIN KAMPF:

> "There is a boy, let us say, of three. This is the age at which a child becomes conscious of his first impressions. In many intelligent people, traces of these early memories are found even in old age." (MK, 42)

Under these circumstances, it will be well for us to inquire into the nature of Hitler's earliest environment and the impressions which he probably formed during this period. Our factual information on this phase of his life is practically nil. In MEIN KAMPF Hitler tries to create the impression that his home was rather peaceful and quiet, his "father a faithful civil servant, the mother devoting herself to the cares of the household and looking after her children with eternally the same loving care." It would seem that if this is a true representation of the home environment there would be no reason for his concealing it so scrupulously. This is the only passage in a book of a thousand pages in which he even intimates that there were other children for his mother to take care of. No brother and no sister are mentioned in any other connection and even to his asociates he has never admitted that there were other children besides his half-sister, Angela. Very little more is said about his mother, either in writing or speaking. This concealment in itself would make us suspicious about the truth of the statement quoted above. We become even more suspicious when we find that not a single patient manifesting Hitler's character traits has grown up in such a well-ordered and peaceful home environment.

If we read on in MEIN KAMPF we find that Hitler gives us a description of a child's life in a lower-class family. He says:

> "Among the five children there is a boy, let us say, of three. . . . When the parents fight almost daily, their brutality leaves nothing to the imagination; then the results of such visual education must slowly but inevitably become apparent to the little one. Those who are not familiar with such conditions can hardly imagine the results, especially when the mutual differences express themselves in the form of brutal attacks on the part of the father towards the mother or to assaults due to drunkenness. The poor little boy, at the age of six, senses things which would make even a grown-up person shudder . . . . The other things the little fellow hears at home do not tend to further his respect for his surroundings." (MK, 42)

Hitler at the age of two years

100

BRAUNAU
STADTGRABEN 318

In view of the fact that we now know that there were five children in the Hitler home and that his father liked to spend his spare time in the village tavern where he sometimes drank so heavily that he had to be brought home by his wife or children, we begin to suspect that in this passage Hitler is, in all probability, describing conditions in his own home as a child.

If we accept the hypothesis that Hitler is actually talking about his own home when he describes conditions in the average lower-class family, we can obtain further information concerning the nature of his home environment. We read:

> "... things end badly indeed when the man from the very start goes his own way and the wife, for the sake of the children stands up against him. Quarreling and nagging set in, and in the same measure in which the husband becomes estranged from his wife, he becomes familiar with alcohol .... When he finally comes home ... drunk and brutal, but always without a last cent or penny, then God have mercy on the scenes which follow. I witnessed all of this personally in hundreds of scenes and at the beginning with both disgust and indignation." (MK, 38)

When we remember the few friends that Hitler has made in the course of his life, and not a single intimate friend, one wonders where he had the opportunity of observing these scenes personally, hundreds of times, if it was not in his own home. And then he continues:

> "The other things the little fellow hears at home do not tend to further his respect for his surroundings. Not a single good shred is left for humanity, not a single institution is left unattacked; starting with the teacher, up to the head of the State, be it religion, or morality as such, be it the State or society, no matter which, everything is pulled down in the nastiest manner into the filth of a depraved mentality." (MK, 43)

All of this agrees with information obtained from other sources whose veracity might otherwise be open to question. With this as corroborating evidence, however, it seems safe to assume that the above passages are a fairly accurate picture of the Hitler household and we may surmise that these scenes did arouse disgust and indignation in him at a very early age.

These feelings were aggravated by the fact that when his father was sober he tried to create an entirely different impression. At such times he stood very much on his dignity and prided himself on his position in the civil service. Even after he had retired from this service he always insisted on wearing his uniform when he appeared in public. He was scrupulous about his appearance and strode down the village street in his most dignified manner. When he spoke to his neighbors or acquaintances he did so in a very condescending manner and always demanded that they use his full title when they addressed him. If one of them happened to omit a part of it, he would call attention to their omission. He carried this to the point where, so informants tell us, he became a source of amusement to the other villagers and their children. At home he demanded that the children address him as Herr Vater instead of using one of the intimate abbreviations or nicknames that children commonly do.

Father's Influence on Hitler's Character.

We know from our study of many cases that the character of the father is one of the major factors determining the character of the child, particularly that of a boy. In cases in which the father is a fairly well-integrated individual and presents a consistent pattern of behavior which the small boy can respect, he becomes a model which the child strives to emulate. The image the child has of his father becomes the cornerstone of his later character-structure and with its help he is able to integrate his own behavior along socially accepted lines. The importance of this first step in character development can scarcely be over-estimated. It is almost a prerequisite for a stable, secure and well-integrated personality in later life.

In Hitler's case, as in almost all other neurotics of his type, this step was not feasible. Instead of presenting an image of a consistent, harmonious, socially-adjusted and admirable individual which the child could use as a guide and model, the father showed himself to be a mass of contradictions. At times he played the role of "a faithful civil servant" who respected his position and the society he served, and demanded that all others do likewise. At such times he was the soul of dignity, propriety, sternness and justice. To the outside world he tried to appear as a pillar of society whom all should respect and obey. At home, on the other hand, particularly after he had been drinking, he appeared the exact opposite. He was brutal, unjust and inconsiderate. He had no respect for anybody or anything. The world was all wrong and an unfit place in which to live. At such times he also played the part of the bully and whipped his wife and children who were unable to defend themselves. Even the dog comes in for his share of this sadistic display.

Under such circumstances the child becomes confused and is unable to identify himself with a clear-cut pattern which he can use as a guide for his own adjustment. Not only is this a severe handicap in itself but in addition the child is given a distorted picture of the world around him and the nature of the people in it. The home, during these years, is his world and later he judges the outside world in terms of it. In Hitler's case we would expect that the whole world would appear as extremely dangerous, uncertain and unjust and the child's impulse would be to avoid it as far as possible because he felt unable to cope with it. His feelings of insecurity would be enhanced inasmuch as he could never predict beforehand how his father would behave when he came home or what he could expect from him. The person who should give him love, support and a feeling of security fills him with anxiety, uneasiness and uncertainty.

His Search for a Competent Guide.

As a child Hitler must have felt this lack very keenly for throughout his later life we find him searching for a strong masculine figure whom he can respect and emulate. The men with whom he had contact during his childhood evidently could not fill the role of guide to his complete satisfaction. There is some evidence that he attempted to regard some of his teachers in this way but whether it was the influence of his father's ranting or the shortcomings of the teachers themselves, his attempts always miscarried. Later he attempted to find great men in history who could fill this need. Caesar, Napoleon and Frederick the Great are only a few of the legion to whom he became attached. Although historic figures serve an important role of this kind in the life of almost every child, they are in themselves inadequate. Unless a fairly solid foundation already exists in the mind of the child these heroes never become flesh and blood people inasmuch as the relationship is one-sided and lacks reciprocation. The same is also true of the political figures with which Hitler sought to identify himself during the Vienna period. For a time Schoenerer and Lueger became his heroes and although they were instrumental in forming some of his political beliefs and channeling his feelings, they were still too far removed from him to play the role of permanent guides and models.

During his career in the army we have an excellent example of Hitler's willingness to submit to the leadership of strong males who were willing to guide him and protect him. Throughout his army life there is not a shred of evidence to show that Hitler was anything but the model soldier as far as submissiveness and obedience are concerned. From a psychological point of view his life in the army was a kind of substitute for the home life he had always wanted but could never find, and he fulfilled his duties willingly and faithfully. He liked it so well that after he was wounded, in 1916, he wrote to his commanding officer and requested that he be called back to front duty before his leave had expired.

After the close of the war he stayed in the army and continued to be docile to his officers. He was willing to do anything they asked, even to the point of spying on his own comrades and then condemning them to death. When his officers singled him out to do special propaganda work because they believed he had a talent for speaking, he was overjoyed. This was the beginning of his political career, and here too we can find many manifestations of his search for a leader. In the beginning he may well have thought of himself as the "drummer-boy" who was heralding the coming of the great leader. Certain it is that during the early years of his career he was very submissive to a succession of impor-

C02571145

tant men to whom he looked for guidance—von Kahr, Ludendorff and Hindenburg, to name only a few.

It is true that in the end he turned upon them one after another and treated them in a despicable fashion, but usually this change came after he discovered their personal shortcomings and inadequacies. As in many neurotic people of Hitler's type who have a deep craving for guidance from an older man, their requirements grow with the years. By the time they reach maturity they are looking for, and can only submit to, a person who is perfect in every respect—literally a super-man. The result is that they are always trying to come in contact with new persons of high status in the hope that each one, in turn, will prove to be the ideal. No sooner do they discover a single weakness or shortcoming than they depose him from the pedestal on which they have placed him. They then treat their fallen heroes badly for having failed to live up to their expectations. And so Hitler has spent his life looking for a competent guide but always ends with the discovery that the person he has chosen falls short of his requirements and is fundamentally no more capable than himself. That this tendency is a carry-over from his early childhood is evidenced by the fact that throughout these years he has always laid great stress on addressing these persons by their full titles. Shades of his father's training during early childhood!

It may be of interest to note at this time that of all the titles that Hitler might have chosen for himself he is content with the simple one of "Fuehrer". To him this title is the greatest of them all. He has spent his life searching for a person worthy of the role but was unable to find one until he discovered himself. His goal now is to fulfill this role to millions of other people in a way in which he had hoped some person might do for him. The fact that the German people have submitted so readily to his leadership would indicate that a great many Germans were in a similar state of mind as Hitler himself and were not only willing, but anxious, to submit to anybody who could prove to them that he was competent to fill the role. There is some sociological evidence that this is probably so and that its origins lie in the structure of the German family and the dual role played by the father within the home as contrasted with the outside world. The duality, on the average is, of course, not nearly as marked as we have shown it to be in Hitler's case, but it may be this very fact which qualified him to identify the need and express it in terms which the others could understand and accept.

There is evidence that the only person in the world at the present time who might challenge Hitler in the role of leader is Roosevelt. Informants are agreed that he fears neither Churchill nor Stalin. He feels that they are sufficiently like himself so that he can understand their psychology and defeat them at the game. Roosevelt, however, seems to be an enigma to him. How a man can lead a nation of 130,000,000 people

146

and keep them in line without a great deal of name-calling, shouting, abusing and threatening is a mystery to him. He is unable to understand how a man can be the leader of a large group and still act like a gentleman. The result is that he secretly admires Roosevelt to a considerable degree, regardless of what he publicly says about him. Underneath he probably fears him inasmuch as he is unable to predict his actions.

Hitler's Mother and Her Influence.

Hitler's father, however, was only a part of his early environment. There was also his mother who, from all reports, was a very decent type of woman. Hitler has written very little and said nothing about her publicly. Informants tell us, however, that she was an extremely conscientious and hard-working individual whose life centered around her home and children. She was an exemplary housekeeper and there was never a spot or speck of dust to be found in the house—everything was very neat and orderly. She was a very devout Catholic and the trials and tribulations that fell upon her home she accepted with Christian resignation. Even her last illness, which extended over many months and caused her great pain, she endured without a single complaint. We may assume that she had to put up with much from her irascible husband and it may be that at times she did have to stand up against him for the welfare of her children. But all of this she probably accepted in the same spirit of abnegation. To her own children she was always extremely affectionate and generous although there is some reason to suppose that that she was mean at times to her two step-children.

In any event, every scrap of evidence indicates that there was an extremely strong attachment between herself and Adolph. As previously pointed out, this was due in part to the fact that she had lost two, or possibly three, children before Adolph was born. Since he, too, was frail as a child it is natural that a woman of her type should do everything within her power to guard against another recurrence of her earlier experiences. The result was that she catered to his whims, even to the point of spoiling him, and that she was over-protective in her attitude towards him. We may assume that during the first five years of Adolph's life, he was the apple of his mother's eye and that she lavished affection on him. In view of her husband's conduct and the fact that he was twenty-three years her senior and far from having a loving disposition, we may suppose that much of the affection that normally would have gone to him also found its way to Adolph.

The result was a strong libidinal attachment between mother and son. It is almost certain that Adolph had temper tantrums during this time but that these were not of a serious nature. Their immediate purpose was to get his own way with his mother and he undoubtedly succeeded in achieving this end. They were a technique by which he could dominate her whenever he wished, either out of fear that she would lose his love or out of fear that if he continued he might become like his father. There is reason to suppose that she frequently condoned behavior of which the father would have disapproved and may have become a partner in forbidden activities during the father's absence. Life with his mother during these early years must have been a veritable Paradise for Adolph except for the fact that his father would intrude and disrupt the happy relationship. Even when his father did not make a scene or lift his whip, he would demand attention from his wife which prevented her participation in pleasurable activities. It was natural, under these circumstances, that Adolph should resent the intrusion into his Paradise and this undoubtedly aggravated the feelings of uncertainty and fear which his father's conduct aroused in him.

As he became older and the libidinal attachment to his mother became stronger, both the resentment and fear undoubtedly increased. Infantile sexual feelings were probably quite prominent in this relationship as well as fantasies of a childish nature. This is the Oedipus complex mentioned by psychologists and psychiatrists who have written about Hitler's personality. The great amount of affection lavished upon him by his mother and the undesirable character of his father served to develop this complex to an extraordinary degree. The more he hated his father the more dependent he became upon the affection and love of his mother, and the more he loved his mother the more afraid he became of his father's vengeance should his secret be discovered. Under these circumstances, little boys frequently fantasy about ways and means of ridding the environment of the intruder. There is reason to suppose that this also happened in Hitler's early life.

Influences Determining His Attitude Towards Love, Women, Marriage.

Two other factors entered into the situation which served to accentuate the conflict still further. One of these was the birth of a baby brother when he was five years of age. This introduced a new rival onto the scene and undoubtedly deprived him of some of his mother's affection and attention, particularly since the new child was also rather sickly. We may suppose that the newcomer in the family also became the victim of Adolph's animosity and that he fantasied about getting rid of him as he had earlier contemplated getting rid of his father. There is nothing abnormal in this except the intensity of the emotions involved.

The other factor which served to intensify these feelings was the fact that as a child he must have discovered his parents during intercourse. An examination of the data makes this conclusion almost inescapable and from our knowledge of his father's character and past history it is not at all improbable. It would seem that his feelings on this occasion were very mixed. On the one hand, he was indignant at his father for what he considered to be a brutal assault upon his mother. On the other hand, he was indignant with his mother because she submitted

C02571145

so willingly to the father, and he was indignant with himself because he was powerless to intervene. Later, as we shall see, there was an hysterical re-living of this experience which played an important part in shaping his future destinies.

Being a spectator to this early scene had many repercussions. One of the most important of these was the fact that he felt that his mother had betrayed him in submitting to his father, a feeling which became accentuated still further when his baby brother was born. He lost much of his respect for the female sex and while in Vienna, Hanisch reports, he frequently spoke at length on the topic of love and marriage and that "he had very austere ideas about relations between men and women". Even at that time he maintained that if men only wanted to they could adopt a strictly moral way of living. "He often said it was the woman's fault if a man went astray" and "He used to lecture us about this, saying every woman can be had." In other words, he regarded woman as the seducer and responsible for man's downfall and he condemned them for their disloyalty. These attitudes are probably the outcome of his early experiences with his mother who first seduced him into a love relationship and then betrayed him by giving herself to his father. Nevertheless, he still continued to believe in an idealistic form of love and marriage which would be possible if a loyal woman could be found. As we know, Hitler never gave himself into the hands of a woman again with the possible exception of his niece, Geli Raubal, which also ended in disaster. Outside of that single exception he has lived a loveless life. His distrust of both men and women is so deep that in all his history there is no record of a really intimate and lasting friendship.

The outcome of these early experiences was probably a feeling of being very much alone in a hostile world. He hated his father for his brutality, he distrusted his mother for her lack of loyalty, and despised himself for his weakness. The immature child finds such a state of mind almost unendurable for any length of time and in order to gain peace and security in his environment these feelings are gradually repressed from his memory.

This is a normal procedure which happens in the case of every child at a relatively early age. This process of repression enables the child to re-establish a more or less friendly relationship with his parents without the interference of disturbing memories and emotions. The early conflicts, however, are not solved or destroyed by such a process and we must expect to find manifestations of them later on. When the early repression has been fairly adequate these conflicts lie dormant until adolescence when, due to the process of maturation, they are re-awakened. In some cases they reappear in very much their original form, while in others they are expressed in a camouflaged or symbolic form.

In Hitler's case, however, the conflicting emotions and sentiments were so strong that they could not be held in complete abeyance

149

during this entire period. Quite early in his school career we find his conflicts appearing again in a symbolic form. Unfortunately, the symbols
he unconsciously chose to express his own inner conflicts were such that
they have seriously affected the future of the world. And yet these symbols fit his peculiar situation so perfectly that it was almost inevitable
that they would be chosen as vehicles of expression.

His Early Conflicts Expressed in Symbolic Form.

Unconsciously, all the emotions he had once felt for his mother
became transferred to Germany. This transfer of affect was relatively
easy inasmuch as Germany, like his mother, was young and vigorous
and held promise of a great future under suitable circumstances.
Furthermore, he felt shut off from Germany as he now felt shut off
from his mother, even though he secretly wished to be with her. Germany
became a symbol of his ideal mother and his sentiments are clearly
expressed in his writings and speeches. A few excerpts will serve to illustrate the transfer of emotion:

> "The longing grew stronger to go there (Germany) where
> since my early youth I had been drawn by secret wishes and
> secret love."
>
> "What I first had looked upon as an impassable chasm now
> spurred me on to greater love for my country than ever
> before."
>
> "An unnatural separation from the great common Mother-
> land."
>
> "I appeal to those who, severed from the Motherland, . . . and
> who now in painful emotion long for the hour that will allow
> them to return to the arms of the beloved mother."

It is significant that although Germans, as a whole, invariably refer to
Germany as the "Fatherland", Hitler almost always refers to it as the
"Motherland."

Just as Germany was ideally suited to symbolize his mother, so
was Austria ideally suited to symbolize his father. Like his father Austria
was old, exhausted, and decaying from within. He therefore transferred
all his unconscious hatred from his father to the Austrian state. He could
now give vent to all his pent-up emotions without exposing himself to the
dangers he believed he would have encountered had he expressed these
same feelings towards the persons really involved. In MEIN KAMPF
he frequently refers to the Austrian state, for example, in terms such
as these:

> ". . . an intense love for my native German-Austrian country
> and a bitter hatred against the Austrian state."
>
> "With proud admiration I compared the rise of the Reich
> with the decline of the Austrian state."

The alliance between Austria and Germany served to symbolize the
marriage of his mother and father. Over and over again we find references

to this alliance and we can see clearly how deeply he resented the marriage of his parents because he felt that his father was a detriment to his mother and only through the death of the former could the latter obtain her freedom and find her salvation. A few quotations will illustrate his sentiments:

> "And who could keep faith with an imperial dynasty which betrayed the cause of the German people for its own ignominious ends, a betrayal that occurred again and again."

> "What grieved us most was the fact that the whole system was morally protected by the alliance with Germany, and thus Germany herself . . . walked by the side of the corpse."

> ". . . It suffices to state here that from my earliest youth I came to a conviction which never deserted me, but on the contrary grew stronger and stronger: that the protection of the German race presumed the destruction of Austria . . . that above all else, the Royal House of Hapsburg was destined to bring misfortune upon the German nation."

> "Since my heart had never beaten for an Austrian monarchy but only for a German Reich, I could only look upon the hour of the ruin of this state as the beginning of the salvation of the German nation."

When we have grasped the significance of this transference of affect we have made a long step in the direction of understanding Hitler's actions. Unconsciously he is not dealing with nations composed of millions of individuals but is trying to solve his personal conflicts and rectify the injustices of his childhood. Unable to enter into a "give-and-take" relationship with other human beings which might afford him an opportunity of resolving his conflicts in a realistic manner, he projects his personal problems on great nations and then tries to solve them on this unrealistic level. His microcosm has been inflated into a macrocosm.

We can now understand why Hitler fell on his knees and thanked God when the last war broke out. To him it did not mean simply a war, as such, but an opportunity of fighting for his symbolic mother, of proving his manhood and of being accepted by her. It was inevitable that he would seek enlistment in the German Army rather than in the Austrian Army and it was also inevitable, under these circumstances, that he would be a good and obedient soldier. Unconsciously it was as though he were a little boy who was playing the part of a man while his mother stood by and watched him. Her future welfare was his great concern and in order to prove his love he was willing, if need be, to sacrifice his own life for her. His relationship to Germany was, in effect, the sexless, idealistic marriage he longed for.

The Effects of Germany's Defeat.

Everything went smoothly as long as he felt sure that all would turn out well in the end. He never complained about the hardships that were imposed on him and he never grumbled with the other men. He was happy in what he was doing and met the trials and tribulations of army life with his chin up until he discovered that things were going badly and that his symbolic mother was about to be degraded as he had imagined his real mother had been degraded in his childhood. To him it was as if his mother was again the victim of a sexual assault. This time it was the November Criminals and the Jews who were guilty of the foul deed and he promptly transferred his repressed hate to these new perpetrators.

When he became fully aware of Germany's defeat he reacted in a typically hysterical manner. He refused to accept or adjust to the situation on a reality level. Instead, he reacted to this event as he probably reacted to the discovery of his parents in intercourse. He writes:

> "'I stumbled and tottered rearwards with burning eyes . . . . Already a few hours later the eyes had turned into burning coals; it had become dark around me."

In another place he writes:

> "While everything began to go black again before my eyes, stumbling, I groped my way back to the dormitory, threw myself on my cot and buried my burning head in the covers and pillows."

At the time this happened he had been exposed to a slight attack of mustard gas. He immediately believed that he was blinded and speechless. Although he spent several weeks in the hospital, neither his symptoms nor the development of the illness corresponded to those found in genuine gas cases. It has been definitely established that both the blindness and the mutism were of an hysterical nature. The physician who treated him at that time found his case so typical of hysterical symptoms in general that for years after the war he used it as an illustration in his courses given at a prominent German medical school. We know from a great many other cases that during the onset of such attacks the patient behaves in exactly the same manner as he did earlier in his life when confronted by a situation with the same emotional content. It is as though the individual were actually reliving the earlier experience over again. In Hitler's case this earlier experience was almost certainly the discovery of his parents in intercourse and that he interpreted this as a brutal assault in which he was powerless. He refused to believe what his eyes told him and the experience left him speechless.

That this interpretation is correct is evidenced by his imagery in dealing with the event later on. Over and over again we find figures of speech such as these:

> ". . . by what wiles the soul of the German has been raped."
> ". . . our German pacifists will pass over in silence the most bloody rape of the nation."

which illustrate his sentiments very clearly.

The Origins of His Belief in His Mission and His Longing for Immortality.

It was while he was in the hospital suffering from hysterical blindness and mutism that he had the vision that he would liberate the Germans from their bondage and make Germany great. It was this vision that set him on his present political career and which has had such a determining influence on the course of world events. More than anything else it was this vision which convinced him that he was chosen by Providence and that he had a great mission to perform. This is probably the most outstanding characteristic of Hitler's mature personality and it is this which guides him with the "precision of a sleep-walker."

From an analysis of many other other cases we know that such convictions never result from an adult experience alone. In order to carry conviction they must reawaken earlier beliefs which have their roots far back in childhood. It is, of course, nothing unusual for a child to believe that he is some special creation and destined to do great things before he dies. One can almost say that every child passes through such a period on his way to growing up. In many people remnants of such early beliefs are observable inasmuch as they feel or believe that Fate or Luck or Providence or some other extra-natural power has chosen them for special favors. In most of these cases, however the adult individual only half believes that this is really so even when a whole series of favorable events may make the hypothesis plausible. Only rarely do we find a firm conviction of this kind in adulthood and then only when there were extenuating circumstances in childhood which made such a belief necessary and convincing.

In Hitler's case the extenuating circumstances are relatively clear. Mention has already been made of the fact that his mother had given birth to at least two and possibly three children, all of whom had died prior to his own birth. He, himself, was a frail and rather sickly infant. Under these circumstances, his mother undoubtedly exerted herself to the utmost to keep him alive. He was unquestionably spoiled during this period and his survival was probably the great concern of the family as well as of the neighbors. From his earliest days there was, no doubt, considerable talk in the household about the death of the other children and constant comparisons between their progress and his own.

Children first become aware of death as a phenomenon very early in life and in view of these unusual circumstances it may have dawned on Hitler even earlier than with most children. The thought of death in itself, is inconceivable to a small child and they usually are able to form only the vaguest conception of what it means or implies before they push it out of their minds, for later consideration. In Hitler's case, however, it was a living issue and the fears of the mother were in all likelihood communicated to him. As he pondered the problem in his immature way, he probably wondered why the others died while he continued to live. The natural conclusion for a child to draw would be that he was favored in some way or that he was chosen to live for some particular purpose. The belief that he was the "chosen one" would have been reinforced by the fact that as far as his mother was concerned he was very much the chosen one in comparison with her two step-children who were also living in the home at that time.

This belief must have been strengthened considerably when, at the age of five, his baby brother was born. This baby brother has undoubtedly played a much more important role in Adolph's life than has been acknowledged by his biographers. The pertinent fact at the moment, however, is that this brother too died before he was six years old. It was Adolph's first real experience with death and it must have brought up the problem of death again in a much more vivid form. Again, we can surmise, he asked himself why they died while he continued to be saved. The only plausible answer to a child at that age would be that he must be under divine protection. This may seem far-fetched and yet, as an adult Hitler tells us that he felt exactly this way when he was at the front during the war, even before he had the vision. Then too, he speculated on why it is that comrades all around him are killed while he is saved and again he comes to the conclusion that Providence must be protecting him. Perhaps the exemplary courage he displayed in carrying messages at the front was due to the feeling that some kindly Fate was watching over him. Throughout MEIN KAMPF we find this type of thinking. It was Fate that had him born so close to the German border; it was Fate that sent him to Vienna to suffer with the masses; it was Fate that caused him to do many things. The experience he reports at the front, when a voice told him to pick up his plate and move to another section of the trench just in time to escape a shell which killed all his comrades, must certainly have strengthened this belief to a marked degree and paved the way for his vision later on.

The Messiah Complex.

Another influence may have helped to solidify this system of belief. Among patients we very frequently find that children who are spoiled at an early age and establish a strong bond with their mother tend to question their paternity. Eldest children in particular are prone to such doubts and it is most marked in cases where the father is much older than the mother. In Hitler's case the father was twenty-three years older, or almost twice the age of the mother. Just why this should be is not clear, from a psychological point of view, but in such cases there is a strong tendency to believe that their father is not their real father and to ascribe their birth to some kind of supernatural conception. Usually such beliefs are dropped as the child grows older. It can be observed in young children, however, and can often be recovered in adults under suitable conditions. Due to the unsympathetic and brutal nature of his father we may suppose that there was an added incentive in Hitler's case for rejecting him as his real father and postulating some other origin to himself.

118

C02571145

The problem is not important in itself at the moment except insofar as it may help to throw some light on the origins of Hitler's conviction in his mission and his belief that he is guided by some extra-natural power which communicates to him what he should or should not do under varying circumstances. This hypothesis is tenable in view of the fact that during his stay in Vienna, when still in his early twenties, he grew a beard and directly after the war when he again grew a Christ-like beard. Then, too, when he was a student at the Benedictine school his ambition was to join the Church and become an abbot or priest. All of these give some indication of a Messiah complex long before he had started on his meteoric career and become an open competitor of Christ for the affections of the German people.

Fear of Death and Desire for Immortality.

Although beliefs of this kind are common during childhood they are usually dropped or are modified as the individual becomes older and more experienced. In Hitler's case, however, the reverse has taken place. The conviction became stronger as he grew older until, at the present time, it is the core of his thinking. Under these circumstances, we must suppose that some powerful psychological stream continued to nourish these infantile modes of thought. This psychological stream is probably, as it is in many other cases, a fear of death. It seems logical to suppose that in the course of his early deliberations on the deaths of his brothers his first conclusion was probably that all the others die and that consequently he too would die. His fear would not be allayed by his mother's constant concern over his well-being, which he may have interpreted as an indication that the danger was imminent. Such a conclusion would certainly be a valid one for a child to make under the circumstances. The thought of his own death, however, is almost unbearable to a small child. Nothing is quite so demoralizing as the constant dread of self-annihilation. It gnaws away day and night and prevents him from enjoying the good things that life affords.

To rid himself of this devastating fear becomes his major objective. This is not easily accomplished, especially when all available evidence seems to corroborate the validity of the fear. In order to offset its potency he is almost driven to deny its reality by adopting the belief that he is of divine origin and that Providence is protecting him from all harm. Only by use of such a technique is the child able to convince himself that he will not die. We must also remember that in Hitler's case there was not only the unusual succession of deaths of siblings, but there was also the constant menace of his father's brutality which helped to make the fear more intense than in most children. This danger could easily be exaggerated in Hitler's mind due to a sense of guilt concerning his feelings towards his respective parents and what his father might do to him if he discovered his secret. These feelings would tend to increase

113

155

C02571145

his fear of death at the same time that they caused him to reject his father. Both tendencies would serve to nourish the belief that he was of divine origin and was under its protection.

It is my belief that this basic fear of death is still present and active in Hitler's character at the present time. As time goes on and he approaches the age when he might reasonably expect to die, this infantile fear asserts itself more strongly. As a mature, intelligent man he knows that the law of nature is such that his physical self is destined to die. He is still not able, however, to accept the fact that he as an individual, his psyche, will also die. It is this element in his psychological structure which demands that he become immortal. Most people are able to take the sting out of this fear of death through religious beliefs in life after death, or through the feeling that a part of them, at least, will continue to go on living in their children. In Hitler's case, both of these normal channels have been closed and he has been forced to seek immortality in a more direct form. He must arrange to go on living in the German people for at least a thousand years to come. In order to do this, he must oust Christ as a competitor and usurp his place in the lives of the German people.

In addition to evidence drawn from experience with patients which would make this hypothesis tenable, we have the evidence afforded by Hitler's own fears and attitudes. We have discussed these in detail in Section IV. Fear of assassination, fear of poisoning, fear of premature death, etc., all deal with the problem of death in an uncamouflaged form. One can, of course, maintain that in view of his position all these fears are more or less justified. There is certainly some truth in this contention but we also notice that as time goes on these fears have increased considerably until now they have reached the point where the precautions for his own safety far exceed those of any of his predecessors. As long as he could hold a plebescite every now and then and reassure himself that the German people loved him and wanted him, he felt better. Now that this is no longer possible, he has no easy way of curbing the fear and his uncertainty in the future becomes greater. There can be little doubt concerning his faith in the results of the plebescites. He was firmly convinced that the 98% vote, approving his actions, really represented the true feelings of the German people. He believed this because he needed such reassurance from time to time in order to carry on with a fairly easy mind and maintain his delusions.

When we turn to his fear of cancer we find no justification whatever for his belief, especially in view of the fact that several outstanding specialists in this disease have assured him that it is without foundation. Nevertheless, it is one of his oldest fears and he continues to adhere to it in spite of all the expert testimony to the contrary. This fear becomes intelligible when we remember that his mother died following an operation for cancer of the breast. In connection with his fear of death we must not forget his terrifying nightmares from which he awakes in a cold sweat and acts as though he were being suffocated. If our hypothesis is correct, namely, that a fear of death is one of the powerful unconscious streams which drive Hitler on in his mad career, then we can expect that as the war progresses and as he becomes older the fear will continue to increase. With the progress of events along their present course, it will be more and more difficult for him to feel that his mission is fulfilled and that he has successfully cheated death and achieved immortality in the German people. Nevertheless, we can expect him to keep on trying to the best of his ability as long as a ray of hope remains. The great danger is that if he feels that he cannot achieve immortality as the Great Redeemer he may seek it as the Great Destroyer who will live on in the minds of the German people for a thousand years to come. He intimated this in a conversation with Rauschning when he said:

> "We shall not capitulate — no, never. We may be destroyed, but if we are, we shall drag a world with us — a world in flames."

With him, as with many others of his type, it may well be a case of immortality of any kind at any price.

Sexual Development.

Closely interwoven with several of the themes which have already been elaborated is the development of his sexual life. From what we know about his mother's excessive cleanliness and tidiness we may assume that she employed rather stringent measures during the toilet training period of her children. This usually results in a residual tension in this area and is regarded by the child as a severe frustration which arouses feelings of hostility. This facilitates an alliance with his infantile aggression which finds an avenue for expression through anal activities and fantasies. These usually center around soiling, humiliation and destruction, and form the basis of a sadistic character.

Here, again, we may assume that the experience was more intense in Hitler's case than in the average due to the strong attachment and spoiling of his mother in early infancy. Unaccustomed to minor frustrations which most children must learn to endure, prior to the toilet training, he was poorly equipped to deal with this experience which plays an important role in the life of all infants. Even now, as an adult, we find Hitler unable to cope with frustrating experiences on a mature level. That a residual tension from this period still exists in Hitler is evidenced by the frequency of imagery in his speaking and writing which deal with dung and dirt and smell. A few illustrations may help to clarify his unconscious preoccupation with these subjects:

> "You don't understand: we are just passing a magnet over a dunghill, and we shall see presently how much iron was in the dunghill and has clung to the magnet." (By 'dunghill' Hitler meant the German people.)

C02571145

"And when he (the Jew) turns the treasures over in his hand they are transformed into dirt and dung."

"... One's hands seize slimy jelly; it slips through one's fingers only to collect again in the next moment."

"Charity is sometimes actually comparable to the manure which is spread on the field, not out of love for the latter, but out of precaution for one's own benefit later on."

"... dragged into the dirt and filth of the lowest depths."

"Later the smell of these caftan wearers made me ill. Added to this were their dirty clothes and their none too heroic appearance."

"...The rottenness of artificially nurtured conditions of peace has more than once stunk to high heaven."

His libidinal development however, was not arrested at this point, but progressed to the genital level at which the Oedipus complex, already referred to, developed. This complex, as we have seen, was aggravated by his mother's pregnancy at precisely the age when the complex normally reaches its greatest intensity. In addition to accentuating his hatred for his father and estranging him from his mother, we can assume that this event at this particular time served to generate an abnormal curiosity in him. He, like all children at this age, must have wondered how the unborn child got into the mother's stomach and how it was going to get out.

These three reactions have all played an important part in Hitler's psychosexual development. It would seem from the evidence that his aggressive fantasies towards the father reached such a point that he became afraid of the possibility of retaliation if his secret desires were discovered. The retaliation he probably feared was that his father would castrate him or injure his genital capacity in some way — a fear which is later expressed in substitute form in his syphilophobia. Throughout MEIN KAMPF he comes back to the topic of syphilis again and again and spends almost an entire chapter describing its horrors. In almost all cases we find that a fear of this sort is rooted in a fear of genital injury during childhood. In many cases this fear was so overpowering that the child abandoned his genital sexuality entirely and regressed to earlier stages of libidinal development. In order to maintain these repressions later in life he uses the horrors of syphilis as a justification for his unconscious fear that genital sexuality is dangerous for him, and also as a rationalization for his avoidance of situations in which his earlier desires might be aroused.

In abandoning the genital level of libidinal development the individual becomes impotent as far as heterosexual relations are concerned. It would appear, from the evidence, that some such process took place during Hitler's early childhood. Throughout his early adult life, in Vienna, in the Army, in Munich, in Landsberg, no informant has reported a heterosexual relationship. In fact, the informants of all these periods make a point of the fact that he had absolutely no interest in women or any contact with them. Since he has come to power his peculiar relationship to women has been so noticeable that many writers believe that he is completely asexual. Some have surmised that he suffered a genital injury during the last war, others that he is homosexual. The former hypothesis, for which there is not a shred of real evidence, is almost certainly false. The second hypothesis we will examine later on.

The Diffusion of the Sexual Instinct.

When a regression of this kind takes place the sexual instinct usually becomes diffuse and many organs which have yielded some sexual stimulation in the past become permanently invested with sexual significance. The eyes, for example, may become a substitute sexual organ and seeing then takes on a sexual significance. This seems to have happened in Hitler's case for a number of informants have commented on his delight in witnessing strip-tease and nude dancing numbers on the stage. On such occasions he can never see enough to satisfy him even though he uses opera glasses in order to observe more closely. Strip-tease artists are frequently invited to the Brown House, in Munich, to perform in private and there is evidence that he often invites girls to Berchtesgaden for the purpose of exhibiting their bodies. On his walls are numerous pictures of obscene nudes which conceal nothing and he takes particular delight in looking through a collection of pornographic pictures which Hoffmann has made for him. We also know the extreme pleasure he derives from huge pageants, circus performances, opera, and particularly the movies of which he can never get enough. He has told informants that he gave up flying not only because of the danger involved but because he could not see enough of the country. For this reason, automobile travel is his favorite form of transportation. From all of this it is evident that seeing has a special sexual significance for him. This probably accounts for his "hypnotic glance" which has been the subject of comment by so many writers. Some have reported that at their first meeting Hitler fixated them with his eyes as if "to bore through them." It is also interesting that when the other person meets his stare, Hitler turns his eyes to the ceiling and keeps them there during the interview. Then, too, we must not forget that in the moment of crisis his hysterical attack manifested itself in blindness.

In addition to the eyes, the anal region has also become highly sexualized and both faeces and buttocks become sexual objects. Due to early toilet training, certain inhibitions have been set up which prevent their direct expression. However, we find so many instances of imagery of this kind, particularly in connection with sexual topics, that we must assume that this area has taken on a sexual significance. The nature of this significance we will consider in a moment.

The mouth, too, seems to have become invested as an erogenous zone of great importance. Few authors or informants have neglected to mention Hitler's peculiar dietary habits. He consumes tremendous quantities of sweets, candies, cakes, whipped cream, etc., in the course of a day in addition to his vegetable diet. On the other hand, he refuses to eat meat, drink beer or smoke, all of which suggest certain unconscious inhibitions in this area. In addition, he has a pathological fear of poisoning by mouth, and has shown an obsessional preoccupation at times with mouth washing. These suggest a reaction formation or defense against an unacceptable tendency to take something into his mouth or get something out which from one point of view appears to be disgusting. In this connection we must not forget his resolve to starve himself to death after the failure of the Beer Hall Putsch, his hysterical mutism at the end of the last war, and his love of speaking. The significance of these we shall consider later on.

Disturbance of Love Relations.

The second effect of his mother's pregnancy was his estrangement from her. The direct result of this was, on the one hand, an idealization of love but without a sexual component and, on the other hand, the setting up of a barrier against intimate relationships with other people, particularly women. Having been hurt once, he unconsciously guards himself against a similar hurt in the future. In his relationship to his niece Geli, he tried to overcome this barrier but he was again disappointed and since then has not exposed himself to a really intimate relationship either with man or woman. He has cut himself off from the world in which love plays any part for fear of being hurt and what love he can experience is fixated on the abstract entity — Germany, which, as we have seen, is a symbol of his ideal mother. This is a love relationship in which sex plays no direct part.

Origins of His Perversion.

The third outcome of his mother's pregnancy was to arouse an excessive curiosity. The great mystery to children of this age, who find themselves in this situation, is how the unborn child got into the mother's stomach and how it is going to get out. Even in cases where the children have witnessed parental intercourse, this event is rarely linked with the ensuing pregnancy. Since, in their limited experience, everything that gets into their stomach enters by way of the mouth and everything that comes out usually does so by way of the rectum, they are prone to believe that conception somehow takes place through the mouth and that the child will be born via the anus. Hitler, as a child, undoubtedly adhered to this belief but this did not satisfy his curiosity. He evidently wanted to see for himself how it came out and exactly what happened.

This curiosity laid the foundation for his strange perversion which brought all three of his sexualized zones into play. In her description of sexual experiences with Hitler, Geli stressed the fact that it was of utmost importance to him that she squat over him in such a way that he could see everything. It is interesting that Roehm, in an entirely different connection, once said:

> "He (Hitler) is thinking about the peasant girls. When they stand in the fields and bend down at their work so that you can see their behinds, that's what he likes, especially when they've got big round ones. That's Hitler's sex life. What a man."

Hitler, who was present, did not stir a muscle but only stared at Roehm with compressed lips.

From a consideration of all the evidence it would seem that Hitler's perversion is as Geli has described it. The great danger in gratifying it, however, is that the individual might get faeces or urine into his mouth. It is this danger that requires that suitable inhibitions be instituted.

Return to the Womb.

Another possibility in infantile thinking presents itself in this connection. When the home environment is harsh and brutal, as it was in Hitler's case, the small child very frequently envies the position of passivity and security the unborn child enjoys within the mother. This, in turn, gives rise to fantasies of finding a way in to the longed-for claustrum and ousting his rival in order that he may take his place. These fantasies are usually of very brief duration because, as the child believes, if he succeeded he would have nothing to eat or drink except faeces and urine. The thought of such a diet arouses feelings of disgust and consequently he abandons his fantasies in order to avoid these unpleasant feelings. In many psychotics, however, these fantasies continue and strive to express themselves overtly. The outstanding bit of evidence in Hitler's case that such fantasies were present is to be found in the Kehlstein or Eagle's Nest which he has built for himself near Berchtesgaden. Interestingly enough, many people have commented that only a madman would conceive of such a place, let alone try to build it. From a symbolic point of view one can easily imagine that this is a materialization of a child's conception of the return to the womb. First there is a long hard road, then a heavily guarded entrance, a trip through a long tunnel to an extremely inaccessible place. There one can be alone, safe and undisturbed, and revel in the joys that Mother Nature bestows. It is also interesting to note that very few people have ever been invited there and many of Hitler's closest associates are either unaware of its existence or have only seen it from a distance. Extraordinarly enough, Francois-Poncet is one of the few people who was ever invited to visit there. In the French Yellow Book, he gives us an extremely vivid description of the place, a part of which may be worthwhile quoting:

> "The approach is by a winding road about nine miles long, boldly cut out of the rock . . . the road comes to an end in front of a long underground passage leading into the

mountain, enclosed by a heavy double door of bronze. At the far end of the underground passage a wide lift, panelled with sheets of copper, awaits the visitor. Through a vertical shaft of 330 feet cut right through the rock, it rises up to the level of the Chancellor's dwelling place. Here is reached the astonishing climax. The visitor finds himself in a strong and massive building containing a gallery with Roman pillars, an immense circular hall with windows all around . . . . It gives the impression of being suspended in space, an almost overhanging wall of bare rock rises up abruptly. The whole, bathed in the twilight of the autumn evening, is grandiose, wild, almost hallucinating. The visitor wonders whether he is awake or dreaming." (943)

If one were asked to plan something which represented a return to the womb, one could not possibly surpass the Kehlstein. It is also significant that Hitler often retires to this strange place to await instructions concerning the course he is to pursue.

Vegetarianism.

We can surmise from the psychological defenses Hitler has set up, that there was a period during which he struggled against these tendencies. In terms of unconscious symbolism meat is almost synonomous with faeces and beer with urine. The fact that there is a strict taboo on both would indicate that these desires are still present and that it is only by refraining from everything symbolizing them that he can avoid arousing anxieties. Rauschning reports that Hitler, following Wagner, attributed much of the decay of our civilization to meat eating. That the decadence "had its origin in the abdomen — chronic constipation, poisoning of the juices, and the results of drinking to excess." This assertion suggests decay (contamination, corruption, pollution, and death) as the resultant of constipation, that is, faeces in the gastro-intestinal tract, and if this is so, decay might be avoided both by not eating anything resembling faeces and by taking purges or ejecting as frequently as possible. It has been reported that Hitler once said that he was confident that all nations would arrive at the point where they would not feed any more on dead animals. It is interesting to note that according to one of our most reliable informants Hitler only became a real vegetarian after the death of his niece, Geli. In clinical practice, one almost invariably finds compulsive vegetarianism setting in after the death of a loved object.

We may, therefore, regard Hitler's perversion as a compromise between psychotic tendencies to eat faeces and drink urine on the one hand, and to live a normal socially adjusted life on the other. The compromise is not, however, satisfactory to either side of his nature and the struggle between these two diverse tendencies continues to rage unconsciously. We must not suppose that Hitler gratifies his strange perversion frequently. Patients of this type rarely do and in Hitler's case it is highly probable that he has permitted himself to go this far only with

C02571145

his niece, Geli and possibly with Henny Hoffmann. The practice of this perversion represents an extreme form of masochistic degradation.

Masochistic Gratifications.

In most patients suffering from this perversion the unconscious forces only get out of control to this degree when a fairly strong love relationship is established and sexuality makes decisive demands. In other relationships where the love component is less strong the individual contents himself with less degrading activities. This is brought out clearly in the case of Rene Mueller who confided to her director, Zeissler (921), who had asked her what was troubling her after spending an evening at the Chancellory, "that the evening before she had been with Hitler and that she had been sure that he was going to have intercourse with her; that they had both undressed and were apparently getting ready for bed when Hitler fell on the floor and begged her to kick him. She demurred but he pleaded with her and condemned himself as unworthy, heaped all kinds of accusations on his own head and just grovelled around in an agonizing manner. The scene became intolerable to her and she finally acceded to his wishes and kicked him. This excited him greatly and he begged for more and more, always saying that it was even better than he deserved and that he was not worthy to be in the same room with her. As she continued to kick him he became more and more excited . . . ." Rene Mueller committed suicide shortly after this experience. At this place it might be well to note that Eva Braun, his present female companion, has twice attempted suicide, Geli was either murdered or committed suicide and Unity Mitford has attempted suicide. Rather an unusual record for a man who has had so few affairs with women.

Hanfstaengl, Strasser and Rauschning, as well as several other informants, have reported that even in company when Hitler is smitten with a girl, he tends to grovel at her feet in a most disgusting manner. Here, too, he insists on telling the girl that he is unworthy to kiss her hand or to sit near her and that he hopes she will be kind to him, etc. From all of this we see the constant struggle against complete degradation whenever any affectionate components enter into the picture. It now becomes clear that the only way in which Hitler can control these coprophagic tendencies or their milder manifestations is to isolate himself from any intimate relationships in which warm feelings of affection or love might assert themselves. As soon as such feelings are aroused, he feels compelled to degrade himself in the eyes of the loved object and eat their dirt figuratively, if not literally. These tendencies disgust him just as much as they disgust us, but under these circumstances they get out of control and he despises himself and condemns himself for his weakness. Before considering further the effects of this struggle on his manifest behavior, we must pause for a moment to pick up another thread.

Femininity.

We notice that in all of these activities Hitler plays the passive role. His behavior is masochistic in the extreme inasmuch as he derives sexual pleasure from punishment inflicted on his own body. There is every reason to suppose that during his early years, instead of identifying himself with his father as most boys do, he identified himself with his mother. This was perhaps easier for him than for most boys since, as we have seen, there is a large feminine component in his physical makeup. His mother, too, must have been an extremly masochistic individual or she never would have entered into this marriage nor would she have endured the brutal treatment from her husband. An emotional identification with his mother would, therefore, carry him in the direction of a passive, sentimental, abasive and submissive form of adjustment. Many writers and informants have commented on his feminine characteristics — his gait, his hands, his mannerisms and ways of thinking. Hanfstaengl reports that when he showed Dr. Jung a specimen of Hitler's handwriting, the latter immediately exclaimed that it was a typically feminine hand. His choice of art as a profession might also be interpreted as a manifestation of a basic feminine identification.

There are definite indications of such an emotional adjustment later in life. The outstanding of these is perhaps his behavior towards his officers during the last war. His comrades report that during the four years he was in service he was not only over-submissive to all his officers but frequently volunteered to do their washing and take care of their clothes. This would certainly indicate a strong tendency to assume the feminine role in the presence of a masculine figure whenever this was feasible and could be duly rationalized. His extreme sentimentality, his emotionality, his occasional softness and his weeping, even after he became Chancellor, may be regarded as manifestations of a fundamental feminine pattern which undoubtedly had its origin in his relationship to his mother. His persistent fear of cancer, which was the illness from which his mother died, may also be considered as an expression of his early identification with her.

Although we cannot enter into a discussion concerning the frequency of this phenomenon in Germany, it may be well to note that there is sociological evidence which would indicate that it is probably extremely common. If further research on the subject should corroborate this evidence, it might prove of extreme value to our psychological warfare program insofar as it would give us a key to the understanding of the basic nature of the German male character, and the role that the Nazi organization plays in their inner life.

Homosexuality.

The great difficulty is that this form of identification early in life carries the individual in the direction of passive homosexuality. Hit-

C02571145

ler has for years been suspected of being a homosexual, although there is no reliable evidence that he has actually engaged in a relationship of this kind. Rauschning reports that he has met two boys who claimed that they were Hitler's homosexual partners, but their testimony can scarcely be taken at its face value. More condemning would be the remarks dropped by Foerster, the Danzig Gauleiter, in conversations with Rauschning. Even here, however, the remarks deal only with Hitler's impotence as far as heterosexual relations go without actually implying that he indulges in homosexuality. It is probably true that Hitler calls Foerster "Bubi," which is a common nickname employed by homosexuals in addressing their partners. This alone, however, is not adequate proof that he has actually indulged in homosexual practices with Foerster, who is known to be a homosexual.

The belief that Hitler is homosexual has probably developed (a) from the fact that he does show so many feminine characteristics, and (b) from the fact that there were so many homosexuals in the Party during the early days and many continue to occupy important positions. It does seem that Hitler feels much more at ease with homosexuals than with normal persons, but this may be due to the fact that they are all fundamentally social outcasts and consequently have a community of interests which tends to make them think and feel more or less alike. In this connection it is interesting to note that homosexuals, too, frequently regard themselves as a special form of creation or as chosen ones whose destiny it is to initiate a new order. The fact that underneath they feel themselves to be different and ostracized from normal social contacts usually makes them easy converts to a new social philosophy which does not discriminate against them. Being among civilization's discontents, they are always willing to take a chance of something new which holds any promise of improving their lot, even though their chances of success may be small and the risk great. Having little to lose to begin with, they can afford to take chances which others would refrain from taking. The early Nazi party certainly contained many members who could be regarded in this light. Even today Hitler derives sexual pleasure from looking at men's bodies and associating with homosexuals. Strasser tells us that his personal bodyguard is almost always 100% homosexuals. He also derives considerable pleasure from being with his Hitler Youth and his attitude towards them frequently tends to be more that of a woman than that of a man.

There is a possibility that Hitler has participated in a homosexual relationship at some time in his life. The evidence is such that we can only say there is a strong tendency in this direction which, in addition to the manifestations already enumerated, often finds expression in imagery concerning being attacked from behind or being stabbed in the back. His nightmares, which frequently deal with being attacked by a man and being suffocated, also suggest strong homosexual tendencies and a fear of them. From these indications, however, we would conclude that for the most part these tendencies have been repressed, which would speak against the probability of their being expressed in overt form. On the other hand, persons suffering from his perversion sometimes do indulge in homosexual practices in the hope that they might find sexual gratification. Even this perversion would be more acceptable to them than the one with which they are afflicted.

Early School Years.

   The foundations of all the diverse patterns we have been considering were laid during the first years of Hitler's life. Many of them, as we have seen, were due primarily to the peculiar structure of the home, while others developed from constitutional factors or false interpretations of events. Whatever their origins may have been, they did set up anti-social tendencies and tensions which disturbed the child to a high degree. From his earliest days it would seem he must have felt that the world was a pretty bad place in which to live. To him it must have seemed as though the world was filled with insurmountable hazards and obstacles which prevented him from obtaining adequate gratifications, and dangers which would menace his well-being if he attempted to obtain them in a direct manner. The result was that an unusual amount of bitterness against the world and the people in it became generated for which

Hitler as a pupil in Grade IV

124

166

he could find no suitable outlets. As a young child he must have been filled with intense feelings of inadequacy, anxiety and guilt which made him anything but a happy child.

It would seem, however, that he managed to repress most of his troublesome tendencies and make a temporary adjustment to a difficult environment before he was six years old, because at that time he entered school and for the next years he was an unusually good student. All of the report cards that have been found from the time he entered school until he was eleven years old, show an almost unbroken line of "A's" in all his school subjects. At the age of eleven the bottom dropped right out of his academic career. From an "A" student he suddenly dropped to a point where he failed in almost all his subjects and had to repeat the year. This amazing about-face only becomes intelligible when we realize that his baby brother died at that time. We can only surmise that this event served to reawaken his earlier conflicts and disrupt his psychological equilibrium.

In Hitler's case we may suppose that this event affected him in at least two important ways. First, it must have reawakened fears of his own death which, in turn, strengthened still further the conviction that he was the "chosen one" and under divine protection. Second, it would seem that he connected the death of his brother with his own thinking and wishing on the subject. Unquestionably, he hated this intruder and frequently thought of how nice it would be if he were removed from the scene. Unconsciously, if not consciously, he must have felt that the brother's death was the result of his own thinking on the subject. This accentuated his feelings of guilt on the one hand, while it strengthened still further his belief in special powers of Divine origin on the other. To think about these things was almost synonomous with having them come true. In order to avoid further guilt feelings he had to put a curb on his thinking processes. The result of this inhibition on thinking was that Hitler the good student was transformed into Hitler the poor student. Not only did he have to repeat the school year during which the brother died, but ever after his academic performance was mediocre, to say the least. When we examine his later report cards we find that he does well only in such subjects as drawing and gymastics, which require no thinking. In all the other subjects such as mathematics, languages or history, which require some thinking, his work is on the borderline — sometimes satisfactory and sometimes unsatisfactory.

We can easily imagine that it was during this period that the father's ire was aroused and he began to bring pressure on the boy to apply himself in his school work and threatened dire consequences if he failed to do so. From sociological evidence it would seem that this is about the age at which most German fathers first take a real interest in their sons and their education. If Hitler's father followed this general pattern, we can assume that he had cause to be irate at his son's performance. The constant struggle between himself and his father, which he describes in MEIN KAMPF, is probably true although the motivations underlying his actions were in all likelihood quite different from those he describes. He was approaching the adolescent period and this, together with his little brother's death, served to bring many dormant attitudes nearer the surface of consciousness .

Many of these attitudes now found expression in the father-son relationship. Briefly enumerated these would be (a) rejection of the father as a model; (b) an inhibition against following a career which demanded thinking; (c) the anal tendencies which found an outlet of expression in smearing; (d) his passive, feminine tendencies, and (e) his masochistic tendencies and his desire to be dominated by a strong masculine figure. He was not, however, ready for an open revolt for he tells us in his autobiography that he believed passive resistance and obstinacy were the best course and that if he followed them long enough, his father would eventually relent and allow him to leave school and follow an artist's career. As a matter of fact, his brother Alois, in 1930, before the Hitler myth was well established, reported that his father never had any objecttions to Adolph's becoming an artist but that he did demand that Adolph do well in school. From this we might surmise that the friction between father and son was not determined so much by his choice of a career as by unconscious tendencies which were deriving satisfaction from the antagonism.

Later School Career.

He carried the same pattern into the schools where he was forever antagonizing his teachers and the other boys. He has tried to create the impression that he was a leader among his classmates, which is almost certainly false. More reliable evidence indicates that he was unpopular among his classmates as well as among his teachers who considered him lazy, uncooperative and a trouble-maker. The only teacher during these years with whom he was able to get along was Ludwig Poetsch, an ardent German Nationalist. It would be an error, however, to suppose that Poetsch inculcated these nationalist feelings in Hitler. It is much more logical to assume that all these feelings were present in Hitler before he came in contact with Poetsch and that his nationalist teachings only offered Hitler a new outlet for the expression of his repressed emotions. It was probably during this period that he discovered a resemblance between the young state of Germany and his mother, and between the old Austrian monarchy and his father. At this discovery he promptly joined the Nationalist group of students who were defying the authority of the Austrian state. In this way he was able to proclaim openly his love for his mother and advocate the death of his father. These were feelings he had had for a long time but was unable to express. Now he was able to obtain partial gratification through the use of symbols.

The Death of His Father.

This probably served to increase the friction between father and son, for in spite of what Hitler says the best evidence seems to indicate that the father was anti-German in his sentiments. This again placed father and son on opposite sides of the fence and gave them new cause for hostility. There is no telling how this would have worked out in the long run because while the struggle between the two was at its height, the father fell dead on the street. The repercussions of this event must have been severe and reinforced all those feelings which we have described in connection with the brother's death. Again, it must have seemed like a fulfillment of a wish and again, there must have been severe feelings of guilt, with an additional inhibition on thinking processes.

His school work continued to decline and it seems that in order to avoid another complete failure, he was taken from the school at Linz and sent to school in Steyr. He managed to complete the year however, with marks which were barely satisfactory. It was while he was there that the doctor told him that he had a disease from which he would never recover. His reaction to this was severe since it brought the possibility of his own death very much into the foreground and aggravated all his childhood fears. The result was that he did not return to school and finish his course, but stayed at home where he lived a life which was marked by passivity. He neither studied nor worked but spent most of his time in bed where he was again spoiled by his mother who catered to his every need despite her poor financial circumstances.

One could suppose that this was the materialization of his conception of Paradise inasmuch as it reinstated an earlier childhood situation which he had always longed for. It would seem from his own account, however, that things did not go too smoothly, for he writes in MEIN KAMPF:

> "When at the age of fourteen, the young man is dismissed from school, it is difficult to say which is worse; his unbelievable ignorance as far as knowledge and ability are concerned, or the biting impudence of his behavior combined with an immorality which makes one's hair stand on end .... The three year old child has now become a youth of fifteen who despises all authority . . . now he loiters about, and God only knows when he comes home."

We can imagine the deaths of his brother and his father in rapid succession had filled him with such guilt that he could not enjoy this idyllic situation to the full. Perhaps the situation aroused desires in him which he could no longer face on a conscious level and he could only keep these in check by either remaining in bed and playing the part of a helpless child or absenting himself from the situation entirely. In any case, he must have been a considerable problem to his mother who died four years after his father. Dr. Bloch informs us that her great concern in dying was: "What would become of poor Adolph, he is still so young." At this time Adolph was eighteen years of age. He had failed at school and had not gone to work. He describes himself at this time as a milk-sop, which he undoubtedly was.

Admission Examinations to Academy of Art.

Two months before his mother's death he had gone to Vienna to take the entrance examinations for admission to the Academy of Art. At this time he knew that his mother was in a critical condition and that it was only a matter of a few months before death would overtake her. He knew, therefore, that his easy existence at home would shortly come to an end and that he would then have to face the cold, hard world on his own. It is sometimes extraordinary how events in the lifetime of an individual fall together. The first day's assignment on the examination was to draw a picture depicting "The Expulsion from Paradise". It must have seemed to him that Fate had chosen this topic to fit his personal situation. On the second day he must have felt that Fate was rubbing it in when he found the assignment to be a picture depicting "An Episode of the Great Flood". These particular topics in his situation must have aroused such intense emotional reactions within him that he could hardly be expected to do his best. Art critics seem to feel that he has some artistic talent even though it is not outstanding. The comment of the examiners was: "Too few heads." We can understand this in view of the circumstances under which he had taken the examination.

Death of His Mother.

He returned home shortly after the examinations. He helped to look after his mother who was rapidly failing and in extreme pain. She died on December 21, 1907 and was buried on Christmas Eve. Adolph was completely broken and stood for a long time at her grave after the remainder of the family had left. Dr. Bloch says: "In all my career I have never seen anyone so prostrate with grief as Adolph Hitler." His world had come to an end. Not long after the funeral he left for Vienna in order to follow in his father's footsteps and make his own way in the world. He made a poor job of it, however. He could not hold a job when he had one, and sunk lower and lower in the social scale until he was compelled to live with the dregs of society.

Vienna Days.

As he writes about these experiences in MEIN KAMPF one gets the impression that it was a terrific struggle against overwhelming odds. From what we now know of Adolph Hitler it would seem more likely that this existence yielded him considerable gratification in spite of its hardships. It is perfectly clear from what Hanisch writes that with a very small amount of effort he could have made a fair living and improved his condition by painting water colors. He refused to make this effort and

Specimens of Hitler's Artistic Talent

preferred to live in the filth and poverty which surrounded him. There must have been something in this that he liked, consciously or unconsciously. When we examine Hanisch's book carefully, we find the answer. Hitler's life in Vienna was one of extreme passivity in which activity was held at the lowest level consistent with survival. He seemed to enjoy being dirty and even filthy in his appearance and personal cleanliness. This can mean only one thing, from a psychological point of view, namely, that his perversion was in the process of maturation and was finding gratification in a more or less symbolic form. His attitude during this period could be summarized in the following terms: "I enjoy nothing more than to lie around while the world defecates on me." And he probably delighted in being covered with dirt, which was tangible proof of the fact. Even in these days he lived in a flophouse which was known to be inhabited by men who lent themselves to homosexual practices, and it was probably for this reason that he was listed on the Vienna police record as a "sexual pervert."

Nobody has ever offered an explanation of why he remained in Vienna for over five years if his life there was as distasteful and the city disgusted him to the degree that he claims in his autobiography. He was free to leave whenever he wished and could have gone to his beloved Germany years earlier if he had so desired. The fact of the matter is that he probably derived great masochistic satisfaction from his miserable life in Vienna, and it was not until his perversion became full-blown and he realized its implications that he fled to Munich at the beginning of 1913.

Anti-Semitism.

With the development of his perverse tendencies we also find the development of his anti-Semitism. There is absolutely no evidence that he had any anti-Semitic feelings before he left Linz or that he had any during the first years of his stay in Vienna. On the contrary, he was on the very best terms with Dr. Bloch while he was in Linz and sent him post cards with very warm sentiments for some time after he went to Vienna. Furthermore, his closest friends in Vienna were Jews, some of whom were extremely kind to him. Then, too, we must remember that his godfather, who lived in Vienna, was a Jew and it is possible that during his first year there he might have lived with this family. Most of the records of his mother's death are incorrect and place the event exactly one year after it had happened. During this year Hitler lived in Vienna but we have no clue as to what he did or how he managed to live without money during this intervening year. All we know is that he had time for painting during this period for he submitted the work he had done to the Academy of Art the following October. He was not admitted to the examination, however, because the examiners found the work of this period unsatisfactory. Shortly afterwards, he applied for admission to the School of Architecture but was rejected. The cause of his rejection was

C02571145

probably inadequate talent rather than the fact that he had not completed his course in the Realschule. It is only after this happened that we find him going to work as a laborer on a construction job, and from then on we have a fairly complete picture of his activities.

We know that he had very little money when he left Linz, certainly not enough to live on for almost an entire year while he spent his time in painting. Since the date of his mother's death has been so universally distorted, it would seem that efforts were being made to cover something which happened during this intervening year. My guess would be that he lived with his Jewish godparents who supported him while he was preparing work for the Academy. When he failed to be admitted at the end of a year, they put him out and made him go to work. There is one bit of evidence for this hypothesis. Hanisch, in his book, mentions in passing that when they were particularly destitute he went with Hitler to visit a well-to-do Jew whom Hitler said was his father. The wealthy Jew would have nothing to do with him and sent him on his way again. There is scarcely a possibility that Hitler's father was a Jew living in Vienna at this time, but Hanisch might easily have understood him to say father when he said godfather. This would certainly make much more sense and would indicate that Hitler had contact with his godparents before the visit and that they were fed up with him and would help him no further.

Projection.

Hitler's outstanding defense mechanism is one commonly called *projection*. It is a technique by which the ego of an individual defends itself against unpleasant impulses, tendencies or characteristics by denying their existence in himself while he attributes them to others. Innumerable examples of this mechanism could be cited in Hitler's case, but a few will suffice for purposes of illustration:

> "In the last six years I had to stand intolerable things from states like Poland."
>
> "It must be possible that the German nation can live its life   without being constantly molested."
>
> "Social democracy   directs a bombardment of lies and calumnies towards the adversary who seemed most danger-ous, till finally the nerves of those who have been attacked give out and they for the sake of peace, bow down to the hated enemy."
>
> "For this peace proposal of mine I was abused, and personally insulted. Mr. Chamberlain in fact spat upon me before the eyes of the world . . . ."
>
> "   It was in keeping with our own harmlessness that England took the liberty of some day meeting our peaceful activity with the brutality of the violent egoist."
>
> "   The outstanding features of Polish character were cruelty and lack of moral restraint."

131

173

From a psychological point of view it is not too far-fetched to suppose that as the perversion developed and became more disgusting to Hitler's ego, its demands were disowned and projected upon the Jew. By this process the Jew became a symbol of everything which Hitler hated in himself. Again, his own personal problems and conflicts were transferred from within himself to the external world where they assumed the proportions of racial and national conflicts.

Forgetting entirely that for years he not only looked like a lower class Jew but was as dirty as the dirtiest and as great a social outcast, he now began to see the Jew as a source of all evil. The teachings of Schoenerer and Lueger helped to solidify and rationalize his feelings and inner convictions. More and more he became convinced that the Jew was a great parasite on humanity which sucked its life-blood and if a nation was to become great it must rid itself of this pestilence. Translated back into personal terms this would read: "My perversion is a parasite which sucks my life-blood and if I am to become great I must rid myself of this pestilence." When we see the connection between his sexual perversion and anti-Semitism, we can understand another aspect of his constant linking of syphilis with the Jew. These are the things which destroy nations and civilizations as a perversion destroys an individual.

The greater the demands of his perversion became, the more he hated the Jews and the more he talked against them. Everything which was bad was attributed to them. Here was his political career in an embryo state. He now spent most of his time reading books, attending political talks and reading newspapers in cafe houses. He himself tells us in so many words that he skipped through this material and only took out those parts which were useful to him. In other words, he was not reading and listening in order to become educated sufficiently to form a rational judgment of the problem. This would have been a violation of his earlier inhibition on thinking. He read only in order to find additional justification for his own inner feelings and convictions and to rationalize his projections. He has continued this technique up to the present time. He does a great deal of reading on many diverse subjects but he never forms a rational opinion in the light of the information but only pays attention to those parts which convince him that he was right to begin with.

In the evening he would return to his flophouse and harangue his associates with political and anti-Semitic speeches until he became a joke. This, however, did not disturb him too much. On the contrary, it seemed to act as a stimulant for further reading and the gathering of more arguments to prove his point of view. It was as though in trying to convince others of the dangers of Jewish domination, he was really trying to convince himself of the dangers of being dominated by his perversion. Perhaps Hitler is really referring to his perversion when he writes:

"During the long pre-war years of peace certain pathological features had certainly appeared .... There were many signs of decay which ought to have stimulated serious reflection."
(MK, 315)

The same may also be true when he says:

"How could the German people's political instincts become so morbid? The question involved here was not that of a single symptom, but instances of decay which flared up now in legion . which like poisonous ulcers ate into the nation now here, now there. It seemed as though a continuous flow of poison was driven into the farthest blood vessels of this one-time heroic body by a mysterious power, so as to lead to ever more severe paralysis of sound reason and of the simple instinct of self-preservation." (MK, 201)

As time went on the sexual stimulation of the Viennese environment seemed to aggravate the demands of his perversion. He suddenly became overwhelmed by the role that sex plays in the life of the lower classes and the Jews. Vienna became for him "the symbol of incest" and he suddenly left it to seek refuge with his ideal mother, Germany. But his pre-war days in Munich were not different from those he left behind in Vienna. His life was still one of extreme passivity and although we know little about them we can surmise that his days were filled with inner troubles.

The First World War.

Under these circumstances, we can understand why he thanked God for the first World War. For him it represented an opportunity of giving up his individual war against himself in exchange for a national war in which he would have the help of others. It also represented to him, on an unconscious level, an opportunity of redeeming his mother and assuming a masculine role for himself. Even at that time, we may suppose, he had inklings that he was destined to be a Great Redeemer. It was not only his mother he was going to redeem, but also himself.

His advent in the German Army was really his first step in attempting to redeem himself as a social human being. No longer was he to be the underdog for he was joining forces with those who were determined to conquer and become great. Activity replaced his earlier passivity to a large degree. Dirt, filth, and poverty were left behind and he could mingle with the chosen people on an equal footing. But for him this was not enough. As we have pointed out in an earlier section, he was not content to be as clean as the average soldier. He had to go to the other extreme and become exceedingly clean. Whenever he returned from the front he immediately sat down and scrupulously removed every speck of mud from his person, much to the amusement of his comrades. Mend, his comrade during this time, relates an experience at the front when Hitler upbraided one of the other men for not keeping himself clean and called him a "manure pile", which sounds very much like a memory of himself in Vienna.

During this period, as previously mentioned, his passive feminine tendencies were finding an outlet in his abasive conduct toward his officers. It looks as though he had not progressed sufficiently far in his conquest of himself to maintain a wholly masculine role. But with the help of others and the guidance of his respected officers he was making some progress toward what appeared to be a social adjustment. The final defeat of Germany, however, upset his well-laid plans and shattered his hopes and ambitions.

The Defeat of Germany.

Nevertheless, it was this event which proved to be the turning-point in his life and determined that he would be an outstanding success rather than a total failure. Unconscious forces, some of which had been dormant for years, were now reawakened and upset his whole psychological equilibrium. His reaction to this event was an hysterical attack which manifested itself in blindness and mutism. Although the hysterical blindness saved him from witnessing what he regarded as an intolerable spectacle, it did not save him from the violent emotional reactions it aroused. These emotions, we may assume, were similar to those which he had experienced as a child when he discovered his parents in intercourse. It seems logical to suppose that at that time he felt his mother was being defiled before his eyes but in view of his father's power and brutality he felt himself utterly helpless to redeem her honor or to save her from future assaults. If this is true, we would expect that he swore secret vengeance against his father and, as has been shown, there is evidence to this effect.

Now the same thing was happening again but instead of his real mother it was his ideal mother, Germany, who was being betrayed, corrupted and humiliated and again he was unable to come to her rescue. A deep depression set in of which he writes:

> "What now followed were terrible days and even worse nights. Now I knew that everything was lost .... In those nights my hatred arose, the hatred against the originators of this deed."

But again he was weak and helpless — a blind cripple lying in a hospital. He struggled with the problem:

> "How shall our nation be freed from the chains of this poisonous embrace?"

It would seem that the more he thought about it, the more his intellect told him that all was lost. He probably despised and condemned himself for his weakness and as his hatred continued to rise in the face of this frustrating experience he vowed then and there:

Hitler in Munich crowd at outbreak of World War I

177

"To know neither rest nor peace until the November Criminals had been overthrown . . . ."

Undoubtedly his emotions were extremely violent and would serve as a powerful motive for much of the retaliation which becomes so prominent in his later behavior. There are, however, many ways of retaliating which do not involve a complete upheaval and transformation of character such as we find in Hitler at this time.

From our experience with patients we know that complete transformations of this kind usually take place only under circumstances of extreme duress which demonstrate to the individual that his present character structure is no longer tenable. Naturally we do not know exactly what went on in Hitler's mind during this period or how he regarded his own position. We do know, however, that under such circumstances very strange thoughts and fantasies pass through the minds of relatively normal people and that in the case of neurotics, particularly when they have strong masochistic tendencies, these fantasies can become extremely absurd. Whatever the nature of these fantasies might have been, we may be reasonably sure that they involved his own safety or well-being. Only a danger of this magnitude would ordinarily cause an individual to abandon or revolutionize his character structure.

It may be that his nightmares will yield a clue. These, it may be remembered, center on the theme of his being attacked or subjected to indignities by another man. It is not his mother who is being attacked, but himself. When he wakes from these nightmares he acts as though he were choking. He gasps for breath and breaks out in a cold sweat. It is only with great difficulty that he can be quieted because frequently there is an hallucinatory after-effect and he believes he sees the man in his bedroom.

Under ordinary circumstances, we would be inclined to interpret this as the result of an unconscious wish for homosexual relations together with an ego revulsion against the latent tendency. This interpretation might apply to Hitler, too, for to some extent it seems as though he reacted to the defeat of Germany as a rape of himself as well as of his symbolic mother. Furthermore, while he was lying helpless in the hospital, unable to see or to speak, he could well have considered himself an easy object for a homosexual attack. When we remember, however, that for years he chose to live in a Vienna flophouse which was known to be inhabited by many homosexuals and later on associated with several notorious homosexuals, such as Hess and Roehm, we cannot feel that this form of attack, alone, would be sufficient to threaten his integrity to such an extent that he would repudiate his former self.

A further clue to his thoughts during this period may be found in his great preoccupation with propaganda which, in his imagery is almost synonomous with poison.

"Slogan after slogan rained down on our people."
". . . the front was flooded with this poison."
". . . for the effect of its language on me was like that of
spiritual vitriol . . . I sometimes had to fight down the rage
rising in me because of this concentrated solution of lies."

This type of imagery probably has a double significance. There is considerable evidence to show that as a child he believed that the man, during intercourse, injected poison into the woman which gradually destroyed her from within and finally brought about her death. This is not an uncommon belief in childhood and in view of the fact that his mother died from a cancer of the breast, after a long illness, the belief may have been more vivid and persisted longer in Hitler than in most children. On the other hand, the importance of poison in connection with his perversion has already been considered. We know about his inhibitions against taking certain substances into his mouth. These were not present during the early days of his career but developed much later in connection with his transformed character.

In view of all this it may not be too far-fetched to suppose that while he was fantasying about what the victors might do to the vanquished when they arrived, his masochistic and perverse tendencies conjured up the thought that they might attack him and force him to eat dung and drink urine (a practice which, it is alleged, is fairly common in Nazi concentration camps). Interestingly enough, this idea is incorporated in the colloquial expression "to eat the dirt of the victors." And in his weakened and helpless condition he would be unable to ward off such an attack. Such an hypothesis gains credence when we review the behavior of Nazi troops in the role of conquerors.

Transformation of Character.

Although a thought of this kind would have certain pleasurable aspects to a masochistic person, it would also arouse fear of consequences together with violent feelings of guilt and disgust. If the thought kept recurring at frequent intervals and refused to be suppressed, we can easily imagine that it might drive an individual into such depths of despair that death would appear as the only solution. Hitler's fear of death has already been reviewed and it is possible that it was this alternative which shocked him out of his former self. Certain it is that in his public utterances, as well as in his actions, he attributes extraordinary powers to the fear of death.

"I shall spread terror by the surprise employment of my
measures. The important thing is the sudden shock of an
overwhelming fear of death."

And in MEIN KAMPF he tells us that:

"In the end, only the urge for self-preservation will eternally
succeed. Under its pressure so-called 'humanity', as the

> expression of a mixture of stupidity, cowardice, and imaginary superior intelligence, will melt like snow under the March sun."

Sentiments of this sort suggest rather strongly that he was brought face to face with the prospect of his own death and that in order to save himself he had to rid himself of a bad conscience as well as the dictates of the intellect. The following quotations illustrate his attitude towards conscience and the need of rendering it inactive:

> "Only when the time comes when the race is no longer overshadowed by the consciousness of its own guilt, then it will find internal peace and external energy to cut down regardlessly and brutally the wild shoots, and to pull up the weeds."

> "Conscience is a Jewish invention. It is a blemish like circumcision."

> "I am freeing men from the restraints of an intelligence that has taken charge; from the dirty and degrading modifications of a chimera called conscience and morality . . . ."

And of the intellect he says:

> "The intellect has grown autocratic and has become a disease of life."

> "We must distrust the intelligence and the conscience and must place our faith in our instincts."

Having repudiated these two important human functions, he was left almost entirely at the mercy of his passions, instincts and unconscious desires. At the crucial moment these forces surged to the fore in the form of an hallucination in which an inner voice informed him that he was destined to redeem the German people and lead them to greatness. This, for him, was a new view of life. It opened new vistas to him particularly in connection with himself. Not only did it confirm the vague feeling he had had since childhood, namely, that he was the "Chosen One" and under the protection of Providence, but also that he had been saved for a divine mission. This revelation served to crystallize his personality on a new pattern. He writes:

> "In the hours of distress, when others despair, out of apparently harmless children, there shoots suddenly heros of death-defying determination and icy coolness of reflection. If this hour of trial had never come, then hardly anyone would ever have been able to guess that a young hero is hidden in the beardless boy. Nearly always such an impetus is needed in order to call genius into action. Fate's hammer-stroke, which then throws the one to the ground, suddenly strikes steel into another, and while now the shell of everyday life is broken, the erstwhile nucleus lies open to the eyes of the astonished world."

In another place he writes:

> "A fire had been lighted, and out of its flames there was bound to come some day the sword which was to regain the

freedom of the Germanic Siegfried and the life of the German nation."

How, one may ask, was it possible for a person with Hitler's past life and abnormal tendencies to take this seriously? The answer is relatively simple. He believed it because he wanted to believe it — in fact, had to believe it in order to save himself. All the unpleasantries of the past he now interpreted as part of a great design. Just as it was Fate which ordained he should be born on the Austrian side of the border, so it was Fate which sent him to Vienna to suffer hardships in order to take the "milk-sop out of him by giving him Dame Sorrow as a foster-mother" and "kept him at the front where any negro could shoot him down when he could have rendered a much more worthwhile service elsewhere," and so it was probably Fate which decreed his past life and tendencies. These were the crosses he had to bear in order to prove his mettle. He might have been speaking about himself when he said of Germany:

> ". . . if this battle should not come, never would Germany win peace. Germany would decay and at the best would sink to ruin like a rotting corpse. But that is not our destiny. We do not believe that this misfortune which today our God sends over Germany has no meaning: it is surely the scourge which should and shall drive us to new greatness, to a new power and glory . . . ."

Before this new greatness, power and glory could be achieved, however, it was necessary to conquer the misfortune. The misfortune, in Hitler's case, so he probably thought, was the emotional identification he had made with his mother during childhood. He had used this as a cornerstone for his personality and it was responsible for his "humanity". But it also carried with it a passive, masochistic form of adjustment which, instead of leading to greatness as he had hoped, had carried him to the brink of degradation, humiliation and self-destruction. It exposed him to untold dangers which were no longer compatible with self-preservation. Consequently, if he were to survive he must rid himself not only of his conscience and intellect but of all the traits which were associated with false "humanity". In its place he must set a personality which was in keeping with the "Law of Nature". Only after he had achieved this transformation could he feel safe from attack. To overcome his weakness and to grow strong became the dominant motive of his life.

> ". . . feels the obligation in accordance with the Eternal Will that dominates this universe to promote the victory of the better and stronger, and to demand the submission of the worse and weaker."

> "A stronger generation will drive out the weaklings because in its ultimate form the urge to live will again and again break the ridiculous fetters of a so-called 'humanity' of the individual, so that its place will be taken by the 'humanity of nature', which destroys weakness in order to give its place to strength."

If our hypothesis concerning his mental processes while he lay helpless in Pasewalk Hospital is correct, we may assume that in order to quiet his fears he sometimes imagined himself as a person who far surpassed his enemies in all the "virile" qualities. Under these circumstances he could conquer his enemies and do to them what he now feared they would do to him. This is, of course, pure wishful thinking, but evidently this play of imagery yielded him so much pleasure that he unconsciously identified himself with this super-man image. We would guess that it was at the moment when this mechanism, which is known as "Identification with the Aggressor", operated, that the aforementioned hallucination was produced. He was no longer the weak and puny individual who was exposed to all kinds of attacks and indignities. On the contrary, he was fundamentally more powerful than all the others. Instead of his being afraid of them, they should be afraid of him.

The image Hitler created was a form of compensation for his own inferiorities, insecurities and guilts. Consequently the image negated all his former qualities and turned them into their opposites and to the same degree. All the human qualities of love, pity, sympathy and compassion were interpreted as weaknesses and disappeared in the transformation.

> "All passivity, all inertia   (became) senseless, inimical to life."
> "The Jewish Christ-creed with its effeminate pity-ethics."
> "Unless you are prepared to be pitiless you will get nowhere."

In their place we find what Hitler's warped mind conceived to be the super-masculine view:

> ". . . if a people is to become free it needs pride and will-power, defiance, hate, hate and once again hate."
> "Brutality is respected. Brutality and physical strength. The plain man in the street respects nothing but brutal strength and ruthlessness."
> "We want to be the supporters of the dictatorship of national reason, of national energy, of national — brutality and resolution."

Anti-Semitism.

When the "Identification with the Aggressor" mechanism is used, however, there is no conscious struggle within the personality in which the new personality gradually overcomes the old one. The identification takes place outside the realm of consciousness and the individual suddenly feels that he is this new person. There is no process of integration or assimilation. The old personality is automatically suppressed and its characteristics are projected onto some external object against which the new personality can carry on the struggle. In Hitler's case, all his undesirable characteristics were projected onto the Jew. To Hitler he became Evil incarnate and responsible for all the world's difficulties, just as Hitler's earlier femininity now appeared to him to be the source of all his personal difficulties. This projection was relatively easy for him to make inasmuch as in his Vienna days the Jew had become for him the symbol of sex, disease and his perversion. Now another load of undesirable qualities was poured upon his head with the result that Hitler now hated and despised the Jew with the same intensity as he hated his former self.

Obviously, Hitler could not rationalize his projection as long as he stood by himself as a single individual, nor could he combat the Jew single-handed. For this he needed a large group which would fit the picture he had created. He found this in defeated Germany as a whole. At the close of the war it was in a position almost identical with his own before the transformation had taken place. It, too, was weak and exposed to further attack and humiliation. It, too, had to be prepared to eat the dirt of the conquerers and during the inflation period it, too, was confused, passive and helpless. It, therefore, made an excellent symbol of his earlier self and Hitler again shifted his personal problems to a national and racial scale where he could deal with them more objectively. Providence had "given" him the spark which transformed him over-night. It was now his mission to transform the remainder of the German people by winning them to his view of life and the New Order. The Jews now played the same role in the life of Germany as his effeminate, masochistic and perverse adjustment had played in his own life. He now resolved to become a politician.

Many writers have expressed the opinion that Hitler's anti-Semitism is motivated primarily by its great propaganda value. Undoubtedly, anti-Semitism is the most powerful weapon in his propaganda arsenal and Hitler is well aware of it. He has even expressed the opinion on several occasions that the Jews would make Germany rich. All our informants who knew him well, however, agree that this is superficial and that underneath he has a sincere hatred for the Jews and everything Jewish. This is in complete agreement with our hypothesis. We do not deny that he often uses anti-Semitism propagandistically when it suits his purpose. We do maintain, however, that behind this superficial motivation is a much deeper one which is largely unconscious. Just as Hitler had to exterminate his former self in order to get the feeling of being great and strong, so must Germany exterminate the Jews if it is to attain its new glory. Both are poisons which slowly destroy the respective bodies and bring about death.

> "All the great cultures of the past perished only because the originally creative race died off through blood poisoning."
> "...alone the loss of purity of the blood destroys the inner happiness forever; it eternally lowers man, and never again can its consequences be removed from body and mind."

C02571145

The symbolism in these quotations is obvious and the frequency with which they recur in his speaking and writing bears testimony to their great importance in his thinking and feeling processes. It would seem from this that unconsciously he felt that if he succeeds in ridding himself of his personal poison, his effeminate and perverse tendencies as symbolized in the Jew, then he would achieve personal immortality.

In his treatment of the Jews we see the "Identification with the Aggressor" mechanism at work. He is now practicing on the Jews in reality the things he feared the victors might do to him in fantasy. From this he derives a manifold satisfaction. First, it affords him an opportunity of appearing before the world as the pitiless brute he imagines himself to be; second, it affords him an opportunity of proving to himself that he is as heartless and brutal as he wants to be (that he can really take it); third, in eliminating the Jews he unconsciously feels that he is ridding himself, and Germany, of the poison which is responsible for all difficulties; fourth, as the masochist he really is, he derives a vicarious pleasure from the suffering of others in whom he can see himself; fifth, he can give vent to his bitter hatred and contempt of the world in general by using the Jew as a scapegoat; and sixth, it pays heavy material and propagandistic dividends.

Early Political Career.

Armed with this new view of life Hitler sought for opportunities to put his resolve to become a politician into effect and start on the long road which would redeem Germany and lead her to new greatness and glory. This was not easy in post-war Germany which was now engaged in violent internal strife. He remained in the Reserve Army for a time where he engaged in his "first political activity"—that of spying on his comrades. His duties were to mingle with the men in his barracks and engage them in political discussions. Those who voiced opinions with a Communistic flavor he reported to his superior officers. Later, when the offenders were brought to trial, it was his job to take the witness stand and give the testimony which would send these comrades to their death. This was a severe trial for his new character but he carried it off in a brazen and unflinching manner. It must have given him tremendous satisfaction to find that he actually could play this new role in such an admirable fashion. Not long afterwards it was discovered that he had a talent for oratory and he was rewarded for his services by being promoted to instructor. The new Hitler, the embryo Fuehrer, was beginning to pay dividends.

"Identification with the Aggressor" is, at best, an unstable form of adjustment. The individual always has a vague feeling that something is not just as it should be, although he is not aware of its origins. Nevertheless, he feels insecure in his new role and in order to rid himself of his uneasiness he must prove to himself, over and over again, that he is

184

really the type of person he believes himself to be. The result is a snow-ball effect. Every brutality must be followed by a greater brutality, every violence by a greater violence, every atrocity by a greater atrocity, every gain in power by a greater gain in power, and so on down the line. Unless this is achieved successfully, the individual begins to feel insecure and doubts concerning his borrowed character begin to creep in together with feelings of guilt regarding his shortcomings. This is the key to an under-standing of Hitler's actions since the beginning of his political activities to the present day. This effect has not escaped the attention of non-psychological observers. Francois-Poncet, for example, writes in the French Yellow Book:

> "The Chancellor chafes against all these disappointments with indignant impatience. Far from conducing him to mod-eration, these obstacles irritate him. He is aware of the enor-mous blunder which the anti-Jewish persecutions of last November have proved to be; yet, by a contradiction which is part of the dictator's psychological make-up, he is said to be preparing to enter upon a merciless struggle against the Church and Catholicism. Perhaps he thus wishes to wipe out the memory of past violence with fresh violence . . . ." (p. 49)

The mechanism feeds on itself and must continue to grow in order to maintain itself. Since it has no real foundations to support it, the indivi-dual can never quite convince himself that he is secure and need fear no longer. The result is that he can brook no delays but must plunge ahead on his mad career.

Hitler's political career shows these tendencies to a marked degree. Scarcely had he affiliated himself with the group which had founded the Party than he connived to get control over it. Then followed a rapid expansion of membership, the introduction of terror, a series of broken promises, collusions and betrayals. Each brought him fresh gains and new power, but the pace was still too slow to satisfy him. In 1923 he believed himself to be strong enough to undertake a Putsch and seize the reins of government. The Putsch failed and Hitler's conduct during it has been the subject of much comment. There are a number of versions concerning what happned. Some report that when the troops fired on them Hitler fell to the ground and crawled through an alley which car-ried him to safety while Ludendorff, Roehm and Goering marched ahead. Some claim that he stumbled, others that he was knocked down by his bodyguard who was killed. The Nazi version is that he stopped to pick up a small child who had run out into the street and been knocked down! Years later they produced a child on the anniversary of the event to prove the story!

From a psychological point of view it would appear that he turned coward on this occasion and that he did fall down and crawl away from the scene of activities. Although he had usurped considerable power and had reason to have faith in his new character, it seems unlikely that it was sufficient for him to actually engage the recognized authority in physical combat. His attitude towards recognized superiors and authority in general would make such a direct attack improbable. Furthermore, his reactions after his escape would seem to indicate that his new role had temporarily failed. He went into a deep depression and was restrained from committing suicide only by constant reassurances. When he was taken to Landsberg prison he went on a hunger strike and refused to eat for three weeks. This was his response to being placed again in the position of the vanquished. Perhaps memories of his fantasies in the hospital were returning to harass him! It was only after he discovered that his jailers were not unkindly disposed to him that he permitted himself to be persuaded to take food.

During his stay in Landsberg he became much quieter. Ludecke says:

> "Landsberg had done him a world of good. Gone from his manner was the nervous intensity which formerly had been his most unpleasant characteristic."

It was during this period that he wrote MEIN KAMPF and we may suppose that his failure in the Putsch made it necessary for him to take a fresh inventory and integrate his new character more firmly. He resolved, at this time, not to try another Putsch in the future but to gain the power by legal means alone! In other words, he would not participate again in an open conflict with the recognized authority.

Leaders of Munich Putsch, Nov. 8, 1923; Left to right: Pernet; Weber; Dr. Frick; Col. Kriebel; Gen. Ludendorff; Hitler; Lt. Brueckner; Capt. Roehm; Judge Poehner.

Hitler in Fortress Landsberg-on-Lech

His Rise to Power.

It is scarcely necessary for us to trace the history of his rise to power and his actions after he achieved it. They all follow along the same general pattern we have outlined. Each successful step served to convince him that he was the person he believed himself to be but brought no real sense of security. In order to attain this he had to go a step higher and give additional proof that he was not deluding himself. Terror, violence and ruthlessness grew with each advance and every recognized virtue was turned into a vice — a sign of weakness. Even after he became the undisputed leader of the nation, he could not rest in peace. He projected his own insecurities onto the neighboring states and then demanded that they bow to his power. As long as there was a nation or a combination of nations more powerful than Germany, he could never find the peace and security he longed for. It was inevitable that this course would lead to war because only by that means could he crush the threat and prove to himself that he need no longer be afraid. It was also inevitable that the war would be as brutal and pitiless as possible for only in this way could he prove to himself that he was not weakening in his chosen course but was made of stuff becoming to his conception of what a victor should be.

Rages.

Although space will not permit a detailed analysis of the operation of the various psychological streams we have enumerated, in the determination of his everyday behavior, a few have aroused sufficient speculation to warrant a place in our study. One of the outstanding of these is his rages. Most writers have regarded these as temper-tantrums, his reaction to minor frustrations and deprivations. On the surface they appear to be of this nature and yet, when we study his behavior carefully, we find that when he is confronted by a real frustration or deprivation, such as failure to be elected to the Presidency or being refused the Chancellorship, his behavior is exactly the opposite. He is very cool and quiet. He is disappointed but not enraged. Instead of carrying on like a spoiled child, he begins immediately to lay plans for a new assault. Heiden, his biographer, describes his characteristic pattern as follows:

> "When others after a defeat would have gone home despondently, consoling themselves with the philosophical reflection that it was no use contending against adverse circumstances, Hitler delivered a second and a third assault with sullen defiance. When others after a success would have become more cautious, because they would not dare put fortune to the proof too often and perhaps exhaust it, Hitler persisted and staked a bigger claim on Destiny with every throw."

This does not sound like a person who would fly into a rage at a trifle.

Nevertheless, we know that he does fly into these rages and launches into tirades on very slight provocation. If we examine the causes of these outbursts, we almost invariably find that the trigger which sets them off is something which he considers to be a challenge of his superman personality. It may be a contradiction, a criticism or even a doubt concerning the truth or wisdom of something he has said or done, or it might be a slight or the anticipation of opposition. Even though the subject may be trifling or the challenge only by implication, or even wholly imagined, he feels called upon to display his primitive character. Francois-Poncet has also detected and described this reaction. He writes:

> "Those who surround him are the first to admit that he now thinks himself infallible and invincible. That explains why he can no longer bear either criticism or contradiction. To contradict him is in his eyes a crime of 'lese-majeste'; opposition to his plans, from whatever side it may come, is a definite sacrilege, to which the only reply is an immediate and striking display of his omnipotence."

As soon as his display has served its purpose and cowed his listeners into submission, it is turned off as suddenly as it was turned on. How great is the insecurity which demands such constant vigilance and apprehension!

Fear of Domination.

We find this same insecurity at work when he is meeting new people and particularly those to whom he secretly feels inferior in some way. Earlier in our study we had occasion to point out that his eyes had taken over a diffuse sexual function. When he first meets the person he fixates him with his eyes as though to bore through the other person. There is a peculiar glint in them on these occasions which many have interpreted as an hypnotic quality. To be sure, he uses them in such a way and tries to overpower the other person with them. If he turns his eyes away, Hitler keeps his fixated directly on him or her but if the other person returns this gaze Hitler turns his away and looks up at the ceiling as long as the interview continues. It is as though he were matching his power against theirs. If he succeeds in overpowering the other person, he rudely follows up his advantage. If, however, the other person refuses to succumb to his glance, he avoids the possibility of succumbing to theirs. Likewise, he is unable to match wits with another person in a straightforward argument. He will express his opinion at length but he will not defend it on logical grounds. Strasser says:

> "He is afraid of logic. Like a woman he evades the issue and ends by throwing in your face an argument entirely remote from what you were talking about."

We might suspect that even on this territory he cannot expose himself to a possible defeat which would mar the image he has of himself. He is, in fact, unable to face real opposition on any ground. He cannot speak to a group in which he senses opposition but walks out on his audience. He has run out of meetings with Ludendorff, Gregor Strasser, Bavarian Industrialists and many others, because he could not risk the possibility

C02571145

of appearing in an inferior light or expose himself to a possible domination by another person. There is reason to suppose that his procrastination is not so much a matter of laziness as it is a fear of coming to grips with a difficult problem. Consequently, he avoids it as long as possible and it is only when the situation has become dangerous and disaster lies ahead that his "inner voice" or intuition communicates with him and tells him what course he should follow. Most of his thinking is carried on subconsciously which probably accounts for his ability to penetrate difficult problems and time his moves. Psychological experiments in this field seem to indicate that on this level the individual is often able to solve very complex problems which are impossible for him on the level of consciousness. Wherever we turn in studying Hitler's behavior patterns we find the spectre of possible defeat and humiliation as one of his dominant motivations.

Monuments.

His passion for constructing huge buildings, stadia, bridges, roads, etc., can only be interpreted as attempts to compensate for his lack of confidence. These are tangible proofs of his greatness which are designed to impress himself as well as others. Just as he must be the greatest man in all the world, so he has a tendency to build the greatest and biggest of everything. Most of the structures he has erected he regards as temporary buildings. They are, to his way of thinking, on a par with ordinary mortals. The permanent buildings he plans to construct later on. They will be much larger and grander and will be designed to last at least a thousand years. In other words, these are befitting monuments to himself who plans on ruling the German people for that period of time through his new view of life.

One of Hitler's monuments

It is also interesting to note the frequency with which he uses gigantic pillars in all his buildings. Most of the buildings are almost surrounded by them and he places them in every conceivable place. Since pillars of this sort are almost universally considered to be phallic symbols, we may regard the size and frequency as unconscious attempts to compensate for his own impotence. His huge pageants serve a similar purpose.

Oratory.

No study of Hitler would be complete without mentioning his oratory talents. His extraordinary gift for swaying large audiences has contributed, perhaps more than any other single factor, to his success and the partial realization of his ideal. In order to understand the power of his appeal, we must be cognizant of the fact that for him the masses are fundamentally feminine in character. To Hanfstaengl and other informants he has frequently said: "Die Masse ist ein Weib," and in MEIN KAMPF he writes:

> "The people, in an overwhelming majority, are so feminine in their nature and attitude that their activities and thoughts are motivated less by sober consideration than by feeling and sentiment."

In other words, his unconscious frame of reference, when addressing a huge audience, is fundamentally that of talking to a woman.

In spite of this, his insecurities assert themselves. He never is the first speaker on the program. He must always have a speaker precede him who warms up the audience for him. Even then he is nervous and jittery when he gets up to speak. Frequently he has difficulty in finding words with which to begin. He is trying to get the "feel" of the audience. If it "feels" favorable, he starts in a rather cautious manner. His tone of voice is quite normal and he deals with his material in a fairly objective manner. But as he proceeds his voice begins to rise and his tempo increases. If the response of the audience is good, his voice becomes louder and louder and the tempo faster and faster. By this time all objectivity has disappeared and passion has taken complete possession of him. The mouth which can never utter a fragment of profanity off the speaker's platform now pours forth a veritable stream of curses, foul names, villification and hatred. Hanfstaengl compares the development of a Hitlerian speech with the development of a Wagnerian theme which may account for Hitler's love for Wagnerian music and the inspiration he derives from it.

This steady stream of filth continues to pour forth until both he and the audiences are in a frenzy. When he stops he is on the verge of exhaustion. His breathing is heavy and uncontrolled and he is wringing wet with perspiration. Many writers have commented on the sexual components in his speaking and some have described the climax as a veritable orgasm.

C02571145

Heyst writes:

> "In his speeches we hear the suppressed voice of passion and wooing which is taken from the language of love; he utters a cry of hate and voluptuousness, a spasm of violence and cruelty. All those tones and sounds are taken from the backstreets of the instincts; they remind us of dark impulses repressed too long."

And Hitler himself says:

> "Passion alone will give to him, who is chosen by her, the words that, like beats of a hammer, are able to open the doors to the heart of a people."

Undoubtedly, he uses speaking as a means of talking himself into the super-man role and of living out the role of "Identification with the Aggressor." He carefully builds up imposing enemies — Jews, Bolsheviks, capitalists, democracies, etc., in order to demolish them without mercy (these are all inventions of the Jews to his way of thinking and consequently in attacking any one of them he is fundamentally attacking the

Hitler leaving hall after 3-hour speech

Jews). Under these circumstances, he appears to the naive and unsophisticated listener as the Great Redeemer of Germany.

But this is only one side of the picture. On the other side we have the sexual attack which, in his case, is of a perverse nature. It finds expression in his speaking but due to the transformation of character everything appears in the reverse. The steady stream of filth he pours on the heads of his "feminine" audience is the reverse of his masochistic perversion which finds gratification in having women pour their "filth" on him. Even the function of the physical organs is reversed. The mouth which, under ordinary circumstances, is an organ of injection and is surrounded with inhibitions and prohibitions, now becomes the organ through which filth is ejected. Hitler's speaking has been aptly described as a "verbal diarrhea." Rauschning describes it as an oral enema. It is probably this unconscious sexual element in his speaking which holds such a fascination for many people.

His Appeal.

A word may be added in connection with the content of his speeches. Strasser sums it up very concisely when he says:

> "Hitler responds to the vibrations of the human heart with the delicacy of a seismograph . . . enabling him, with a certainty with which no conscious gift could endow him, to act as a loudspeaker proclaiming the most secret desires, the least permissible instincts, the sufferings and personal revolts of a whole nation."

We are now in a position to understand how this is possible for him. In regarding his audience as fundamentally feminine in character, his appeal is directed at a repressed part of their personalities. In many of the German people there seems to be a strong feminine-masochistic tendency which is usually covered over by more "virile" characteristics but which finds partial gratification in submissive behavior, discipline, sacrifice, etc. Nevertheless, it does seem to disturb them and they try to compensate for it by going to the other extreme of courage, pugnaciousness, determination, etc. Most Germans are unaware of this hidden part of their personalities and would deny its existence vehemently if such an insinuation is made. Hitler, however, appeals to it directly and he is in an excellent position to know what goes on in that region because in him this side of his personality was not only conscious but dominant throughout his earlier life. Furthermore, these tendencies were far more intense in him than in the average person and he had a better opportunity of observing their operation. In addressing an audience in this way he need only dwell on the longings, ambitions, hopes and desires of his earlier life in order to awaken these hidden tendencies in his listeners. This he does with inordinate skill. In this way he is able to arouse the same attitudes and emotions in his listeners that he himself now experiences in connection with this type of adjustment, and is able to direct these into the same channels that he has found useful. Thus he is able to win them to his new view of life which sets a premium on brutality, ruthlessness, dominance, determination, etc., and which frowns upon all the established human qualities. The key is always to strive to be what you are not and to do your best to exterminate that which you are. The behavior of the German armies has been an outstanding manifestation of this contradiction. To the psychologist it seems as though the brutality expressed towards the people of the occupied countries is motivated not only by a desire to prove to themselves that they are what they are not, but also by a vicarious masochistic gratification which they derive from an identification with their victims. On the whole, one could say of many of the German troops what Rauschning said of Hitler:

> "...there lies behind Hitler's emphasis on brutality and ruthlessness the desolation of a forced and artificial inhumanity, not the amorality of the genuine brute, which has after all something of the power of a natural force."

It is Hitler's ability to play upon the unconscious tendencies of the German people and to act as their spokesman which has enabled him to mobilize their energies and direct them into the same channels through which he believed he had found a solution to his own personal conflicts. The result has been an extraordinary similarity in thinking, feeling and acting in the German people. It is as though Hitler had paralyzed the critical functions of the individual Germans and had assumed the role for himself. As such he has been incorporated as a part of the personalities of his individual supporters and is able to dominate their mental processes. It is this phenomenon which lies at the very root of the peculiar bond which exists between Hitler, as a person, and the German people and places it beyond the control of any purely rational, logical or intellectual appeal. In fighting for Hitler these persons are now unconsciously fighting for what appears to them to be their own psychological integrity.

All of this throws a very interesting light on the underlying psychology of a large part of the German people both in war and in peace and one is forced to suspect that fundamental changes within the German culture itself must be affected before the German people are ready to play a constructive role in a family of nations. A consideration of these aspects of the problem, however, lie beyond the scope of the present study.

Chapter Six

Hitler's Probable Behavior In The Future

"The victor will never be asked if he told the truth."

Adolf Hitler

HITLER'S PROBABLE BEHAVIOR IN THE FUTURE

As the tide of battle turns against Hitler it may be well to consider very briefly the possibilities of his future behavior and the effect that each would have on the German people as well as on ourselves.

1. *Hitler may die of natural causes.* This is only a remote possibility since, as far as we know, he is in fairly good health except for his stomach ailment which is, in all probability, a psychosomatic disturbance. The effect such an event would have on the German people would depend on the nature of the illness which brought about his death. If he would die from whooping cough, mumps, or some other ridiculous disease, it would be a material help in breaking the myth of his supernatural origins.

2. *Hitler might seek refuge in a neutral country.* This is extremely unlikely in view of his great concern about his immortality. Nothing would break the myth more effectively than to have the leader run away at the critical moment. Hitler knows this and has frequently condemned the Kaiser for his flight to Holland at the close of the last war. Hitler might want to escape as he has escaped from other unpleasant situations, but it seems almost certain that he would restrain himself.

3. *Hitler may get killed in battle.* This is a real possibility. When he is convinced that he cannot win, he may lead his troops into battle and expose himself as the fearless and fanatical leader. This would be most undesirable from our point of view because his death would serve as an example to his followers to fight on with fanatical, death-defying determination to the bitter end. This would be what Hitler would want for he has predicted that:

> "We shall not capitulate . . . no, never. We may be destroyed, but if we are, we shall drag a world with us . . . a world in flames."

> "But even if we could not conquer them, we should drag half the world into destruction with us and leave no one to triumph over Germany. There will not be another 1918."

At a certain point he could do more towards the achievement of this goal by dying heroically than he could by living. Furthermore, death of this kind would do more to bind the German people to the Hitler legend and insure his immortality than any other course he could pursue.

4. *Hitler may be assassinated.* Although Hitler is extremely well protected there is a possibility that someone may assassinate him. Hitler is afraid of this possibility and has expressed the opinion that:

> "His own friends would one day stab him mortally in the back . . . . And it would be just before the last and greatest victory, at the moment of supreme tension. Once more Hagen would slay Siegfried. Once more Hermann the Liberator

would be murdered by his own kinsmen. The eternal destiny
of the German nation must be fulfilled yet again, for the
last time."

This possibility too, would be undesirable from our point of view inasmuch as it would make a martyr of him and strengthen the legend.

It would be even more undesirable if the assassin were a Jew for this would convince the German people of Hitler's infallibility and strengthen the fanaticism of the German troops and people. Needless to say, it would be followed by the complete extermination of all Jews in Germany and the occupied countries.

5. *Hitler may go insane.* Hitler has many characteristics which border on the schizophrenic. It is possible that when faced with defeat his psychological structure may collapse and leave him at the mercy of his unconscious forces. The possibilities of such an outcome diminish as he becomes older, but they should not be entirely excluded. This would not be an undesirable eventuality from our point of view since it would do much to undermine the Hitler legend in the minds of the German people.

6. *German Military might revolt and seize him.* This seems unlikely in view of the unique position Hitler holds in the minds of the German people. From all the evidence it would seem that Hitler alone is able to rouse the troops, as well as the people, to greater efforts and as the road becomes more difficult this should be an important factor. One could imagine, however, that as defeat approaches Hitler's behavior may become more and more neurotic and reach a point where it would be well for the military to confine him. In this case, however, the German people would probably never know about it. If they discovered it, it would be a desirable end from our point of view because it would puncture the myth of the loved and invincible leader.

The only other possibility in this connection would be that the German military should decide, in the face of defeat, that it might be wiser to dethrone Hitler and set up a puppet government to sue for peace. This would probably cause great internal strife in Germany. What the ultimate outcome might be would depend largely on the manner in which it was handled and what was done with Hitler. At the present time the possiblity seems rather remote.

7. *Hitler may fall into our hands.* This is the most unlikely possibility of all. Knowing his fear of being placed in the role of the vanquished, we can imagine that he would do his utmost to avoid such a fate. It should, however, be considered as a possibility if for no other reason than that we have a precedent for such behavior in the case of Jan Bockelsson. His early life, character and career bear an uncanny resemblance to that of Hitler. In the final stages of his mad career his

masochistic tendencies got the upper hand and he surrendered to his enemies and proposed to them that they confine him in a cage and exhibit him throughout the country in order that the people, for a small admission fee, might look at him and express their contempt. In Hitler's case such an outcome seems remote but it is difficult to estimate the extent to which an extreme masochist will go in order to gratify these tendencies. From our point of view it would be most desirable to have Hitler fall into our hands and in the long run it would probably be of benefit to the German people as well.

8. *Hitler might commit suicide.* This is the most plausible outcome. Not only has he frequently threatened to commit suicide, but from what we know of his psychology it is the most likely possibility. It is probably true that he has an inordinate fear of death, but being an hysteric he could undoubtedly screw himself up into the super-man character and perform the deed. In all probability, however, it would not be a simple suicide. He has much too much of the dramatic for that and since immortality is one of his dominant motives we can imagine that he would stage the most dramatic and effective death scene he could possibly think of. He knows how to bind the people to him and if he cannot have the bond in life he will certainly do his utmost to achieve it in death. He might even engage some other fanatic to do the final killing at his orders.

Hitler has already envisaged a death of this kind, for he has said to Rauschning:

"Yes, in the hour of supreme peril I must sacrifice myself for the people."

This would be extremely undesirable from our point of view because if it is cleverly done it would establish the Hitler legend so firmly in the minds of the German people that it might take generations to eradicate it.

Whatever else happens, we may be reasonably sure that as Germany suffers successive defeats Hitler will become more and more neurotic. Each defeat will shake his confidence still further and limit his opportunities for proving his own greatness to himself. In consequence he will feel himself more and more vulnerable to attack from his associates and his rages will increase in frequency. He will probably try to compensate for his vulnerability by continually stressing his brutality and ruthlessness.

His public appearances will become less and less for, as we have seen, he is unable to face a critical audience. He will probably seek solace in his Eagle's Nest on the Kehlstein near Berchtesgaden. There among the ice-capped peaks he will wait for his "inner voice" to guide him. Meanwhile, his nightmares will probably increase in frequency and intensity and drive him closer to a nervous collapse. It is not wholly im-

155

198

C02571145

probable that in the end he might lock himself into this symbollic womb and defy the world to get him.

In any case, his mental condition will continue to deteriorate. He will fight as long as he can with any weapon or technique that can be conjured up to meet the emergency. The course he will follow will almost certainly be the one which seems to him to be the surest road to immortality and at the same time wreak the greatest vengeance on a world he despises.

Chapter Seven

Appendix

and

Bibliography

"The great strength of the totalitarian state is that it forces those who fear it to imitate it." Adolf Hitler

BIBLIOGRAPHY

COMPLETE BIBLIOGRAPHY

Names preceded by asterisk have been excerpted and are included in the Hitler Source-Book

ABEL, Theodor: Why Hitler came into Power? New York, Prentice Hall Inc. 1938.
ADAM, Adela M.: Philip alias Hitler. Oxford, 1941, v. 10 p. 105-113.
ALLARD, Paul: Quand Hitler espionne la France, Paris. Les editions de France. 1939. 197 p.
*ANDERNACH, Andreas: Hitler ohne Maske. Muenchen. Der Antifaschist. 1932.
ARBUERSTER, Martin: Adolf Hitler, Blut oder Geist. Zurich. Reso Verlag. 1936. 47 p.
        Kulturpolit. Schriften Heft 7.
ATLANTIC MONTHLY—FAIRWEATHER, N.: Hitler and Hitlerism. 149: 380-87, 509-16,
        March-April 1932.
ATLANTIC MONTHLY—FAIRWEATHER, N.: A man of destiny. 149 vol. 380-87.

BADE, Wilfred: Der Weg des Dritten Reichs. 4 Bande Lubeck Coleman. 1933-38, je 150
        Seiten.
BAINVILLE, Jacques: Histoire de deux peuples, continuee jusqu'a Hitler. Paris. Flam-
        marion. 1938. 155 p.
*BALK, Ernst, Wilhelm: "Mein Fuhrer." Berlin. P. Schmidt. 1933. 15 p.
*BAVARIAN State Police: Report to the Bavarian State Ministry of the Interior Re: Con-
        ditional Parole of Adolf Hitler.
*BAYLES, Will D.: Caesars in Goose Step. New York, Harper Bros. 1940. 262 p.
BAYNES, Helton Godwin: "Germany possessed," London. J. Cape. 1941.
*BEDEL, Maurice: Monsieur Hitler (17 ieme ed.) Paris. Gallimard. 1937. 92 p.
BELGIUM. The Official Account of What Happened. 1939-40. Belgium. New York. 1941.
*BERCHTHOLD, Josef: Hitler Uber Deutschland. Muenchen. F. Eher 1932 88 p.
BEREITSCHAFT fur Adolf Hitler. Wien 1932. 15 p.
*BERLINER ILLUSTRIERTE ZEITUNG. Berlin No. 32. August, 1939. Militarpass Adolf
        Hitlers.
*BERLINER TAGEBLATT. Berlin 2/27/1924. p. 10-26. Putschprozess Hitlers Vernehmung.
*BERLINER TAGEBLATT. Berlin Sept. 6, 1930. Hitler als Zeuge im Leipziger Reichswehr-
        prozess.
*BERTRAND, Louis, M. E.:   . . . Hitler. Paris. Fayard & Cie. 1936.
*BILLINGER, Karl (pseud.). "Hitler is no fool." Modern age books. 1939.
*BILLUNG, R.: Rund um Hitler. Muenchen. 1931. B. Funck.
BLAKE, Leonard: Hitler's last year of Power. London A. Daker's Ltd. 1939.
*BLANK, Herbert: Adolf Hitler, Wilhelm III. Berlin Rowohlt. 1931. 92 p.
BOUHLER, Philipp: . . . Adolf Hitler, Das WERDEN einer Volksbewegung. (Colemans K.
        Biogr. Heft. 11. 1935. 49 p.)
*BOUHLER, Philipp: Adolf Hitler, a short sketch of his life. Terramare office. 1938.
BRADY, Robert A.: The Spirit and Structure of German Fascism. New York. 1937.
BRAUN, Otto: Von Weimar zu Hitler. New York, Europa Verl. 1940.
BREDOW, Klaus: Hitler rast. Der 30. Juni. . .Saarbrucken ? 1934. 72 p.
BRENTANO, Bernard: Der Beginn der Barbarei in Deutschland. Rowohlt. Berlin. 1930.
*BRITISH WAR BLUEBOOK. 1939.
BROOKS, Robert Clarkson: . . . Deliver us from Dictators. University of Penna. Press. 1935,
        245 p.
*BUELOW, Paul: Adolf Hitler und der Bayreuther Kulturkreis. (Aus Deutschlands Werden
        Heft 9. p. 1-16) Leipzig 1933.

CAHEN, Max: Man against Hitler. Dobbs & Merrill. May, 1939.
CANADIAN MONTHLY: LE BOURDAIS, D. M.: Crackpot Chancellor. 91:20-22 April 1939.
CATHOLIC WORLD—CRABITS, P.: Masterstroke of Psychology. 148:190-97 November, 1938.
*CATHOLIC WORLD—Crabits, P.: HUDDLESTON, S.: Hitler the Orator. 149 229/30
        May 1939.
CATHOLIC WORLD—GILLIS, J. M.: Austrian Phaeton. 151:257-65 Jan. 1940.
CHATEAUBRIANT, Alphonse, de: . . . La Gerbe des Forces. Noucelle Allemagne. 1937.
*CHELIUS, Fritz, Heinz: Aus Hitlers Jugendland und Jugendfuss. Leipzig. Schaufuss. 1933.
        30 p.
CHRISTIAN CENTURY—CLINCHY, E. R.: I saw Hitler, too. 49:1131-33 September 21, 1932.
CHRISTIAN CENTURY—HONRIGHAUSEN, E. G.: Hitler and German Religion. 50:418-20
        —March 29, 1933.
CHRISTIAN CENTURY—HUTCHINSON, P.: Portent of Hitler. 50:1299-1301 October 18,
        1933.
CHRISTIAN CENTURY—PENDELL, E. H.: Adolph alias 666.50:759. January 7, 1933. Dis-
        cussion 50:819,849. January 21-28, 1933.
CHRISTIAN CENTURY—RAMSDELL, E. T.: Hitler adored and hated. 51-971. July 25, 1934.
CHRISTIAN CENTURY: How seriously must Hitler be taken. 53.1277 September 30, 1936.
CHRISTIAN CENTURY: Comedy has its limits: Chaplinized. Hitler 57:816-17 January 26,
        1940.
*CIARLATINI, Franco: Hitler e il Fascismo. R. Bemporad, Firenze. 1933 70 p.
CLINCHY, Everett R.: The Strange Case of Herr Hitler. The John Day Pamphlets. No.
        24, 1933. 30 p.
*COLLIER'S—YBARRA, T. R.: Says Hitler, Interview. 29:17, July 1, 1933
COLLIER'S—YBARRA, T. R.: Hitler. 94-50. August 4, 1934.
*COLLIER'S—HANFSTAENGL, E. T. S.: My Leader. 94. 7-9 August 4, 1934.
COLLIER'S—YBARRA, T. R.: Hitler changes his clothes. 95:12/3 April 27, 1935.
COLLIER'S—YBARRA, T. R.: Hitler on High. 100:21/2 September 4, 1937.

COLLIER'S—CHURCHILL, W.: Dictators are Dynamite. 102:16/7 September 3, 1938.
COLLIER'S: Is Hitler Crazy? 103:82 June 17, 1939.
*COLLIER'S—BLOCH, E.: My Patient Hitler. 107:11, March 15, 1941, 69-70, March 22, 1941.
COLLIER'S—OECHSNER, F.: Portable Lair; Fuehrerhauptquartier. 110:26 August 22, 1942.
COMMONWEAL: Quandaries of Herr Hitler. 16:419. August 31, 1932.
COMMONWEAL—BINSSE, H. L.: Complete Hitler. 29:625/6. March 31, 1939.
CONTEMPORARY REVIEW: Adolf Hitler. 140:726-32, December 1931.
CONTEMPORARY REVIEW—EXCERPT. R. of Rs. 85:56/7. February 1932.
CONTEMPORARY REVIEW: Hitler's Age of Heroism. The Advent of Herr Hitler. 143. vol.
     532-41, 143 vol. 366-68, 1933.
CONTEMPORARY REVIEW: Hitler's Cards. Germanicus. 154:190-96, August 1938.
CONTEMPORARY REVIEW: Der Fuhrer Spricht. 155:357-68, March 1939.
CONTEMPORARY REVIEW—STERN-RUBARTH, E.: Heinrich Himmler, Hitler's Fouche,
     Head of Gestapo. 158: 641-45, December 1940.
CONTEMPORARY REVIEW—ALBERT, E.: Hitler and Mussolini. 159:155-61, February,
     1941.
*CRAIN, Maurice: Rulers of the World. New York, 1940.
CURRENT HISTORY—LORRE, L.: Hitler's Bid for German Power. May, 1932.
CURRENT HISTORY—FRITERS, G.: Who are the German Fascists? 35:532-36 January,
     1932.
*CURRENT HISTORY—PHAYRE, I.: Holiday with Hitler. 44:50-58, July 1936.
CURRENT HISTORY: Prosecuted by Hitler, an unbiased Account of a real Expe. 44:83-90,
     June 1936.
CURRENT HISTORY: Mr. Hitler. 48:74/5. January, 1938.
CURRENT HISTORY: Dictatorial Complex; Psychologist analyses the mental pattern of
Europe's strongest strong Men. J. Jastrow. 49:40 December 1, 1938.
CURRENT HISTORY—PANTON, S.: Hitler's New Hiding Place. 50:71/2 April, 1939.
CURRENT HISTORY: Hitler's Escape. 51:12. December, 1939.
CURRENT HISTORY: Hitler as Wotan...Retreat High Bavarian Alps. By T. Lang 51:50.
     February 1, 1940.
CURRENT HISTORY: Stranger in Paris. 51:54 August, 1940.
CURRENT HISTORY: Ascetic Adolf; Hitler's Income. 52:27/28. January 23, 1941.
*CURRENT HISTORY: I Was Hitler's Boss. Volume I. November 1941. p. 193/99.
*CZECH-JOCHBERG, Erich: Adolf Hitler und sein Stab Oldenburg. G. Stalling, 1933.
*CZECH-JOCHBERG: Hitler, eine Deutsche Bewegung. Oldenburg. Stalling, 1936.

D'ABERNON, Edgar, Vincent: Diary of an Ambassador. 1920/26, New York, Doubleday.
*DESCAVES, Pierre: Hitler. Paris. Denel & Steele. 1936.
*DEUEL, Wallace R.: People under Hitler. New York. Harcourt ...1942 p. 92.
DEUTSCHE Juristenzeitung. 330. Oktober, 1924. Muenchener Hochverratsprozess. Graf au
     Dohna.
DEUTSCHE Republik. V.4. 1930. Riesse, G. Hitler und die Armee.
DEUTSCHE Republik. V.358-64. Das Schutzserum gegen die Hitlerei.
DEUTSCHE Republik. IV. 1476-81 Figuren aus dem "Dritten Reich."
DIEBOW, Hans.: Hitler, eine Biographie. W. Kolk, 1931.
*DIETRICH, Otto: Mit Hitler in die Macht. F. Eher Nachfl. Muenchen, 1934. p. 209.
*DOBERT, Eitel Wolf: Convert to Freedom, New York, Putnam's, 1940.
*DODD'S, Ambassador: Diary. 1933-38, New York—Harcourt, 1941. 464 p.
*DODD, Martha: Through Embassy Eyes. New York, Harcourt, 1939. 382 p.
DOERR, Eugen: Mussolini, Hitler. . .Leipzig. S. Schnurpfeil Verlag. 1931, 16 p.
DOKUMENTE DER DEUTSCHEN POLITIK. Berlin, Junker & Dunnhaupt Verlag. 1935-39.
DUHAMEL, Georges: Memoriel de la Guerre Blanche. 1938, Paris, 1939.
*DUTCH, Oswald (pseud.) Hitler's 12 Apostles. London. E. Arnold & Co. 1939, 271 p.
DZELEPY, E.N.: . .Hitler contre la France? Paris. Editions Excelsior, 1933. 59 p.
DZELEPY, E. N.: Le vrai "Combat" de Hitler. . .Paris. L. Vogel. (1936) 317 p.

*ECKART, Dietrich: Der Bolschewismus von Moses bis Lenin. Muenchen, 1925.
*EICHEN, Dr. Carl von: Hitler's Throat. Time Magazine, Nov. 14, 1938.
EINZIG, Paul: Hitler's "New Order" in Europe. London. MacMillan. 1941 147 p.
*EMSEN, Kurt von: Adolf Hitler und die Kommenden. Leipzig. W. R. Lindner (1932) 160 p.
*ENSOR, Robert Charles K.: Who Hitler is. Oxford Pamphlets. No. 20. 1939, 32 p.
ENSOR, Robert Charles K.: Herr Hitler's Self Disclosure in "Mein Kampf." Oxford Pam-
     phlets. No. 3 (1938).
ERCKNER, S.: Hitler's Conspiracy against Peace. London. Gollanz. 1937. 288 p.
ERMARTH, Fritz: The New Germany (Washington, 1936)

FEDER, GOTTRIED: Was will Adolf Hitler? Muenchen. F. Eher. 1931. 23 p.
*FERNSWORTH, Lawrence: Dictators and Democrats, New York, McBride. . .1941.
FICKE, Karl: Auf dem Wege nach Canossa. Klausthal. Selbstverlag. 1931. 47 p.
*FLANNER, Janet: An American in Paris. New York, Simon Schuster (1940).
*FLANNERY, Harry W.: Assignment to Berlin. New York. 1942, 430 p.
*FODOR, M. W.: Plot and Counterplot in Central Europe. (Houghton) Boston, 1937, 317 p.
FOREIGN AFFAIRS: SCHEFFER, P.: Hitler Phenomenon and Portent. 10:382-90, April,
     1932.
FORUM—CLATCHIE, S. M.: Germany Awake. 85:217-24, April, 1931.
FORUM—UMBELL, H. D.: Dept. of brief Biography. Reply to Emil Ludwig. 98 supp. 10/11.
     December, 1937.
FRANCOIS, Jean: L'Affaire Rohm-Hitler. Les Oeuvres Libres. Paris. 1938 v. 209. p. 5-142.
FRATECO (pseud.): M. Hitler, Dictateur. Trad. de l'allemand sur le manuscript, indit.
     Paris. L'eglantine. 1933 275 p.

*FRIED, Hans Ernest: The Guilt of the German Army. New York, MacMillan, 1942. 426 p.
*FROMMER: Blood and Banquets. New York. Harper Bros. 1942. 322 p.
*FRY, Michael: Hitler's Wonderland. London. Murray, 1934.
*FUCHS, Martin: Showdown in Vienna. New York. Putnam's, 1939. 311 p.
FUEHRER, Der. in 100 Buchern. Wir lesen. May, 1939. p. 1-16.

*GANZER, Karl, Rich.: . . .Vom Ringen Hitlers um das Reich. 1924-33. "ZEITGESCHICHTE
    VERLAG." Berlin, 1935.
GEHL, Walter: Der Deutsche Aufbruch. Breslau. Hirt. 1938, 172 p.
*GEORGES-ANQUETIL: Hitler conduit le bal. Paris. Les editions de Lutece. 1939, 632 p.
*GERMAN FOREIGN OFFICE: The German White Paper. June 23, 1940.
GOEBBELS, Dr. Joseph: Kampf um Berlin. NSDAP. Muenchen. 1934.
*GOEBBELS, Dr. Joseph: Vom Kaiserhof zur Reichskanzlei. NSDAP. Muenchen. 1934. 312 p.
GOLDING, Louis: Hitler Through the Ages. London. Soverign Books Ltd. 1940.
GOLLOMB, Joseph: Armies of Spies. New York, MacMillan, 1939, 213 p.
*GOOD HOUSEKEEPING: 109:30/1. October, 1939. ALLEN, J.: Directors of Destiny.
GOREL, Michael: Hitler sans masque.
GRAACH, Heinrich: Freiheitskampf . Saarlouis. Hansen Verlag, 1935 64 p.
GREENWOOD, H.: Hitler's First Year. London, 1934. The spectator booklet No. 5.
GRZESINSKI, Albert: Inside Germany. New York. Dutton. 1939. 374 p.
*GRIMM, Alfred Max: Horoscope Hitler. Toelz. Selbstverlag, 1925.
GRITZBACH, Erich: Hermann Goering. London, 1939.
*GROSS, Felix: Hitler's Girls, Guns and Gangsters. London, Hurst. 1941, 320 p.
*GRUNSKY, Karl: Warum Hitler?. .Der Aufschwung, Deutsche Reihe, 1933.
GUMBEL, Emil Julius: Zwei Jehre Mord. (Kapp Putsch) 1921. Berlin Verlag Neuess Vater-
    land. 63 p.
GUMBEL, Emil Julius: Les crimes politiques en Allemagne. 1919-29. Paris. Gallimard, 1931.
*GUNTHER, John: Inside Europe, New York. Harper Bros., 1936. 470 p.
*GUNTHER, John: The High Cost of Hitler. London, Hamilton, 1939, 126 p.

*HAAKE, Heinz: Das Ehrenbuch des Fuhrers. NSDAP. 1933.
*HADAMOWSKY, Eugen: Hitler kempft um den Frieden Europas. NSDAP. 1936, 210 p.
HADELN, Hajo, Freiherr von: Vom Wesen einer Nationalsozialistischen Weltgeschichte,
    Frankfurt a.M.Osterrieth, 1935, 56 p.
*HAFFNER, S.: GERMANY: Jekyll and Hyde. New York, Dutton, 1941, 318 p.
HAGEN, Paul: Will Germany Crack? New York, 1942, 283 p.
HAMBLOCH, Ernest: Germany Rampant. London. Duckworth, 1939, 297 p.
*HANFSTAENGL, Ernst Franz: Hitler in der Karrikstur der Welt. Berlin. Verlag Braune
    Bucher, 1933. 174 p. (Neue Folge: Tat gegen Tinte. Berlin. O. Rentsch. 1934.
*HANISCH, Reinhold: I was Hitler's Buddy. The New Republic, April 5, 1939, p. 239-242.
    April 12, 1939, p. 270-272; April 19, 1939, p. 297-300.
HANSEN, Henrich: Der Schlussel zum Frieden. Berlin. Klieber, 1938, 48 p.
HANSEN, Henrich: Hitler, Mussolini. . .Diessen. Raumbild Verlag. 1938.
*HARPER MAGAZINE: December, 1934; THOMPSON, Dorothy: "Good Bye to Germany."
    (quoted in Brooks: Deliver us from Dictators.)
HARPER MAGAZINE—GUNTHER, J.: Hitler. 172:/148-59. January, 1936.
HARPER MAGAZINE—ROBERTS, S. H.: Riddle of Hitler. 176:246-54. February, 1938.
    (quoted in book: Roberts: House that Hitler built.)
HARSCH, Joseph C.: Pattern of Conquest. New York. Doubleday. 1941, 309 p.
HAUSER, Heinrich: Hitler vs. Germany. London. Jarrold. 1940.
HAUSER, Heinrich: Time was: Death of a Junker. New York. Reynal. 1942, 308 p.
HAUTEOLOQUE, Xavier de: A l'hombre de la croix gammee. Paris. Les Editions de France.
    1933, 252 p.
*HEIDEN, Konrad: Adolf Hitler. Zurich. Europa Verlag, 1936. 447 p.
*HEIDEN, Konrad: Adolf at School. Living Age. 351:227-29. Nov., 1936.
*HEIDEN, Konrad: Ein Mann gegen Europa. Zurich. Europa Verlag. 1937, 390 p.
HEIDEN, Konrad: Les vepres Hitleriennes. Sorlot. Paris. 1939, 190 p.
*HEINER, Einar, Henrik: Adolf Hitler. . .Torekas. Schweden. Selbstverlag, 1937, 13 p.
*HEINZ, Heinz A.: Germany's Hitler, London, Hurst. 1934.
*HENDERSON, Sir Neville: Failure of a Mission. New York. Putnam's, 1940. 334 p.
HENRY, Ernst. (pseud.): Hitler over Europe. London Dent. 1934. 307 p.
*HEUSS, Theodor: Hitlers Weg. Union Deutsche Verlags Anstalt, 1932, 167 p.
*HEYST, Axel: After Hitler. London, Minerva Publ. Co., 1940, 228 p.
*HINKEL, Hans/BLEY, Wulf: Kabinet Hitler. Verlag Deutsche Kulturwacht. Berlin, 1933.
    (?) 64 p.
HITLER: Ja, aber-was sagt Hitler Selbst? Eine Auswahl v. H. Passow. 1931.
HITLER: und die Deutsche Aufgabe. Zeit-und Streitfragen. Heft 1, 1933.
HITLER'S Wollen. Werner Siebart. NSDAP, 1935.
HITLER: Against the World. .New York. Worker's Library Publ., 1935.
HITLER: The man. (London, 1936) Friends of Europe Publ. No. 34, p. 1-21.
HITLER: Acquarelle. NSDAP. (1936).
HITLER calls this Living. London, 1939., 226 p.
HITLER in Hamburg. Hamburg. 1939.
*HOEPER, Wilhelm: Adolf Hitler, der Erzieher der Deutschen. Breslau, Hirt Verl., 1934,
    179 p.
*HOFFMANN, Heinrich: Deutschlands Erwachen. 1924.
*HOFFMANN, Heinrich: Hitler, wie ihn Keiner Kennt. Berlin, 1932, 96 p.
HOFFMANN, Heinrich: Hitler in seinen Bergen. Berlin. Zeitgeschichte Verlag, (1935).

C02571145

HOFFMANN, Heinrich: Hitler Abseits vom Alltag. Berlin, Zeitgeschichte Verlag, 1937.
HOFFMANN, Heinrich: Hitler in Italien. Muenchen. Verlag Heinrich Hofmann (1938) 96 p.
HOFFMANN, Heinrich: Hitler in seiner Heimat. Berlin. Zeitgeschichte Verlag, 1938.
*HOFFMANN, Heinrich: Hitler baut Grossdeutschland, 1938, 311 p.
HOFFMANN, Heinrich: Hitler befreit Sudetendeutschland. Berlin, Zeitgeschichte Verlag, 1938.
HOFFMANN, Heinrich: Hitler in Polen. Berlin, Zeitgeschichte Verlag, 1939, 48 p.
HOFFMANN, Heinrich: Hitler in Bohmen. Berlin, Zeitgeschichte Verlag, 1939.
*HOLBECK, K.: Kaiser, Kanzler, Kampfer. Leipzig. A. Hoffmann, 1933, 41 p.
HOLT, John G.: Under the Swastika. (Chapel Hill, 1936)
*HOOVER, Calvin B.: Germany enters the Third Reich, New York, 1933.
*HUDDLESTON, Sisley: In my Time. London. J. Cape (1938), 411 p.
*HUSS, Pierre, J.: The Foe we Face. New York, Doubleday, 1942, 300 p.
HUTTON, Graham: Survey after Munich, Boston, 1939.

IL POPOLO D'ITALIA: 7-5-29. Hitler: Un processo intentato. . .15-5-29. I diffamatori. . .
    condannati. . .
INDIAN REVUE, the: Chancellor Hitler. (KK Sr. Iyengar) 34 vol. 246.

JONES, Ernest J.: Hitler, the Jews and Communists. Sydney, 1933.
JOSEPHSON, Matthew: Nazi Culture . . . The John Day Pamphlets, 1933, 32 p.

*KEMP, C. D. Jr.: Adolph Hitler and the Nazis, New York, Cook, 1933, 32 p.
KERNAN, Thomas: France on Berlin Time, New York, Lippincott. 1941, 312 p.
KING, Joseph: The German Revolution. London, 1933.
*KLOTZ, Helmut: The Berlin Diaries. London, 1935.
*KNICKERBOCKER, H. R.: Is Tomorrow Hitler's? New York, Reynal, 1941, 382 p.
*KOEHLER, Hansjurgen: Inside information. Pallas Publ. London, 1940, 269 p.
*KOEHLER, Hansjurgen: Inside the Gestapo. Hitler's Shadows over the World. Pallas
    Publ. Co., Ltd. London, 1940.
*KOEHLER, Pauline: The Women lived in Hitler's House. Sheridan House.
KOERBER, Adolf-Victor von: Adolf Hitler, sein Leben und seine Reden. Muenchen. E.
    Boepple, 1923, 112 p.
*KRAUSS, Helene: Des Fuhrers Jugendstatten. Wien Kuhne, 1938.
KREBS, Hans: Wir Sudetendeutsche, Berlin, Runge, 1937, 168 p.
KREBS, Hans: Sudetendeutschland Marschiert: Berlin, Osmer. 1939.
KRUEGER, Kurt MD: "Inside Hitler," New York, Avalon Press, 1941, 445 p.

*LADIES' HOME JOURNAL: Story of the Two Mustaches, 57:18, July, 1940.
LANDAU, Rom: Hitler's Paradise, London, Faber, 1941.
*LANIA, Leo: Today We are Brothers, New York, 1942, 344 p.
*LASWELL, H. D.: Psychology of Hitlerism. Political Quarterly, vol. 4, 373-384.
*LAURIE, Arthur Pillans: The Case for Germany, Berlin, 1939.
LEE, John Alexander: Hitler, The Auckland Serv. print. 1940.
LEERS, Johann v.: Adolf Hitler. Leipzig. 1932, 95 p. (Manner und Machte)
*LEFEBVRE, Henri: Hitler au pouvoir. Paris, Bureau d'Uditions, 1938, 87 p.
*LE GRIX, Francois:. . .20 jours chez Hitler Paris, Grasse, 1933.
*LENGYEL, Emil: Hitler, New York, 1932, 256 p.
*LESKE, Gottfried: I was a Nazi Flier, New York, Dialpress, 1941. 351 p.
LEWIS, Wyndham: Hitler, London, Chatto & Windus, 1931. 202 p.
*LEWIS, Wyndham: The Hitler Cult. London, 1939, 267 p.
LICHTENBERGER, Henri: The Third Reich. New York, 1937.
LIFE: Adolf Hitler's Rise to Power, 9:61-67, August 19, 1940.
*LITERARY DIGEST: Misfire of the German Mussolini. 76:23, March 17, 1923.
*LITERARY DIGEST: Hitler, Germany's Would-Be Mussolini. 107:15/6, October 11, 1930.
*LITERARY DIGEST: Handsome Adolf, The Man Without a Country. 107:34, October 18, 1930.
LITERARY DIGEST: Dangerous Days in Europe. 107:14/5. October 25, 1930.
*LITERARY DIGEST: Adolf Hitler States His Case. 111:15, Nov. 21, 1931.
LITERARY DIGEST: Hitler's astounding Outburst. 111:10. Dec. 19, 1931.
*LITERARY DIGEST: Transformation of Adolf Hitler, 112:13/4, Jan. 9, 1932
LITERARY DIGEST: Freud's Fears of Hitler, 113:15, April 23, 1932.
LITERARY DIGEST: Hitler's Star still in the Ascendant. 113:12/3, 5/7/32.
LITERARY DIGEST: Hitler's shattered Dream of Dictatorship, 114:13/4 November 19, 1932.
LITERARY DIGEST: Gregor Strasser, Big Hitlerite Rebel. 115:13, 1/28/33.
*LITERARY DIGEST: When Hitler Hit the Ceiling. 115:30, February 18, 1933.
LITERARY DIGEST: Bewildering Magic of Fuehrer Hitler. 115:10/1, 5/13/33.
*LITERARY DIGEST: Comic Aspects of Hitler's Career. 116:13, August 26, 1933.
*LITERARY DIGEST—HIGH, S.: The Man who leads Germany. 116:5, Oct. 21, 1933.
LITERARY DIGEST: Chancellor-Reichsfuhrer. Watching his Step. 118:12, August 18, 1934.
LITERARY DIGEST: Abbe Dinnet Gives His Views of Two Dictators. 118:18, November 17, 1934.
LITERARY DIGEST: They Stood out from the Crowd in 1934. 118:7, 12/29/34.
*LITERARY DIGEST—HIGH, Stanley: Hitler and the New Germany, Oct. 7, 1933.
*LITTEN, Irmgard: Beyond Tears, New York, Alliance Book Corp., 1940, 325 p.
*LIVING AGE, GOETZ, F.: How Hitler Failed, 320:595-99, March 29, 1924.
LIVING AGE: From Six to Six Millions. 339:243-45. November, 1930.
*LIVING AGE, MILTENBERG, W. von: Handsome Adolf. 304:14/5, March, 1931. Handsome
    Adolf, reply R. von WISTINGHAUSEN, Living Age, 341:185/6, October, 1931.
LIVING AGE, UNRUH, Fritz v.: Hitler in Action, August, 1931, p. 551.

205

LIVING AGE, HITLER, Adolf: To Victory and Freedom, National Socialism, Labor Party, 342:24/5, March, 1932.
LIVING AGE: Hitler speaks. 344:114-16, April, 1933.
LIVING AGE: Hitler and His Gang. 344:419-22, June 22, 1933.
*LIVING AGE: W.W.C.: Hitler's Salad Days, 345:44-48, Sept., 1933.
LIVING AGE, HENRY, Ernst: The Man Behind Hitler. October, 1933, p. 117.
LIVING AGE: Why I Like Hitler. 349:303-6, December, 1935 (Dr. K. Scharping.)
*LIVING AGE, MORRELL, S.: Hitler's Hiding Place, 352:486-8, August, 1937.
*LIVING AGE, YEATS-BROWN, F.: A Tory Looks at Hitler. 354:512-4, August, 1938.
LIVING AGE, AGHA KHAN: Faith in Hitler, 355:299-302, December, 1938.
LIVING AGE, KORNEY: The Man Who made Hitler rich. 355:337-41, December, 1938.
LIVING AGE: Hitler's Palace in the Clouds on the Top of the Kehlstein, 356:32/3, March, 1939.
*LIVING AGE: Men Whom Hitler Obeys. 356:142-5, April, 1939.
*LIVING AGE: Hitler at 50. 356:451-3, June, 1939.
LIVING AGE, MANN, K: Cowboy Mentor of the Fuhrer, Karl May. 359:217-222, November, 1940.
*LIVING AGE: Hitler's Private Rabbit Warren. Reichschancellery, 360:321 June, 1941.
*LOCHNER, Louis P.: What about Germany? New York, Dodd, 1942, 395 p.
LOEWENSTEIN, Hubert Prinz zu: On Borrowed Peace, New York, 1942.
LOEWENSTEIN, Karl: Hitler's Germany, New York, MacMillan, 1936, 176 p.
LORANT, Stefan: I was Hitler's Prisoner, London, Gollancz, 1935. 318 p.
*LORIMER,, Emily D.: What Hitler Wants, Penguin Book, 1939.
*LUCCHINI, Pierre: (Pierre Dominic pseud.) Deux jours chez Ludendorff, Paris, 1924.
*LUDECKE, Kurt Georg W.: I Knew Hitler, New York, Scribner, 1937, 814 p.
*LUDWIG, Emil: Three Portraits; Hitler, Mussolini, Stalin. New York, 1940 127 p.
LUDWIG, Emil: The Germans. Boston, Little. 1941, 509 p.
*LURKER, Otto: Hitler hinter Festungsmauern. Berlin, Mittler, 1933, 71 p.

MARION, Paul: Leur Combat   Hitler. Paris. Fayard, 1939, 347 p.
MASON, John Brown: Hitler's First Foes. Minneapolis, 1936, 118 p.
*MASSIS, Henry: "Chefs," Paris, Plon., 1939.
MAUGHAM, Fred, Herbert: Lies as Allies; New York, Oxford University Press, 1941, 64 p.
MAUPAS, Jacques: Le Chancelier Hitler et les elections allemandes (Correspondant, 1933. N.S. tome 294, p. 836-853).
MELVILLE, Cecil F.: The Truth about the New Party. London. Wishart, 1931.
*MEND, Hans: Adolf Hitler im Felde. Diessen, Huber. Verlag, 1931, 192 p.
*MEYER, Adolf: Mit Hitler im Bayerischen Infanterie Regt. Neustadt. Aupperle Verlag. 1934, 109 p.
*MILLER, Douglas: You can't do Business with Hitler! Boston, Little, 1941. 329 p.
*MITTEILUNGEN des Deutschvolkischen Turnvereins Urfahr; Adolf Hitler in Urfahr. Felge 67:12. Jehrgang. (Austria).
MOELLER van den Bruck: Das Dritte Reich. Hamburg. Manseatisce Verlags Anstalt. 1931, 321 p.
MORVILLIERS, Roger:... Face A Hitler at A Mein Kampf. Serves en vente chez l'auteur. 1939.
*MOWRER, Edgar Ansell: Germany puts the Clock Back. New York, 1933. (London. Penguin Book, 1938.)
*MOWRER, Lilian: Rip Tide of Aggression. New York, Morrow, 1942, 247 p.
MUHLEN, Norbert: Hitler's Magician: Schacht. London, 1938, 228 p.
*MURPHY, James Bumgardner: Adolf Hitler, the Drama of his Career. London, Chapman, 1934.

NAAB, Ingbert: Ist Hitler ein Christ? Muenchen, Zeichenring Verlag, 1931, 47 p.
*NATION: DENNY, C.: France and the German Counter-Revolution, 116:295-7 March 14, 1923.
NATION: HORLE, W. H.: Ten Years of Hitler, Hundred of Goethe, 134:307-8 March 16, 1932.
NATION: RADEK, K.: Hitler. 134:462-64. April 20, 1932.
NATION: VILLARD, O.G.: Folly of Adolf Hitler. 136:392, April 12, 1933.
NATION: JASZI, O.: Hitler Myth, a forecast. 136:553/4, May, 1933.
NATION: VILLARD, O. G.: Nazi Child-mind. 137:614, November 29, 1933.
NATION: LENGYEL, E.: Hitler and the French Press. 138:216-7, February 21, 1934.
NATION: VILLARD, O.G.: Hitler's Me and Gott. 139:119, August, 1934.
NATION: Can Hitler Be Trusted? 140:645, June 5, 1935.
NATION: VILLARD, O.G.: Issues and Men. 143:395, October 3, 1936.
NATION: Hitler goes to Rome. 146:520, May 7, 1938.
NATIONALSOZIALISMUS, das wahre Gesicht des. Bund deutscher Kriegsteilnehmer. Magdeburg, 59 p.
*NATIONALSOZIALISTISCHE MONATSHEFTE: Jehrgang, 327, vol. 4, Heft 39.33, BUCH, Walter: Der Fuhrer, p. 248-51.
NATIONALSOZIALISTISCHE MONATSHEFTE: Vol. 5. Heft 46.34. p. 2. ANACKER, H.: Ritter Ted und Teufel.
NATIONALSOZIALISTISCHE MONATSHEFTE: Vol. 3. Heft 32.32. p. 511-13, CABALLERO, G. E.: Das Geheimnisdes Nationalsozialismus.
NATIONALSOZIALISTISCHE MONATSHEFTE: Vol. 5. Heft 54, p. 848-9, Adolf Hitler, 1925 in Gera.
*NATIONALSOZIALISTISCHE MONATSHEFTE: Vol. 5. Heft 55, p. 954-58, LINKE: Wie der Modies den Hitler zum Schweigen brachte.

*NATIONALSOZIALISTISCHE MONATSHEFTE: Vol. 5. Heft 54. Geschichten aus der KAMPFZEIT.
NAZI PRIMER, the: Official Handbook. New York, Harper, 1938.
NEUMANN, Franz L.: Behemoth. New York, Oxford University Press, 1942, 532 p.
*NEW REPUBLIC: Is Hitler Crazy? 97:2/3, November 9, 1938.
NEW REPUBLIC: HANISCH, R.: I was Hitler's Buddy. 98:239-42, 270-72, 297-300, April 5-19, 1939.
*NEW REPUBLIC: (Medicus) A Psychiatrist Looks at Hitler. 98:326-8, April 26, 1939.
NEWS WEEK: Nazis Protest Use of Baby Snapshot. 3:31, March 3, 1934.
NEWS WEEK: Hitler and Mussolini Meet. 3:10-12, June 23, 1934.
NEWS WEEK: Hitler Tells How He Directed Merciless Bloodstroke, 4:10-11, July 21, 1934.
NEWS WEEK: Hitler's First Great Crisis. 3:3-4, June 30, 1934.
NEWS WEEK: Hitler at Bavarian Retreat. 5:12-3, March 2, 1935.
*NEWS WEEK: Cocksure Dictator Takes Timid-Soul Precautions. 5:16, April 6, 1935.
NEWS WEEK: Reichsfuhrer. . .What Hitler Is. . .7:27, May 16, 1936.
*NEWS WEEK: Hitler and Mussolini Put Their Heads Together. 10:11-13, October 4, 1937.
*NEWS WEEK: Adolf Hitler's Roman Holiday   11:15-6, May 16, 1938.
*NEWS WEEK: When Hitler Started. 13:22, February 6, 1939.
NEWS WEEK: Adolf Hitler's Double. 13:43, March 13, 1939.
*NEWS WEEK: Hitler Enthroned. . . . 13:21, May 1, 1939.
*NEWS WEEK: To the Fuhrer, Hitler is Terrific. 19:42, June 22, 1942.
NEWS WEEK: Phony Fuhrer, Impersonator Dryden. 20:61-2, July 20, 1942.
*NEW YORK TIMES: November 21, 12:1. Rise as Idol. 1922.
*NEW YORK TIMES: December 14, 5:7. Mrs. Andre Elendt Aids Cause. 1922.
NEW YORK TIMES: May 19, LLL. 8:8. Hitler Wins Libel Suit in Munich   1929.
*NEW YORK TIMES: October 15, 1930. Interview.
NEW YORK TIMES: May 2, 12:4. Sincerity, praised by V. F. Ridder, 1933.
NEW YORK TIMES: December 3. IV. 2:2. Hitler Stories Told in Vienna, 1933.
*NEW YORK TIMES: December 26, 17:5. Gives Rides and Overcoats to Hitchhikers, 1933.
NEW YORK TIMES: March 11, VI, 1934. Feature article. Personality and Private Life: see Tolischus.
NEW YORK TIMES: August 12, IV. 1:7, 1934.
*NEW YORK TIMES: January 28. 6:3. Interviewed by Lord Allen of Hurtwood, 1935.
*NEW YORK TIMES: September 17, 4:4. Alois Hitler Opens Tea Room in Berlin, 1937.
*NEW YORK TIMES: September 19, IV. 2:3. Portrait Adolf Hitler, 1937.
*NEW YORK TIMES: April 16, 6:3. Gruenscheder says He is Older than Record Shows, 1938.
NEW YORK TIMES: March 31. 2:3 Relatives visit U.S.: William Patrick, 1939.
NEW YORK TIMES: October 6, 10:4. Miss Daniels Interview on her dance performance before him, 1939.
NEW YORK TIMES: November 17, VIII. 2:4. Report to have sought Dr. Stekel to interpret dream of undisclosed nature, 1940.
NEW YORK TIMES: January 3.9:1. January 4. 9:2. January 7. 5:6. Reports about arrival of U. Freeman Mitford—illness in England, 1940.
NEW YORK TIMES: January 26. 2:2. German Official as Honduran Foreign Office to ban book, "I was Hitler's Waitress," 1941.
NEW YORK TIMES: June 30. 5:3 and June 25. 4:3. Reports about William Patrick and Mrs. Bridget arrivals, activities in Canada and U.S., 1941.
NEW YORK TIMES MAGAZINE: TOLISCHUS; Portrait of a Revolutionary, p. 3, May 19, 1940.
NEW YORK TIMES MAGAZINE: PETERS, C. B.: In Hitler's Chalet. p. 9, 3/16/41.
*NEW YORKER STAATSZEITUNG und Herold: Various articles, April, 1939; December, 1940.
*NEW YORKER STAATSZEITUNG: Allerhand Merkwurdiges aus Privatleben. Preston Grover, January 2, 1941.
NIEKISCH, Ernst: Hitler-Ein Deutsches Verhaengnis. Berlin. Widerstands Verlag, 1932.
*NINETEENTH CENTURY: WILSON, Sir Arnold: October, 1936. p. 503-512.
NORTH AMERICAN REVUE: Herr Hitler comes to Bat. 1932, 234, vol. 104-9.

*OECHSNER, Frederick: This is the Enemy. Boston, Little, 1942, 364 p.
OEHME, Walter: Kommt das Dritte Reich? Berlin, Rowohlt, 1930.
*OLDEN, Rudolf: Hitler, Amsterdam, Querido, 1935, 364 p.
*OTTO, Carl A. G.: Der Krieg ohne Waffen. Wird Hitler Deutschlands Mussolini. Senitas Verlag. 1930, 69 p.
OTTWALT, Ernst: Deutschland Erwache! Vienna, 1932, Hess & Co.
OWNE, Frank: The Three Dictators   Hitler. London, Allen, 1940.
OUTLOOK: BINSSE, H. L.: Hitler, German Hypnotist, 156, vol. 256, 1931.

*PARISER TAGES ZEITUNG: April 20, 1937. Das Ratsel um Hitlers, E.K.I.
*PARISER TAGES ZEITUNG: Jan. 28, 1939. Der Prozess der Brigitte Hitler.
*PARISER TAGES ZEITUNG: Sept. 29, 1939. Article about the Iron Cross.
*PARISER TAGES ZEITUNG: Jan. 23, 1940. Vom Wahne besessen.
PASCAL, Roy: The Nazi Dictatorship. London, 1934.
*PAULI, Ernst: Die Sendung Adolf Hitlers. Verlag fur VOLKSKUNST, 1934.
*PAULS, Eilhard, Erich: Ein Jahr Volkskanzler. (Aus Deutschlands Werden, Heft 21/2. 1934, 31 p.)
PERNOT, Maurice: L'Allemagne de Hitler, Paris, 1933.
*PHILLIPS, Henry Albert: Germany Today and Tomorrow, New York, Dodd.
*PICTORIAL REVIEW: RADZIWILL, C./ZIERKURSCH, T. v.: Three Women Behind the Demagogue, 34:7, July, 1933.

*PLESSMAYR, Hermann: Der Nationalsozialismus   Stuttgart, Mahler, 1933, 104 p.
POLLOCK, James Kerr: The Government of Greater Germany, New York, Nostrand, 1938, 104 p.
*POPE, Ernest R.: Munich Playground, New York, Putnam's, 1941, 260 p.
POPPELREUTER, Walther: Hitler. Langensalza. 1934 (Heft, 1931 v. Friedr. Mann' padagog. Magazin, p. 1-41).
POTTMANN, Karl: Hitler-Entwicklungsmoglichkeiten. Oxford, 1933, vol. 14, p. 450-54. Blackfriars.
*PRICE, George Ward: I know these Dictators. London, Harrap., 1937, 262 p.

*RALEIGH, John McCutcheon: Behind the Nazi Front. New York, Dodd, 1940, 307 p.
RAUSCHNING, Anna: No Retreat. New York, Bobbs Merrill, 1942, 309 p.
*RAUSCHNING, Hermann: The Voice of Destruction same as "Gesprache mit Hitler."
*RAUSCHNING, Hermann: The Revolution of Nihlisme. New York, Alliance Book Corp., 1939, 300 p.
*RAUSCHNING, Hermann: Gesprache mit Hitler. New York, Europa Verlag, 1940, 272 p.
RAUSCHNING, Hermann: Hitler and the War. American Council on Public Affairs, 1940, 11 p.
RAUSCHNING, Hermann: The Conservative Revolution. New York, Putnam's, 1941, 280 p.
RAUSCHNING, Hermann: The Beast from the Abyss. London, Heinemann, 1941, 170 p.
*RAUSCHNING, Hermann: Men of Chaos, New York, Putnam's, 1942, 341 p.
READER'S DIGEST: SPIWAK, J. L.: Hitler's Racketeers, 28:52-4, March, 1936.
REICH, Albert: Aus Adolf Hitlers Heimst. 1933, 128 p.
*REVEILLE, Thomas (pseud.): The Spoil of Europe, New York, Norton, 1941. 344 p.
REVUE HEBDOMADAIRE: Vingt jours chez Hitler. (F. LeGrix), Paris, 42 A. 4. 94-118.5. 84-98.
*REYNOLDS, Bernard Talbot: Prelude to Hitler. London, J. Cape, 1933, 288 p.
RIBBENTROP, Manfred v.: Um den Fuhrer. (Volkische Reihe im Winterverlag Heft 1) 1933, 32 p.
*RIESS, Curt: The Self-Betrayed. Putnam's, New York, 1942, 402.
*RITTER, Walther: Adolf Hitler   Leipzig. Verlag Nationalsoz Front, 1933, 32 p.
ROBERT, Karl: (pseud.) Hitler's Counterfeit Reich. New York, Alliance Book Corp. 1941, 122 p.
*ROBERTS, Stephen H.: The House that Hitler Built. New York, 1938, 364 p.
*ROCH, Hans: Gott segne den Kanzler. 20. April 1933. 11 p. Rundfunkrede.
*ROEHM, Ernst: Die Geschichte eines Hochverraters. Muenchen, F. Eher, 1933, 367 p.
ROGGE, Heinrich: Hitlers Friedenspolitik. Berlin, Schlieffen. 1935, 127 p.
ROPER, Edith (und Clara Leiser): Skeleton of Justice, New York, Dutton, 1941. 346 p.

*SANTORO, Cesare: Hitler Deutschland   Berlin. Inter. Nat. Verl. 1938. 440 p.
*SANTORO, Cesare: Vier Nahre Hitlerdeutschland. . . 1937.
*SATURDAY EVENING POST—SONDERN, F. Jr.: Schuschnigg's terrible two hours. 211:23. August 13, 1938.
*SATURDAY EVENING POST—NORBURT, R.: Is Hitler Married? 212:14/5. December 16, 1939.
SATURDAY EVENING POST—ULLSTEIN, H.: We Blundered Hitler into Power. 213:12/3, July 13, 1940.
*SATURDAY EVENING POST—McKELWAY, St. C.: Who Was Hitler? 213:12/3. July 20, 1940.
SATURDAY EVENING POST—WALDECK, Countess: Girls Did Well Under Hitler. 215:18, September 26, 1942.
SATURDAY REVIEW (of London): Mann, H.: A German View of Hitler. 153 vol. 314/5, 1932.
SATURDAY REVIEW (of London): MAXWELL, N.: Hitler's He Men and the Gash. 156 vol. 142, 1933.
SATURDAY REVIEW OF LITERATURE: BAKER, J. E.: Carlyle Rules the Reich. 10:291, November 25, 1933.
SATURDAY REVIEW OF LITERATURE: JOSEPHSON, M.: Making of a Demagogue. 10.213/4. Oct. 28, 1933.
*SCHACHER, Gerhard: He wanted to Sleep in the Kremlin. New York, 1942. 261 p.
SCHEID, O.: Les Memoires de Hitler. Paris, Perrin, 1933.
*SCHIRACH, Baldur v.: Die Pioniere des Dritten Reichs. Essen, 1933.
*SCHMIDT-PAULI, Edgar v.: Hitlers Kampf um die Macht. Berlin, 1933, 205 p.
*SCHMIDT-PAULI, Edgar v.: Die Manner um Hitler. Verlag fur Kulturpolitik. Berlin, 1932 (Neue organzte Ausgabe, 1935, 190 p.)
*SCHMIDT-PAULI, Edgar v.: Adolf Hitler, Berlin, De VO Verlag, 1934, 126 p.
SCHOLASTIC: Hitler Crushes Foes   25:15. September 22, 1934.
*SCHOTT, Georg: Das Volksbuch vom Hitler. Muenchen. Eher. 1933, 307 p.
SCHRADER, Fred Franklin: The New Germany.   New York. Deutscher Weckruf & Beobachter. 1937.
*SCHROEDER, Arno: Hitler geht auf die Dorfer. National. Soz. Verlag, 1938, 212 p.
*SCHULTZE-PFAELZER, Gerhard: Hindenburg und Hitler. Berlin, Stollberg, 1933, 96 p.
*SCHULZE, Kurt: Adolf Hitler, London, Harrap, 1935, 80 p.
*SCHUMANN, Frederick Lewis: Hitler and the Nazi Dictatorship, London, 1936.
SCHWARZSCHILD, Leopold: World in Trance, New York, 1942, 445 p.
SCIENCE NEWS LETTER: LASWELL, H. D.: Hitler Rose to Power Because he Felt Personally Insecure. 33:195. March 26, 1938.
SCIENCE NEWS LETTER: Hitler's Personality Called: Paranoid, infantile sadistic. 34:227/8. October 8, 1938.
*SCRIBNER: WHITE, W. C.: Hail Hitler. M. 9:229-31, April, 1932.

SCYLER, J. P.:   Hitler et son troisieme empire. Paris, L'Eglantine, 1933.
*SEEHOFER, Herbert: Mit dem Fuhrer unterwegs! NSDAP, 1939, 228 p.
SENDER, Toni: A Fighter for Peace. New York, Vanguard, 1939.
*SHIRER, William L.: Berlin Diary, New York, Knopf. 1941, 605 p.
*SHUSTER, George N.: Strong Man Rules. (New York, 1934).
SIMONE, Andre: Men of Europe. New York, Modern Age, 1941, 330 p.
*SMITH, Howard K.: Last train from Berlin. New York. 1942, 359 p.
*SNYDER, Louis: Hitleriam   by Nordicus (pseud.) New York, Mohawk Press, 1932.
SPENCER, Franz: Battles of a Bystander. New York, Liveright, 1941, 260 p.
*STARHEMBERG, Ernst, Rudiger, Prinz: Between Hitler and Mussolini. London, Hodder
        1942. 281 p.
STARK, Johannes: Adolf Hitlers Ziele   Deutscher Volksverlag, 1930, 32 p.
STATIST, the: Hitler's Day. London, 1934, 123 vol. 161.
STEED, Henry Wickham: Hitler Whence and Whither? London, Nisbet, 1934, 189 p.
STEEL, Johannes: Hitler als Frankenstein. London, 1933, 185 p.
*STEYRER ZEITUNG: Adolf Hitler als Schuler in Steyr. April 17, 1938.
*STODDARD, Lothrop: Into the Darkness. New York, Duell, 1940, 311 p.
STRASSER, Otto: Aufbau des deutschen Sozialismus. Prag. I., Heinrich Grunow, 1936.
*STRASSER, Otto: Hitler and I. Boston, Houghton, 1940, 248 p.
STRASSER, Otto: Free Germany Against Hitler, Brooklyn, N. Y., 1941, 15 p.
*STRASSER, Otto: Die deutsche Bartholomausnacht. Zurich Reso Verlag, 1935, 242 p.
*STRASSER, Otto: Flight from Terror.
STRESEMANN, Gustav: Letters and Diaries. London, MacMillan, 1935-40.
SURVEY, the: (J. P. Gavit) Much ado about Hitler. 68 vol. 239.

TACITUS REDIVIVUS (pseud.) Die Grosse Trommel. 155 p.
*TAGEBUCH, das—TSCHUPPIK, Karl: Hitler spricht. 498, 1927.
TAGEBUCH, das—SCHER, Pet.: Hitlergesandter bei Ford. VII. 628, 1928.
*TAGEBUCH, das—HEIDEN: Hitler klagt. X. 816, 1929.
TAGEBUCH—SCHWARZSCHILD, L: Ave Adolf: XII, 1808. (1931).
*TAT, die: ROTHE, M.: Siogesallee II, (A. Hitler) 21. J. 780-4.
TAYLOR, Edmond: The Strategy of Terror. Boston, Houghton, 1940. 277 p. (1942 revised
        edition).
*TEELING, William: Know Thy Enemy! London, Nicholson, 1939, 313 p.
TENNANT, E. W. D.: Herr Hitler and His Policy, March, 1933. English Review, v. 56, p. 362,
        375.
TESSON, Francois de: Voici Adolf Hitler. Paris. Flammarion, 1936, 284 p.
THYSSEN, F.: I made a Mistake When I Backed Hitler. American Magazine, 130:16-7.
        July, 1940.
*THYSSEN, F.: I Paid Hitler. New York, Farrar, 1941, 281 p.
*THOMPSON, Dorothy: I Saw Hitler. New York, 1932.
*TIME: Let's Be Friends. 27:21-2, March 9, 1936.
TIME: Critic Hitler, 30. August 2, 1937 (p. 32-A.2).
TIME: Hitler Comes Home. 31: 18-22, March 21, 1938.
*TIME: Hitler's Throat. 32:55. November 14, 1938.
*TIME: Man of the Year. 33:11-14. January 2, 1939.
TIME: Office and Official Residence   33:17/8. January 23, 1939.
TIME: Fuhrer's Next. 33:22 March 13, 1939.
*TIME: Hitler vs. Hitler, 33:20, April 10, 1939.
*TIME: Aggrandizer's Anniversary, 33:23/4, May 1, 1939.
TIME: Two Diagnoses, 33:22, May 8, 1939.
TIME: Eleven Minutes: Hitler's Narrow Escape. 34:21/2, November 20, 1939.
TIME: Mississippi Frontier, K. H. v. Wiegand's Interview, 35:37-8, June 24, 1940.
*TIME: Happy Hitler. 36:18, July 15, 1940.
TIME: Hitler Takes a Trip. 36:28, Nov. 4, 1940.
TIME: Orator Hitler. 37:19, Jan. 13, 1941.
*TIME: Dictator's Hour. 37:26-8 April 14, 1941.
TIME: Happy Birthday. 37:22/3. April 28, 1941.
TIME: Inside Hitler. 39:43, June 22, 1942.
*TOLISCHUS, Otto D.: They Wanted War. New York, Reynolds, 1940, 340 p.
*TOURLEY, Robert (et Z. Lvovsky): Hitler. Paris, Editions due siecle. 1932, 200 p.
*TROSSMAN, Karl: Hitler und Rom. Nurnberg. Sebaldus Verlag, 1931.
TROTZKY, Leon: What Hitler Wants. New York, John Bay Co., 1933, 31 p.
TROTZKY, Leon: How Long Can Hitler Stay? (American Mercury v. 31. p. 1-17), 1934.
TURNER, James: Hitler and the Empire. London, 1937, 40 p.

VERGES, Ferni: El Pangermanisme abans de Hitler. Revista de Catalunya. 1938. juny 15, p.
        213-225).
VIE des Peuples. Adolf Hitler. Annee 4, p. 536-44, Paris, 1923.
*VOIGTS, F. A.: Unto Caesar. New York. Putnam, 1938, 303 p.
VORWAERTS: GOETZ, F.: Ein Offizier Hitlers erzahlt. 3.2.24.
*VORWAERTS: GOETZ, F.: Report on Putsch Prozess. February 26, 1924.

*WAGNER, Ludwig: Hitler, Man of Strife. New York. Norton, 1942, 331 p.
*WALLACH, Sidney: Hitler, Menace to Mankind. Emerson Books, 1933.
*WELTBUEHNE—LANIA, L.: Hitler-Prozess. 20. J. 298-301, 1924.
WELTBUEHNE: Mit Gott fur Hitler und Vaterland. 21. J. 720, 1925.
*WELTBUEHNE: Hitler und die Japaner. 22 J. I. 672, 1926.
WELTBUEHNE: Hitler und Kirdirf (Morus) 26. J. II. 245.
WELTBUEHNE: Begrussung Hitlers auf literarischem Gebiet. (Walter Mehring) 507.

C02571145

WELTBUEHNE: Reichskanzler Hitler. (Toller, E.) 537.
WELTBUEHNE: 1931. 27 J. Zu diesem Hitler. 45 (Borne, L.)
WELTBUEHNE: 1931. Brutus schlaft. 157-60. (Ossietzky, C. v.)
WELTBUEHNE: 1931. Hitler. Winterkonig. 235-37 (Ossietzky, C. v.)
WELTBUEHNE: 1931. Hitlers Horoskop. 607-11. (Ossietzky, C. v.)
WELTBUEHNE: 1931. Grossreinemachen bei Hitler. 483. (Ossietzky, C. v.)
WELTBUEHNE: 1931. Geldgeber der Nazis. (Citron, B.) II. 72.
WELTBUEHNE: 1931. Hitlers Vorlaufer. 814-17. (Gerlach, H. v.)
WELTBUEHNE: 1931. Kommt Hitler doch? 875-80 (Ossietzky, C. v.)
WELTBUEHNE: 1931. Aktive Abwehr gegen Hitler. 880. (Muhsam, E.)
WELTBUEHNE: 1931. Hitlers Fliegerei. 918-20. (Wieland, H.)
WELTBUEHNE: 1931. Illusionen uber Hitler. 950-54 (Gerstorff, K. L.)
WELTKAMPF—HAUPTMANN, R.: An den Pranger mit Hitler! . . .VIII 154-63, 1931.
*WENDEL, Friedrich: Der Gendarm von Hildburghausen. Berlin, Dietz, 1932.
WHAT Hitler Did not Want the English Speaking Countries to Know. Centre d'Information
   documentaire Paris, Pamphlets 5.
*WHEELER-BENNETT, John: The Wooden Titan. 1936.
WHITTLESEY, Derwent: German Strategy of World Conquest. New York, 1942.
*WHO: JACOB, Hans: Hitler's Ear and Tongue. Vol. 1. No. 2., May, 1941, p. 37-8.
*WIEGAND, Karl v.: Hitler Foresees His End. Cosmopolitan, April, 1939, p. 28 ff. and May
   p. 48 ff.
WILD, Alfons: Hitler und das Christentum. Augsburg. Hass., 1931, 85 p.
WIR fliegen mit Hitler. Berlin. Deutsche Kulturwacht, 1934, 184 p.
WOLF, John: Nazi Germany. London, 1934.
WYL, Hans von: Ein Schweizer erlebt Deutschland. Zurich, Europa Verlag, 1938.

*YOUNG, William Russel: Berlin Embassy, 1941, 280 p.

*ZIEMER, Gregor: Education for Death, New York, Oxford University Press, 1941, 208 p.
*ZIEMER, Patsy: 2010 Days of Hitler, New York, Harper, 1940, 312 p.

210

Chapter Eight

Hitler's Certificate of Marriage, Private Will and Last Political Testament

"Who says I am not under the special protection of God?"

Adolf Hitler

The following documents were recovered by US military Intelligence months after the fall of Germany and presented to President Harry S. Truman in March 1946 by Robert P. Patterson then Secretary of War.

WAR DEPARTMENT
WASHINGTON

19 March 1946

Dear Mr. President:

Our Military Intelligence personnel, through information furnished by the British Intelligence Service, recovered Adolf Hitler's personal and political wills, his marriage certificate, and a letter transmitting these documents to Admiral Doenitz, signed by Martin Bormann. The unique character of these papers and their historic significance prompt me to forward them to you as a matter of personal interest. A laboratory test by the Federal Bureau of Investigation indicates that these documents are authentic.

Hitler's final anti-Semitic tirade, his frantic attempt to maintain a semblance of German government, and what amounts to a suicide pact between himself and Eva Braun vividly illustrate the closing hours of the Nazi regime. These are matters of great public interest. Might I suggest that these documents be placed on display in the Library of Congress or other suitable establishment.

Sincerely yours,

Secretary of War

The President

The White House

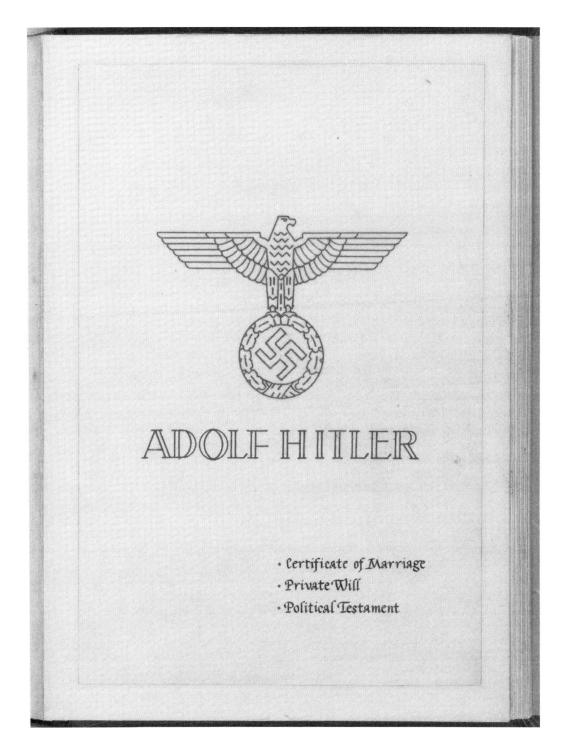

ADOLF HITLER

- Certificate of Marriage
- Private Will
- Political Testament

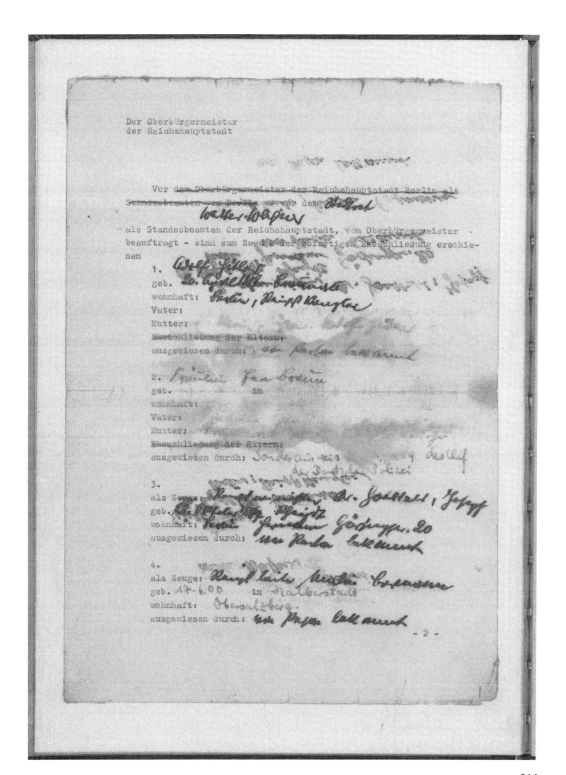

Der Oberbürgermeister
der Reichshauptstadt

Vor dem Oberbürgermeister der Reichshauptstadt Berlin als
Standesbeamten von Berlin — vor dem *Walter Wagner*

als Standesbeamten der Reichshauptstadt, vom Oberbürgermeister
beauftragt - sind zum Zwecke der sofortigen Eheschließung erschie-
nen

1. *Adolf Hitler*
geb. *20. April 1889 in Braunau*
wohnhaft: *Berlin, Reichskanzlei*
Vater:
Mutter:
Eheschließung der Eltern:
ausgewiesen durch: *der Person bekannt*

2. *Fräulein Eva Braun*
geb.
wohnhaft:
Vater:
Mutter:
Eheschließung der Eltern:
ausgewiesen durch: *Sonderausweis*

3.
als Zeuge: *Reichsminister Dr. Goebbels, Josef*
geb.
wohnhaft: *Berlin, Hermann Göringstr. 20*
ausgewiesen durch: *der Person bekannt*

4.
als Zeuge: *Reichsleiter Martin Bormann*
geb. *17.6.00 in Halberstadt*
wohnhaft: *Obersalzberg.*
ausgewiesen durch: *der Person bekannt*

- 2 -

The Mayor
of the Capital of the Reich

Before Walter Wagner, City Councillor, as the appointed Registrar of the Capital of the Reich appeared, for the purpose of joining in marriage.

1. Adolf Hitler

Born 20 April 1889 at Braunau

Residence: Berlin, Reich Chancellory

Father:

Mother:

Marriage of the parents

Identified by: Personnally known

2. Miss Eva Braun

Born on the 6th of February 1910 in Munich, Wasserburgerst No. 8

Residence: Munich Wasserburgerst No. 12

Father: Friedrich Braun

Mother: Franciska Braun, Nee Dronburger

Marriage of the parents

Identified by: Special identity card dated 4 April 39 issued by the Chief of the German Police.

3.

Witness: Reich-Minister Dr. Goebbels, Joseph

Born 26 October 1897 Rheydt

Residence: Berlin, Hermann Goeringst 20

Identified by: Personally known

4.

Witness: Reichs Leiter Martin Bormann

Born 17 June 1900 in Halberstadt

Residence: Obersalzberg

Identified by: Personally known

- 2 -

Die Erschienenen zu 1 und 2 erklären, daß sie rein
arischer Abstammung und mit keiner die Eheschließung aus-
schließenden Erbkrankheiten befallen sind. Sie beantragen
mit Rücksicht auf die Kriegsereignisse wegen außerordentlicher
Umstände die Kriegstrauung und beantragen weiter das Aufgebot
mündlich entgegenzunehmen und von sämtlichen Fristen Abstand
zu nehmen.

Den Anträgen wird stattgegeben. Das mündlich abgegebene
Aufgebot ist geprüft und für ordnungsgemäß befunden worden.

Ich komme nunmehr zum feierlichen Akt der Eheschließung.
In Gegenwart der obengenannten Zeugen zu 3 und 4 frage ich Sie,

Mein Führer Adolf Hitler

ob Sie gewillt sind, die Ehe mit

Fräulein Eva Braun

einzugehen. In diesem Falle bitte ich Sie, mit "ja" zu antworten.

ob Sie gewillt sind, die Ehe mit

Mein Führer Adolf Hitler

einzugehen. In diesem Falle bitte ich auch Sie mit "ja" zu
antworten.

. Nachdem nunmehr beide Verlobte die Erklärung abgegeben
haben die Ehe einzugehen, erkläre ich die Ehe vor dem Gesetz
rechtmäßig für geschlossen.

Berlin, am 29. April 1945

Vorgelesen und unterschrieben:

1.) Ehemann:

2.) Ehefrau: *Eva Hitler geb. Braun*

3.) Zeuge zu 1: *Dr. Joseph Goebbels*

4.) Zeuge zu 2:

5.) *Bormann.*

als Standesbeamter

- 2 -

The persons mentioned under 1 and 2 state, that they are of pure Aryan descent and that they are not infected with inheritable diseases which would exclude them from marriage. Considering the war situation and the special circumstances they apply for marriage under special war time laws. They also ask to accept an oral publication of the bans and to disregard all legal delays.

The application is accepted. The oral publication of the bans is checked. The findings are in order.

I come now to the ceremonial act of marriage.

In the presence of the witnesses mentioned under 3 and 4 I ask you,

My Fuehrer Adolf Hitler

Are you willing to take the

Miss Eva Braun

As your wife.

If you are, answer "I Do"

Now I ask you

Miss Eva Braun

Are you willing to take

Our Fuehrer Adolf Hitler

As your husband

If you are, answer "I Do"

Since both newly weds have stated their intentions, I declare this marriage as legal before the law.

Berlin, 29 April 1945

Read and Signed:

1.) Husband: (Signed) Adolf Hitler

2.) Wife: Eva Hitler nee Braun

3.) Witness 1:   Joseph Goebbels

4.) Witness 2:   M. Bormann

5-) (Signed) Wagner

As Registrar

ADOLF HITLER

Mein privates Testament.

   Da ich in den Jahren des Kampfes
glaubte, es nicht verantworten zu können, eine
Ehe zu gründen, habe ich mich nunmehr vor Be-
endigung dieser irdischen Laufbahn entschlossen, jenes Mädchen zur Frau zu nehmen, das
nach langen Jahren treuer Freundschaft aus
freiem Willen in die schon fast belagerte Stadt
hereinkam, um ihr Schicksal mit dem meinen zu
teilen. Sie geht auf ihren Wunsch als meine
Gattin mit mir in den Tod. Er wird uns das er-
setzen, was meine Arbeit im Dienst meines Volkes
uns beiden raubte.

   Was ich besitze, gehört - soweit es
überhaupt von Wert ist - der Partei. Sollte
diese nicht mehr existieren, dem Staat, sollte

ADOLF HITLER

MY PRIVATE WILL

Since I did not think I should take the
responsibility of entering into marriage during the years of combat, I have decided now
before termination of life on this earth, to
marry the woman who, after many years of
true friendship, entered voluntarily into this
already almost besieged city, to share my
fate. She goes to death with me as my wife,
according to her own desire. Death will
replace for us that of which my work in the
service of my people robbed us.

What I own belongs - as far as it is of
any value at all - to the party. Should the party
no longer exist it will belong to the state. Should

auch der Staat vernichtet werden, ist eine weitere
Entscheidung von mir nicht mehr notwendig.

Ich habe meine Gemälde in den von mir im
Laufe der Jahre angekauften Sammlungen niemals
für private Zwecke, sondern stets nur für den
Ausbau einer Galerie in meiner Heimatstadt Linz
a.d.Donau gesammelt.

Dass dieses Vermächtnis vollzogen wird,
wäre mein herzlichster Wunsch.

Zum Testamentsvollstrecker ernenne ich
meinen treuesten Parteigenossen
Martin B o r m a n n .
Er ist berechtigt, alle Entscheidungen endgültig
und rechtsgültig zu treffen. Es ist ihm gestattet,
alles das, was persönlichen Erinnerungswert besitzt,
oder zur Erhaltung eines kleinen bürgerlichen Lebens
notwendig ist, meinen Geschwistern abzutrennen,
ebenso vor allem der Mutter meiner Frau und meinen,
ihm genau bekannten treuen Mitarbeitern und Mit-

the state also be destroyed, any further decision from me is no longer necessary.

The paintings in the collections which
I have bought during the years have never
been acquired for private purposes, but always
exclusively for the creation of an art gallery
in my native town of Linz a.d. Donau.

It is my heartfelt desire that this legacy
shall be fulfilled.

My most faithful party member

Martin B o r m a n n

shall be the executor of this testament. He is
authorized to make all decisions to be final and
legal. He is permitted to take everything which
either has personal souvenir value or which is necessary for the maintenance of a small bourgeois
household and to give it to my brothers and sisters,
and besides especially to the mother of my wife and my

arbeiterinnen, an der Spitze meinen alten Sekre-
tären, Sekretärinnen, Frau Winter, usw., die mich
jahrelang durch ihre Arbeit unterstützten.

Ich selbst und meine Gattin wählen, um
der Schande des Absetzens oder der Kapitulation
zu entgehen, den Tod. Es ist unser Wille, sofort
an der Stelle verbrannt zu werden, an der ich
den grössten Teil meiner täglichen Arbeit im
Laufe eines zwölfjährigen Dienstes an meinem
Volke geleistet habe.

Gegeben zu Berlin, den 29. April 1945, 4.00 Uhr

als Zeugen:

Martin

Or.

als Zeugen:

Nicolaus von Below

faithful co-workers who all are well known to him. There are most of all my old sec-retaries, Mrs Winter etc., who for many years gave me loyal co-operation.

Myself and my wife choose death to escape the disgrace of being forced to re-sign or to surrender. It is our wish to be cremated immediately at the place where I have done the greatest part of my work during the twelve years of service for my people.

Berlin, 29 April 1945, 4:00 hrs

ADOLF HITLER

As witness: As witness:

MARTIN BORMANN   NICOLAUS VON BELOW

DR. GOEBBELS

DER SEKRETÄR DES FÜHRERS
REICHSLEITER MARTIN BORMANN

FÜHRERHAUPTQUARTIER
ANSCHRIFT FÜR POSTSENDUNGEN
MÜNCHEN 33, FÜHRERBAU

29, 4, 45

Lieber Großadmiral!

Da wegen des Ausbleibens aller Divisionen unsere Lage hoffnungslos erscheint, diktierte der Führer in der vergangenen Nacht das anl. politische Testament.

Heil Hitler!

Ihr

The Secretary of The Fuehrer
Reichsleiter Martin Bormann

Headquarters of The Fuehrer
Mailing Address
Munich 33, Fuhrerbau
29 April 45

Dear Grandadmiral!

Since all our Divisions failed to appear our situation seems to be beyond hope.

The Fuehrer dictated last night the attached political testament.

Heil Hitler!
Yours
(Signed) Bormann

ADOLF HITLER

Mein politisches Testament.

Seit ich 1914 als Freiwilliger meine bescheidene Kraft im ersten, dem Reich aufgezwungenen Weltkrieg einsetzte, sind nunmehr über dreissig Jahre vergangen.

In diesen drei Jahrzehnten haben mich bei all meinem Denken, Handeln und Leben nur die Liebe und Treue zu meinem Volk bewegt. Sie gaben mir die Kraft, schwerste Entschlüsse zu fassen, wie sie bisher noch keinem Sterblichen gestellt worden sind. Ich habe meine Zeit, meine Arbeitskraft und meine Gesundheit in diesen drei Jahrzehnten verbraucht.

Es ist unwahr, dass ich oder irgendjemand anderer in Deutschland den Krieg im Jahre

ADOLF HITLER

MY POLITICAL TESTAMENT

Since 1914, when, as a volunteer, I employed my modest powers in the first World
War forced upon the Reich, more than thirty
years have passed.

In these three decades love and faith for
my people have been the only mainsprings of
all my thinking, acting, and living. These ide-
als gave me the power to make the most difficult decisions, such as no mortal has yet had to
face. I have exhausted my time, my working
energy and my health in these three decades.

It is not true that I or anybody else
in Germany wanted the war in the year

1939 gewollt haben. Er wurde gewollt und ange-
stiftet ausschliesslich von jenen internationalen
Staatsmännern, die entweder jüdischer Herkunft
waren oder für jüdische Interessen arbeiteten.
Ich habe zuviele Angebote zur Rüstungsbeschrän-
kung und Rüstungsbegrenzung gemacht, die die
Nachwelt nicht auf alle Ewigkeiten wegzuleugnen
vermag, als dass die Verantwortung für den Ausbruch dieses Krieges auf mir lasten könnte. Ich
habe weiter nie gewollt, dass nach dem ersten
unseligen Weltkrieg ein zweiter gegen England
oder gar gegen Amerika entsteht. Es werden Jahrhunderte vergehen, aber aus den Ruinen unserer
Städte und Kunstdenkmäler wird sich der Hass gegen das, letzten Endes verantwortliche Volk immer wieder erneuern, dem wir das alles zu verdan-
ken haben: Dem internationalen Judentum und seinen
Helfern!

Ich habe noch drei Tage vor Ausbruch des
deutsch-polnischen Krieges dem britischen Bot-
schafter in Berlin eine Lösung der deutsch-polnischen Probleme vorgeschlagen - ähnlich der im
Falle des Saargebietes unter internationaler
Kontrolle. Auch dieses Angebot kann nicht weg-
geleugnet werden. Es wurde nur

1939. It was desired and provoked
entirely by those international statesmen who were either of Jewish origin
or who worked in the Jewish interest.
I have made so many offers for the
reduction and limitation of armaments,
which posterity cannot explain away
for all eternity, that the responsibility
for the outbreak of this war cannot
rest on me. Furthermore, I never desired that after the first terrible World
War a second war should arise against
England or even against America.
Centuries may pass, but out of the ruins
of our cities and art-monuments the
hatred will arise and be constantly re-
newed against the people which is alone
ultimately responsible: International
Jewry and its assistants!

As late as three days before the
outbreak of the German-Polish war, I proposed to the British Ambassador in Berlin
a solution of the German-Polish problem -
similar to the case of the Saar area, under
international control. This offer cannot be

verworfen, weil die massgebenden Kreise der eng-
lischen Politik den Krieg wünschten, teils der
erhofften Geschäfte wegen, teils getrieben durch
eine, vom internationalen Judentum veranstaltete
Propaganda.

Ich habe aber auch keinen Zweifel darüber
gelassen, dass, wenn die Völker Europas wieder
nur als Aktienpakete dieser internationalen Geld-
und Finanzverschwörer angesehen werden, dann auch
jenes Volk mit zur Verantwortung gezogen werden
wird, das der eigentlich Schuldige an diesem mör-
derischen Ringen ist: Das Judentum! Ich habe weiter keinen darüber im Unklaren gelassen, dass dieses Mal nicht nur Millionen Kinder von Europäern
der arischen Völker verhungern werden, nicht nur
Millionen erwachsener Männer den Tod erleiden und
nicht nur Hunderttausende an Frauen und Kindern
in den Städten verbrannt und zu Tode bombardiert
werden dürften, ohne dass der eigentlich Schuldige, wenn auch durch humanere Mittel, seine Schuld
zu büssen hat.

Nach einem sechsjährigen Kampf, der einst
in die Geschichte trotz aller Rückschläge als ruhm-

explained away either. It was only rejected because the responsible circles in English politics
wanted war, partly because of the expected business, partly driven by a propaganda arranged by
international Jewry.

But I left no doubt about the fact that the
real culprit in this murderous struggle, Jewry,
would also have to pay for it, if the people of
Europe were again to be treated as so many
packages of shares by these international money
and finance conspirators. Furthermore, I left
no doubt that it would not be tolerated this time
that millions of European children of the Aryan
people should starve to death, that millions of
grown-up men should suffer death, and that
hundreds of thousands of women and children
should be burnt and bombed to death in the cities,
without the real culprit suffering his due punishment, even though through more humane methods.

After six years of struggle, which in spite of all
reverses, will go down in history as the most glorious

vollste und tapferste Bekundung des Lebenswillens
eines Volkes eingehen wird, kann ich mich nicht von
der Stadt trennen, die die Hauptstadt dieses Reiches
ist. Da die Kräfte zu gering sind, um dem feindli-
chen Ansturm gerade an dieser Stelle noch länger
standzuhalten, der eigene Widerstand aber durch
ebenso verblendete wie charakterlose Subjekte
allmählich entwertet wird, möchte ich mein Schicksal mit jenem teilen, das Millionen anderer auch
auf sich genommen haben, indem ich in dieser Stadt
bleibe. Ausserdem will ich nicht Feinden in die
Hände fallen, die zur Erlustigung ihrer verhetz-
ten Massen ein neues, von Juden arrangiertes Schau-
spiel benötigen.

Ich hatte mich daher entschlossen, in
Berlin zu bleiben und dort aus freien Stücken in
dem Augenblick den Tod zu wählen, in dem ich glaube,
dass der Sitz des Führers und Kanzlers selbst
nicht mehr gehalten werden kann. Ich sterbe mit
freudigem Herzen angesichts der mir bewussten un-
ermesslichen Taten und Leistungen unserer Soldaten
an der Front, unserer Frauen zuhause, den Leistungen unserer Bauern und Arbeiter und dem in der Geschichte einmaligen Einsatz unserer Jugend, die
meinen Namen trägt.

and most courageous manifestation of a people's
will to live, I cannot separate myself from the
city which is the capital of this Reich. Because
the forces are too small to further resist the
enemy assault just at this point, and because
individual resistance is rendered valueless by
blinded and characterless scoundrels, I desire
to share the fate which millions of others have
taken upon themselves, in that I remain in this
city. Furthermore, I do not want to fall into the
hands of enemies who need another show, arranged
by Jews, for the amusement of their ill-guided
masses.

I have therefore resolved to remain in
Berlin and there to choose death of my own
free will, at that moment in which I ever believe
that this seat of the Fuehrer and Chancellor can
no longer be defended. I die with a glad heart
in view of my awareness of the immeasurable deeds
and accomplishments of our soldiers at the front, of
our women at home, of accomplishments of our farm-
ers and workers, and of the sacrifice - outstanding
in history - of the youth which bears my name.

Dass ich ihnen allen meinen aus tiefstem
Herzen kommenden Dank ausspreche, ist ebenso
selbstverständlich wie mein Wunsch, dass sie
deshalb den Kampf unter keinen Umständen aufgeben
mögen, sondern, ganz gleich wo immer, ihn gegen
die Feinde des Vaterlandes weiterführen, getreu
den Bekenntnissen eines grossen Clausewitz. Aus
dem Opfer unserer Soldaten und aus meiner eigenen
Verbundenheit mit ihnen bis in den Tod, wird in
der deutschen Geschichte so oder so einmal wieder
der Samen aufgehen zur strahlenden Wiedergeburt
der nationalsozialistischen Bewegung und damit
zur Verwirklichung einer wahren Volksgemeinschaft.

Viele tapferste Männer und Frauen haben
sich entschlossen, ihr Leben bis zuletzt an das
meine zu binden. Ich habe sie gebeten und ihnen
endlich befohlen, dies nicht zu tun, sondern am
weiteren Kampf der Nation teilzunehmen. Die Führer
der Armeen, der Marine und der Luftwaffe bitte ich,
mit äussersten Mitteln den Widerstandsgeist unserer Soldaten im nationalsozialistischen Sinne zu
verstärken unter dem besonderen Hinweis darauf,
dass auch ich selbst, als der Gründer und Schöpfer
dieser Bewegung, den Tod dem feigen Absetzen oder
gar einer Kapitulation vorgezogen habe.

That I give them all my thanks from the bottom of my heart is as self-evident as that therefore they should not give up the fight under any circumstance. They shall continue the struggle, wherever it may be, against the enemies of the fatherland, faithful to the great Clausewitz. In one manner or another in the course of history, the seed for a bright resurrection of the National-Socialist movement and for the realization of a true community of the people will grow out of the sacrifice of our soldiers and out of my own solidarity with them in death.

Many very brave men and women decided to tie their lives to mine to the very end. I asked them, and finally ordered them, not to do this but to continue to participate in the nation's struggle. I ask the leaders of the armies, the navy and the air force to fortify the National-Socialist spirit of resistance of our soldiers with all possible means, pointing out especially that I too, as the founder and creator of this movement, have preferred death to cowardly withdrawal or even capitulation.

Möge es dereinst zum Ehrbegriff des
deutschen Offiziers gehören - so wie dies in
unserer Marine schon der Fall ist - dass die
Übergabe einer Landschaft oder einer Stadt
unmöglich ist und dass vor allem die Führer
hier mit leuchtendem Beispiel voranzugehen
haben in treuester Pflichterfüllung bis in den
Tod.

May it be one day a part of the code of honor of the German officer as it is already in our Navy - that the surrender of a district or a town is impossible, and that in this respect the leader above all should give a shining example of faithful performance of duty unto death.

Zweiter Teil des politischen Testaments.

Ich stosse vor meinem Tode den früheren Reichsmarschall Hermann G ö r i n g aus der Partei aus und entziehe ihm alle Rechte, die sich aus dem Erlass vom 29. Juni 1941 sowie aus meiner Reichstagserklärung vom 1. September 1939 ergeben könnten. Ich ernenne an Stelle dessen den Großadmiral D ö n i t z zum Reichspräsidenten und Obersten Befehlshaber der Wehrmacht.

Ich stosse vor meinem Tode den früheren Reichsführer-SS und Reichsminister des Innern, Heinrich H i m m l e r aus der Partei sowie aus allen Staatsämtern aus. Ich ernenne an seiner Stelle den Gauleiter Karl H a n k e zum Reichsführer-SS und Chef der deutschen Polizei und den Gauleiter Paul G i e s l e r zum Reichsminister des Innern.

Göring und Himmler haben durch geheime Verhandlungen mit dem Feinde, die sie ohne mein Wissen und gegen meinen Willen abhielten, sowie durch den Versuch, entgegen dem Gesetz, die Macht im

SECOND PART OF THE POLITICAL TESTAMENT

Before my death I expel the former Reichs
Marshall Hermann Goering from the Party and de-
prive him of all rights which may have resulted
from my decree of 29 June 1941, or from my de-
claration before the Reichstag on 1 September 1939.
In his place I appoint Grand Admiral Doenitz as
President of the Reich and as Supreme Commander
of the Armed Forces.

Before my death I expel the former Reichs
Leader of the SS and Reichs Minister of the Interior,
Heinrich Himmler, from the party and all government
offices. In his place I appoint Gauleiter Karl Hanke
Reichs Leader of the SS and Chief of the German
Police and Gauleiter Paul Geisler as Reichs Minister
of the Interior.

Apart from the disloyalty against my person,
Goering and Himmler have inflicted immeasurable
damage upon the country and the entire people through
secret negotiations with the enemy which they have made

Staate an sich zu reissen, dem Lande und dem
gesamten Volk unabsehbaren Schaden zugefügt,
gänzlich abgesehen von der Treulosigkeit gegenüber
meiner Person.

Um dem deutschen Volk eine aus ehrenhaften
Männern zusammengesetzte Regierung zu geben, die
die Verpflichtung erfüllt, den Krieg mit allen
Mitteln weiter fortzusetzen, ernenne ich als
Führer der Nation folgende Mitglieder des neuen
Kabinetts:

Reichspräsident: D ö n i t z
Reichskanzler: Dr. G o e b b e l s
Parteiminister: B o r m a n n
Aussenminister: S e y ß - I n q u a r t
Innenminister: Gauleiter G i e s l e r
Kriegsminister: D ö n i t z
Oberbefehlshaber des Heeres: S c h ö r n e r
Oberbefehlshaber der Kriegsmarine: D ö n i t z
Oberbefehlshaber der Luftwaffe: G r e i m
Reichsführer-SS und Chef der Deutschen Polizei:
        Gauleiter H a n k e
Wirtschaft: F u n k
Landwirtschaft: B a c k e
Justiz: T h i e r a c k
Kultus: Dr. S c h e e l

without my knowledge and against my will,
and also through the attempt to invest
themselves illegally with the power in the
state.

In order to give to the German
people a government which consists of
honorable men who are fulfilling the obligation to continue the war with all means, I
as leader of the nation nominate the following members of the new cabinet:

Reichs President: D o e n i t z

Reichs Chancellor: Dr. G o e b b e l s

Party Minister: B o r m a n n

Foreign Minister: S e y s z - I n q u a r t

Minister of the Interior: Gauleiter G i e s l e r

War Minister: D o e n i t z

C. in C. of the Army: S c h ö r n e r

C. in C. of the Navy: D o e n i t z

C. in C. of the Airforce: G r e i m

Reichs Leader of the SS and Chief of the German

Police: G a u l e i t e r H a n k e

Economics: F u n k

Agriculture: B a c k e

Justice: T h i e r a c k

Church and Education: Dr. S c h e e l

Propaganda: Dr. N a u m a n n
Finanzen: S c h w e r i n - C r o s s i g k
Arbeit: Dr. H u p f a u e r
Rüstung: S a u r
Leiter der Deutschen Arbeitsfront und Mitglied
des Reichskabinetts: Reichsminister Dr. L e y .

Obwohl sich eine Anzahl dieser Männer, wie
Martin Bormann, Dr. Goebbels usw. einschliesslich
ihrer Frauen, aus freiem Willen zu mir gefunden
haben und unter keinen Umständen die Hauptstadt
des Reiches verlassen wollten, sondern bereit
waren, mit mir hier unterzugehen, muss ich sie
doch bitten, meiner Aufforderung zu gehorchen und
in diesem Falle das Interesse der Nation über ihr
eigenes Gefühl zu stellen. Sie werden mir durch
ihre Arbeit und ihre Treue als Gefährten nach dem
Tode ebenso nahestehen, wie ich hoffe, dass mein
Geist unter ihnen weilen und sie stets begleiten
wird. Mögen sie hart sein, aber niemals ungerecht,
mögen sie vor allem nie die Furcht zum Ratgeber
ihres Handelns erheben und die Ehre der Nation über
alles stellen, was es auf Erden gibt. Mögen sie sich
endlich dessen bewusst sein, dass unsere Aufgabe,
des Ausbaus eines nationalsozialistischen Staates
die Arbeit kommender Jahrhunderte darstellt, die

Propaganda: Dr. N a u m a n n

Finance: S c h w e r i n - C r o s s i g k

Labor: Dr. H u p f a u e r

Armament: S a u r

Leader of the German Labor Front and Member
of the Reichs Cabinet: Reichsminister Dr. L e y.

     Several of these men such as Martin
Bormann, Dr. Goebbels and others, as well as
their wives, have joined me by their own free
will, and do not wish to leave the capital of the
Reich under any circumstances but on the contrary are willing to perish here with me. Nevertheless I must ask them to obey my request, and
in this case to put the interest of the nation before
their own feelings. Through their work and
loyalty they will remain just as close to me as companions after my death, just as I hope that my
spirit will be amongst them and will always accompany them. May they be hard but never unjust, and
above all, may they never let fear inspire their
actions, but place the honor of the nation above anything
on this earth. May they finally realize that our task,
the implementation of the National-Socialist state,
represents the work of the coming centuries which

jeden einzelnen verpflichtet, immer dem gemeinsamen
Interesse zu dienen und seine eigenen Vorteile dem-
gegenüber zurückzustellen. Von allen Deutschen,
allen Nationalsozialisten, Männern und Frauen
und allen Soldaten der Wehrmacht verlange ich, daß
sie der neuen Regierung und ihren Präsidenten treu
und gehorsam sein werden bis in den Tod.

Vor allem verpflichte ich die Führung der
Nation und die Gefolgschaft zur peinlichen Ein-
haltung der Rassegesetze und zum unbarmherzigen
Widerstand gegen den Weltvergifter aller Völker,
das internationale Judentum.

Gegeben zu Berlin, den 29. April 1945, 4.00 Uhr.

obligates every individual at all times to serve the common interest and to subordinate his own advantages to it. I demand of all Germans, all National-Socialists, men and women, and all soldiers of the Armed Forces, that they will remain faithful and obedient to the new government and to their President until death.

Above all I obligate the leadership of the nation and its followers to the most minute observation of the racial laws and to pitiless resistance against the universal poisoner of all people, international Judaism.

Given at Berlin, 29 April 1945, 4 a.m.

Adolf Hitler

As witnesses:

Dr. Joseph Goebbels   Wilhelm Burgdorf

Martin Bormann   Hans Krebs

"The world is a dangerous place to live, not because of the people who are evil, but because of the people who don't do anything about it."   Albert Einstein

Printed in Great Britain
by Amazon

64913613R00140